A-78

THE NEAR EAST

BOOKS ON HISTORY
BY ISAAC ASIMOV

THE KITE THAT WON THE REVOLUTION

A SHORT HISTORY OF BIOLOGY

A SHORT HISTORY OF CHEMISTRY

ASIMOV'S BIOGRAPHICAL ENCYCLOPEDIA
OF SCIENCE AND TECHNOLOGY

THE GREEKS

THE ROMAN REPUBLIC

THE ROMAN EMPIRE

THE EGYPTIANS

THE NEAR EAST: 10,000 YEARS OF HISTORY

THE

NEAR EAST

10,000 YEARS OF HISTORY

BY ISAAC ASIMOV c1968 277p.

HOUGHTON MIFFLIN COMPANY BOSTON

To Mary and Henry Blugerman,
more angels than in-laws

CONTENTS

1 THE SUMERIANS

THE FIRST FARMERS 1

THE LIFE-GIVING RIVERS 4

THE GREAT INVENTIONS 10

THE GREATEST INVENTION 13

THE FLOOD 19

WARFARE 22

2 THE AKKADIANS

THE FIRST EMPIRE 28

THE CONQUERING NOMADS 34

THE CITY OF ABRAHAM 37

3 THE AMORITES

ENTER BABYLON 42

THE CHANGING OF THE GODS 45

THE PILLAR OF THE LAW 49

THE COMING OF THE HORSE 53

4   THE ASSYRIANS

THE GREAT HUNTER   59

IRON   63

THE ASSYRIAN HITLER   66

THE HORSE GROWS LARGER   71

THE QUEEN THAT WASN'T   76

THE POLICY OF EXILE   78

THE LAST DYNASTY   82

FRUSTRATIONS AND FURY   86

AT THE PEAK   92

THE ROYAL LIBRARIAN   94

5   THE CHALDEANS

THE END OF NINEVEH   99

THE DIVISION OF THE SPOILS   102

BABYLON IN ITS GLORY   107

THE JEWS IN EXILE   111

THE ROYAL ANTIQUARIAN   115

6   THE PERSIANS

THE GENTLE CONQUEROR   118

THE WAR OF LIGHT AND DARK   123

THE ORGANIZER   128

THE END OF MARDUK   133

THE BATTLE OF THE BROTHERS   136

7 THE MACEDONIANS

UNION AGAINST PERSIA   141

DAVID BEATS GOLIATH   144

EXIT BABYLON   149

THE PULL OF THE WEST   153

8 THE PARTHIANS

EXIT THE SELEUCIDS   160

ENTER ROME   163

THE ARMORED HORSEMEN   166

STAND-OFF   171

ROME AT THE GULF   174

9 THE SASSANIDS

RE-ENTER THE PERSIANS   179

THE PULL OF THE PAST   183

ROMAN RECOVERY   187

THE CHRISTIAN ENEMY   192

A CENTURY OF CONFUSION   198

THE HERETICS   202

THE MOMENT OF
    ENLIGHTENMENT   205

THE MOMENT OF TRIUMPH   209

10 THE ARABS

HISTORY REPEATS ITSELF 214

THE FACTIONS OF ISLAM 218

BAGHDAD 222

THE PUPPET CALIPHS 227

11 THE TURKS

THE HEIRS TAKE OVER 230

END AND BEGINNING OF A DUAL 232

THE ASSASSINS 236

TERROR FROM CENTRAL ASIA 238

THE OTTOMANS 244

12 THE EUROPEANS

THE RETURN OF THE
WESTERNERS 248

THE RUSSIANS 250

THE GERMANS 253

ISRAEL 256

TABLE OF DATES 261

INDEX 271

1

THE SUMERIANS

THE FIRST FARMERS

About nine thousand years ago, a great change began to come over mankind.

Until then, for many thousands of years, men had gathered or hunted food wherever they could find it, pursuing wild animals, and plucking fruits and berries. They had gnawed at roots and had kept an eye out for nuts. Men had to be lucky to survive and winters were starving times.

A given tract of land could not support many families, and human beings were scattered thinly over the surface of the planet. About 8000 B.C. there may not have been more than eight million human beings in existence altogether — just about as many as are in the city of New York today.

Then, through some gradual process, men learned how to prepare food for future use. Instead of hunting animals and killing them on the spot, he kept some alive and took care of

them. He let them breed and multiply, killing a few now and
then. In this way, he not only had meat, but could also get milk
or wool or eggs. He could even make some of the animals work
for him.

In the same way, instead of just gathering what plant food
he could find, he learned to sow plants and care for them, so
that he could be certain the plants would be there when he
needed them. Furthermore, he could sow a much greater con-
centration of useful plants than he was likely to find in a state
of nature.

From being a hunter and food-gatherer, groups of men
learned to become herders and farmers. Those who concentrated more on the use of animals found they had to be on
the move all the time. The animals had to be fed, and this
meant that green pastures had to be sought out from time to
time. Such herders tended to become wandering "nomads"
(from a Greek word meaning "pasture").

Gardening was more complicated. Sowing had to be done
at the right time of the year and in the right way. The growing
plants had to be cared for; weeds had to be cleared away; ma-
rauding animals kept off. It was tedious and back-breaking
work that lacked the careless ease and changing scene of the
nomad. Many people, working in cooperation, had to remain
in one place throughout the growing season, for they had to stay
with the non-moving plants.

Farmers gathered in groups and built permanent dwelling
places near their fields. The dwelling places huddled together
as the farmers kept close for protection against wild animals
and raiding nomads. In this way, towns came to be established.

The cultivation of plants, or "agriculture," made it possible
for a given stretch of land to support many more people than
would be possible if men were food-gatherers, hunters, or even
herdsmen. The amount of food that could be accumulated not
only fed the farmers on the spot but supplied enough for stor-
age through the winter. Indeed, so much food could be produced that the farmers and their families had more than
enough for themselves. There was sufficient left over to feed

people who were not farmers but who supplied farmers with things they wanted or needed.

Some people could devote themselves to making pottery and tools or to designing ornaments out of stone or metal. Some could be priests, some soldiers, and all would be fed by the farmer. Towns grew into cities, and society grew complicated enough in such cities to allow us to speak of "civilization." (The very term is from a Latin word meaning "city.")

Population began to increase. As the system of agriculture spread, as group after group began to learn how to farm, population continued to increase and has been increasing ever since. By A.D. 1800, there were a hundred times as many people on Earth as there had been before agriculture was invented.*

It is hard to tell now just exactly where agriculture got its very first start, so long ago, or just exactly how the discovery came about. Archaeologists are quite certain, though, that the general area of the epoch-making discovery was in what we now call the Middle East — very likely in the region on the borders of the modern nations of Iraq and Iran.

For one thing, barley and wheat grew wild in that region, and it was just these plants that lent themselves ideally to cultivation. They were easily handled and could be thickly grown. The ears of grain they produced could be ground into flour that could be stored for months on end without spoiling and could be baked into a tasty and nutritious bread.

There is a site called Jarmo (jahr'moh), for instance, in northern Iraq. It is a low mound into which, beginning in 1948, the American archaeologist, Robert J. Braidwood dug carefully. He found the remains of an old, old town, showing the foundations of houses built up of thin walls of packed mud and divided into small rooms. It may have held no more than 100 to 300 people.

There evidence of very early agriculture was uncovered. In the lowest and oldest layers, which date back to 8000 B.C., stone

---

* After A.D. 1800, the so-called "Industrial Revolution" began to spread through the world and made it possible for mankind to multiply at a rate that would have been impossible with pre-industrial agriculture alone — but that is another story and beyond the purpose of this book.

tools were used for cutting the wheat and barley, and stone pots were used to hold water. It was only in higher levels that pottery out of baked clay was found. (Pottery represents a considerable advance, for clay is more common than rock in many areas and is certainly easier to work with.) Animals were also tamed. The early farmers of Jarmo had goats, and dogs, too, perhaps.

Jarmo is at the edge of a mountain range, where rising air is cooled and the vapor in that air is condensed out as rain. It was necessary for the earliest farmers to grow their crops in areas of dependable rain. Only in this way could they have the kind of rich harvests they needed to support their growing population.

THE LIFE-GIVING RIVERS

In the foothills where the rain is abundant, soil is apt to be shallow, however, and not very fertile. To the west and south of Jarmo was good, deep, flat soil that would be excellent for the growing of crops — a fertile region indeed.

This broad band of good soil curved north and west from what we now call the Persian Gulf all the way to the Mediterranean Sea. It rimmed the Arabian desert to the south (which was itself much too dry, sandy, and rocky for agriculture) in a huge crescent a thousand miles long. This is usually called "the Fertile Crescent."

What the Fertile Crescent could have used to make it one of the richest and most populous centers of human civilization (which it eventually became) was a dependable rainfall, and this it did not have quite enough of. The land was flat and the warm winds moved over it without dropping their load of moisture till they came to the mountains that rimmed it along the east. What rain fell, came in the winter; the summers were dry.

Yet there was water in the land — if not from the air, then along the ground.

In the mountains north of the Fertile Crescent, abundant

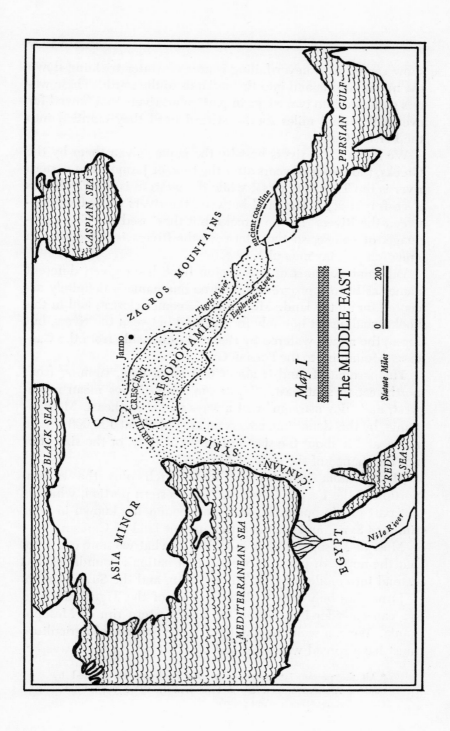

Map I

The MIDDLE EAST

Statute Miles

0   200

CASPIAN SEA

PERSIAN GULF

ancient coastline

ZAGROS MOUNTAINS

Tigris River

Euphrates River

Jarmo

FERTILE CRESCENT

MESOPOTAMIA

SYRIA

CANAAN

BLACK SEA

ASIA MINOR

MEDITERRANEAN SEA

RED SEA

EGYPT

Nile River

snow served as a never-failing source of water trickling down the mountainside and into the flatlands to the south. These waters gathered into two rivers in particular, rivers that flowed for over a thousand miles southeastward until they emptied into the Persian Gulf.

We know these rivers best by the names given them by the Greeks, thousands of years after the time of Jarmo. The eastern river is the Tigris (ty'gris), while the western is the Euphrates (yoo-fray'teez).* The land between the rivers was called "Between-the-Rivers" by the Greeks, but they used the Greek language, of course, so that Between-the-Rivers is Mesopotamia (mes"oh-poh-tay'mee-uh).

Different portions of this region have been given different names as history progressed, and no one name is definitely accepted for all the land. Mesopotamia comes closest, and in this book I shall use it not only for the land between the rivers, but for all the region watered by them on either side from the Caucasus Mountains to the Persian Gulf.

This stretch of land is about 800 miles long, running from northwest to southeast. "Upstream" will always mean northwest, and "downstream" will always mean southeast. Mesopotamia, by this definition, covers an area of about 130,000 square miles, and is about the size and shape of Italy, or the size (but not the shape) of the state of Arizona.

Mesopotamia includes the upper arch plus the eastern portion of the Fertile Crescent. The western portion, which is not part of Mesopotamia, was most commonly known in later times as Syria, and included the ancient land of Canaan.

Most of Mesopotamia is included in what we now call Iraq, but the northern portions overlap that nation's boundaries and extend into modern Syria, Turkey, Iran, and the Soviet Union.

Jarmo lies only about 125 miles east of the Tigris River, so we can consider it to lie on the northeastern rim of Mesopotamia. We can well imagine that the techniques of agriculture must have spread westward and by 5000 B.C., farming was be-

---

* All the pronunciations given in this book are those used by modern Americans, and are not necessarily those used by the Greeks or any other ancient people.

ing practiced along the upper reaches of the two streams and their tributaries. It had been brought not only from Jarmo but from other sites along the hilly rim to the east and north. Improved strains of cereal were grown, and cattle and sheep were domesticated.

The rivers were an even better source of water than rainfall, and the towns that grew up on their banks were larger and more advanced than Jarmo had been. Some of them occupied 3 or 4 acres of land.

Like Jarmo, the towns were built of packed mud. This was only natural, for most of Mesopotamia lacks rock and good timber, while clay exists in profusion. It is warmer in the lowlands than in the hills of Jarmo and the early houses on the rivers were built with thick walls and few openings, in order to keep the heat out.

There were no garbage disposal systems in the early towns, of course, and rubbish gradually accumulated in the streets and was packed down by the comings and goings of men and animals. As the streets grew higher, the floors of houses had to be raised with additional layers of clay.

Every once in a while, storms or floods would beat down or wash out the dried brick. Sometimes an entire town would be devastated. Survivors or newcomers would rebuild the city on top of its ruins. As a result, cities, built over and over, came to stand on mounds above the surrounding countryside. This had some advantages, for it made the town easier to defend from an enemy and more secure against the menace of floods.

Eventually, though, a city would sink into final ruin and only the mounds (called "Tell" in Arabic) would remain. Careful digging into these mounds would reveal layer after layer of habitations, growing steadily more primitive, as one probed deeper. This was true of Jarmo, for instance.

Tell Hassuna (has-soo'nuh), on the upper Tigris about 70 miles west of Jarmo, was excavated in 1943, and its oldest layers were found to contain decorated pottery that was more advanced than anything in old Jarmo. This is considered to be representative of the "Hassuna-Samarra" period of Mesopotamian history, which lasted from 5000 to 4500 B.C.

The mound called Tell Halaf, about 120 miles farther up-stream, revealed the remains of a town with cobbled streets and houses of more advanced brick construction. This "Halaf period" from 4500 to 4000 B.C. showed early Mesopotamian pottery at its height.

As the Mesopotamian culture advanced, the techniques for handling the river water improved. If the rivers were merely taken in a state of nature, only fields immediately along the banks could be used. This limited the useful land sharply. Furthermore, the amount of snow in the northern moun-tains varied from year to year, and so did the rate of melting. There were always floods in the early summer, and if these floods were heavier than usual, there would be far too much water as, at other times, there might be far too little.

It occurred to men that the thing to do was to dig an elaborate set of trenches or ditches inland from either bank of the river. This would lead the water out of the river and, in a fine network, bring it to every field. The ditches could be dug for miles on either side of the river so that inland fields would find themselves on the riverbank after all. What's more, the sides of the canals and of the rivers themselves could be raised into dikes, which the flooding water would not surmount in flood-time, except at desired places.

In this way, therefore, the water could be counted on, gen-erally, to be neither too little nor too much. Of course, if the water level were unusually low, the canals would be ineffective except fairly close to the river. And if the floods were too high, the dikes would be surmounted or broken down. These bad years came but rarely, however.

The water supply was most regular in the lower stretches of the Euphrates River, which had a less erratic shift in level from season to season and year to year than did the turbulent Tigris. The elaborate system of "irrigated agriculture" began along the upper Euphrates about 5000 B.C., worked its way downstream and by 4000 B.C., toward the end of the Halaf period, had reached this desirable section of the lower Euphrates.

It was along the lower Euphrates then that civilization burst into true flower. The cities there became much larger than any-thing that had yet been seen, and some had populations as large as 10,000 by 4000 B.C.

Such cities became too large to run on a tribal system, with everyone related as a family and obeying some patriarchal head. Instead, people without clear family connections had to cling together and work in peaceful cooperation or all would starve. To keep the peace and enforce that cooperation, some leader had to be chosen.

Each city then became a political unit controlling enough farming land in its neighborhood to support its population. It was a "city-state," and at the head of each city-state was a king.

The inhabitants of the Mesopotamian city-states did not really know where the absolutely essential river water came from; why it flooded at some seasons and not at others; why the floods failed in some years and were disastrously high in others. It seemed reasonable to consider it all the handiwork of beings much more powerful than ordinary men — of gods.

Since the water fluctuations seemed to follow no logical sys-tem but were completely capricious, it was easy to suppose that the gods were impulsive and whimsical, like overgrown and extremely powerful children. They had to be cajoled into supplying the proper amount of water; they had to be soothed when angry; and kept in good humor when placid. Rites were devised in which the gods were endlessly praised and propi-tiated.

It was assumed that what pleased men also pleased gods, so the most important method of propitiating the gods was to give them food. They didn't eat as men did, but the smoke of burning food mounted toward the sky where it was imagined the gods lived, and animals were therefore sacrificed as burnt offerings to them.*

In one ancient Mesopotamian poem, for instance, a great flood, sent by the gods, devastates mankind. But the gods, de-

---

* The assumption that the gods lived in the sky may have re-sulted from the fact that the earliest farmers depended upon rain from the heavens rather than upon floods from the river.

prived of sacrifices, grow hungry themselves. When a survivor of the flood sacrifices animals, the gods cluster about eagerly:

> *The gods scented its savor*
> *The gods scented the sweet savor,*
> *Like flies, the gods gathered above the sacrifice*

Naturally, the rules and regulations involved in dealing with the gods were even more complicated and intricate than those involved in dealing with men. A mistake with a man might mean a killing or a blood feud; but a mistake with a god could mean a famine or a flood that would devastate a whole region.

A powerful priesthood therefore grew up in farming communities, much more elaborate than anything that can be found in hunting or nomadic societies. The kings of the Mesopotamian cities were high priests as well, and conducted the sacrifices.

The central structure about which each city revolved was the temple. The priests who occupied the temple were in charge not merely of the relationship of the people and the gods, but also of the records of the city itself. They were the treasurers, the taxers, and the organizers; the civil service; the bureaucracy; the brains and heart of the city.

THE GREAT INVENTIONS

Irrigation isn't the answer to everything. A civilization based on irrigated agriculture has its problems, too. For one thing, river water, flowing through and across soil, contains a bit more salt than rainwater does. This salt gradually accumulates in the soil over long centuries of irrigation and ruins it unless special methods are used to wash it out again.

Some irrigation-civilizations declined back into barbarism for this reason. The Mesopotamians avoided this, but their soil did grow slightly salty. That, in fact, was one reason that barley was their chief crop (and remains so even today), for barley will endure slightly salty soil.

Then, too, the accumulation of food, tools, metal ornaments, and all the good things of life, is a standing temptation to people from the outside who lack agriculture. The history of Mesopotamia is a long succession of ups and downs for this reason. First, civilization builds up in peace, accumulating wealth. Then, nomads swoop down from outside, upsetting civilization and driving it downward, so that there is a decline in material comforts, even a "dark age."

The newcomers learn the ways of civilization and raise material wealth again, often to new heights, only to be overwhelmed by a new influx of barbarians. It happens over and over.

Mesopotamia faced outsiders on two flanks. To the northeast and north were hardy mountaineers. To the southwest and south were equally hardy sons of the desert. From one flank or the other, Mesopotamia was bound to face strife and, possibly, disaster.

Thus, the Halaf period came to an end about 4000 B.C. because nomads swarmed into Mesopotamia from the Zagros Mountains (zag'ros) that mark the limit of the Mesopotamian lowlands to the northeast.

The culture of the period that followed can be studied at Tell el Ubaid (oo-bayd'), a mound near the lower Euphrates. In many ways, what is found shows a decline from the works of the Halaf period, as is to be expected. The "Ubaid period" may have lasted from 4000 to 3300 B.C.

These nomads who established the Ubaid period may well have been the people we call the "Sumerians." They settled along the lowermost section of the Euphrates, and that section of Mesopotamia in that period of history is therefore referred to as "Sumer" (soo'mer) or "Sumeria."

The Sumerians found civilization already established in their new home, with cities and a working system of canals. Once the Sumerians learned the ways of civilization, they struggled back to the level which had existed before their disrupting influence had come upon the scene.

Then, amazingly enough, as the Ubaid period drew to its close, they advanced farther. Over the centuries, they introduced a series of key inventions that we still profit from today.

They developed the art of monumental structures. Coming from mountain lands of adequate rainfall, they were accustomed to the notion of gods in the sky. Feeling the need to get as close to the heavenly gods as possible, in order that their rites be most effective, they built large mounds out of baked clay, and set up their sacrifices on top. It soon occurred to them to build a smaller mound upon the first, a still smaller on the second, and so on, if they could.

Such staged structures are known as "ziggurats" (zig'oo-rats), and they were probably the most impressive structures of their time. Even the Egyptian pyramids did not come till centuries after the first ziggurats.

However, it is the tragedy of the Sumerians (and of the peoples who followed them in Mesopotamia) that they had only clay to work with, while the Egyptians had granite. The Egyptian monuments still stand, at least in part, to enforce the wonder of all subsequent ages, whereas the Mesopotamian monuments washed away in the floods and left nothing behind.

Yet word of the ziggurats reached the modern west through the Bible. The book of Genesis (which reached its present form twenty-five centuries after the close of the Ubaid period) tells of an early time when men "found a plain in the land of Shinar; and they dwelt there" (Genesis 11:2). The land of Shinar is, of course, Sumer. Once there, the Bible says, they said, "Go to, let us build us a city and a tower, whose top may reach unto heaven" (Genesis 11:4). This is the famous "Tower of Babel," a legend based on the ziggurats.

Of course, the Sumerians did try to reach heaven in the sense that they hoped their rites would be more effective on top of the ziggurats than on the ground. Moderns who read the Bible, however, usually tend to think of the phrase as implying the builders of the tower literally tried to reach the sky.

The Sumerians must have used the ziggurats for astronomical observations, since the movements of the heavenly bodies could be interpreted as important guides to the intentions of the gods. They were the first astronomers and astrologers.

Their astronomical work led them to develop mathematics and a calendar. Some of what they devised five thousand years ago and more remains with us today. It was the Sumerians, for instance, who divided the year into twelve months, the day into twenty-four hours, the hour into sixty minutes, and the minute into sixty seconds. They may also have invented the seven-day week.

They also developed an intricate system of trade and commerce. To facilitate trade, they developed an elaborate system of weights and measures, and devised a postal system.

They also invented the wheeled vehicle. Previous to that, heavy weights may have been moved on rollers. Individual rollers, as they were left behind by the moving vehicle, would be brought forward and placed before it again. Such a device was tedious and slow, but it was better than trying to drag a weight across the ground by brute force.

Once a pair of wheel-and-axle combinations were affixed to a cart, however, it was as though it was on two permanent rollers that moved with it. The wheeled cart, pulled by a single donkey, allowed weights to be moved that previously required a dozen men. It was a revolution in transport that was equivalent to the invention of the railroad in modern times.

THE GREATEST INVENTION

The chief cities of Sumeria during the Ubaid period may have been Eridu (ay'rih-doo) and Nippur (nih-poor').

Eridu, perhaps the oldest settlement in the south, dating back to 5300 B.C. or so, was on the shores of the Persian Gulf, probably at the mouth of the Euphrates. Its ruins are some ten miles south of the Euphrates now, for the river's sinuous course changes from one channel to another over the course of the millennia.

The ruins of Eridu are even farther from the Persian Gulf today. In early Sumerian times, the Persian Gulf may have stretched much farther northwest than it does now, and the Euphrates and the Tigris entered it by separate mouths, eighty miles apart.

The two rivers brought silt and muck down from the mountains, however, and deposited it at their mouths, building up rich soil that slowly extended mile after mile southeastward, filling the upper end of the Gulf.

The two rivers, flowing across the new land, gradually approached till they came together and formed a single combined river that flows to what is now the shore of the Persian Gulf — about 120 miles southeast of where it was in the great days of Eridu.

Nippur is a hundred miles upstream from Eridu. Its ruins also are no longer on the fickle Euphrates which now runs twenty miles to the west.

Nippur remained a religious center for the Sumerian city-states long after the Ubaid period, even after it was no longer one of the larger or more powerful cities. Religion is more conservative than any other aspect of human life. A city may become a religious center in the first place because it is a capital. It may then lose its importance, dwindle in size and population, even fall under the control of outsiders, yet still continue to remain a revered religious center. We need only think of the importance of Jerusalem through all the centuries when it was little more than a ruined village.

As the Ubaid period drew to a close, conditions drifted toward the greatest invention of all, the most important one in man's civilized history — that of writing.

One of the factors that led the Sumerians in that direction must have been the very clay they used in building. The Sumerians could scarcely have failed to notice that the soft clay took impressions that remained perfect and permanent after it was baked and hardened into brick.

Some people may well have thought of making marks deliberately as a kind of signature to their own work. In order to prevent "counterfeiting" it might have occurred to some to pre-

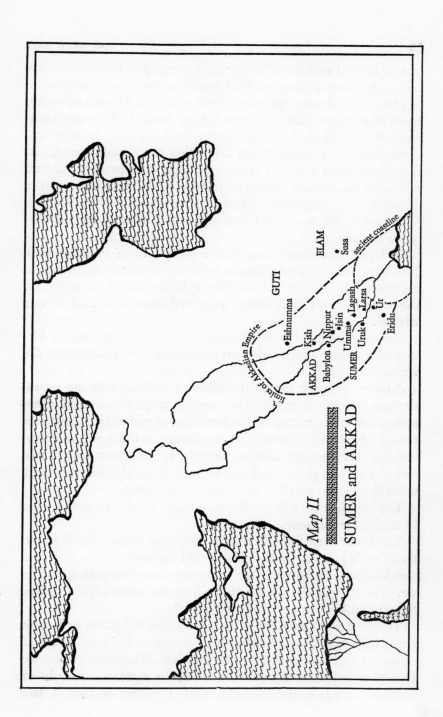

Map II

SUMER and AKKAD

ELAM

GUTI

Susa

ancient coastline

limits of Akkadian Empire

Eshnumma

Kish

AKKAD

Nippur

Babylon

Isin

Umma

Lagash

SUMER

Uruk

Larsa

Ur

Eridu

pare a carved surface which could be stamped into the clay to form a picture or diagram that would serve as a signature.

The next advance occurred in the city of Uruk (oo'rook), some fifty miles upstream from Eridu. Uruk had grown dominant at the end of the Ubaid period and, indeed, the two centuries from 3300 to 3100 B.C. are called the "Uruk period." It may have been because Uruk was busy and prosperous that advances took place there, or it may have been because the advances took place that the city became busy and prosperous. It is hard to tell which is cause and which effect from this distance in time.

In Uruk, the stamp seal was replaced by a cylinder seal. This consisted of a small stone roller on which was carved, in negative relief, some scene. The cylinder could be rolled on the clay to form that scene, repeated over and over if one wished.

Such cylinder seals multiplied in later Mesopotamian history and clearly represented art objects as well as signature devices.

Another impulse in the direction of writing was the necessity for keeping records. The temples were the central storehouses for grain, cattle, and other forms of property. They held the city surplus to be used in sacrificing to the gods, in carrying the city through famine periods, in financing war needs, and so on. The priesthood had to keep track of what they had, what they were getting, and what they issued.

The simplest way to do this is to make marks; to cut notches in sticks, for instance.

The Sumerians lacked an easy supply of sticks, but the matter of seals had shown that clay could be used. Strokes of various kinds could be used for units, for tens, for sixties, and so on. The clay tablet on which such scores were kept could be baked and kept as a permanent record.

To show whether a set of notches stood for cattle or barley, the priests may have made a rough sketch of the head of a bull on one, or of an ear of grain on another. That established the fact that some mark could be made to signify some object. Such a mark is called a "pictograph" ("picture-writing"), and if only all people agreed on the same set of pictographs, they could then communicate without speech — and the communication could be permanently preserved.

Little by little, such signs were agreed upon, as early as 3400 B.C. perhaps. Abstract ideas could next be represented by "ideographs" ("idea-writing"). Thus a round circle with rays might represent the sun; it could also represent light. A crude drawing of a mouth could stand for hunger as well as for the mouth itself; combined with another crude drawing of an ear of grain, it could stand for eating.

As time went on, the signs grew more and more schematic and resembled the original objects they were modeled on less and less. Indeed, for the sake of speed, the scribes took to making the signs by jabbing the sharp edge of their instrument into the soft clay in such a way as to make a narrow, triangular mark, one that looked like a wedge. The signs were built up out of these marks, which we now call "cuneiform," (from the Latin, meaning "wedge-formed").

By 3100 B.C., at the end of the Uruk period, the Sumerians had a completely developed written language, the first in the world. The Egyptians, whose villages dotted the Nile River in northwestern Africa, 900 miles west of the Sumerian cities, heard of the system. They borrowed the idea, but in some ways improved on it. They used papyrus, sheets made out of the pith of a river reed, as a writing surface; something that was much less bulky and much more easy to handle than clay. They covered the papyrus with symbols much more attractive than the coarse cuneiform of the Sumerians.

The Egyptian symbols were carved on stone monuments and painted on the interior walls of tombs. These stayed in plain view, while the cuneiform-covered bricks remained hidden underground. It was therefore long thought that the Egyptians were the first to make use of writing. Now, however, the honor is given the Sumerians.

The existence of writing in Sumeria meant revolutionary changes in the social system. It increased the power of the priests still further, for they had the secret of writing; they could read the records and ordinary laymen could not.

The reason this was so was that learning to read was no easy task. The Sumerians never got beyond the notion of separate symbols for each basic word, and they ended with over two thousand different ideographs. This represented a serious memorizing problem.

To be sure, one could break words down into simple sounds and represent each of these sounds by a separate mark. Such sound-signs ("letters") need be only two dozen in number and could be put together to form any conceivable word. However, such a system of letters, or "alphabet," was not developed till many centuries after the Sumerian invention of writing, and then by Canaanites at the western end of the Fertile Crescent, and not by the Sumerians.

Writing strengthened the power of the king too, for he could put his own view of matters into writing and carve it upon monumental structures, together with carved scenes. The opposition would find it difficult to compete with this earliest written propaganda.

Business affairs were also made easier. Contracts could be preserved as written documents witnessed by priests. Laws could be placed in writing. Society grew more stable and orderly when the rules governing it were permanent instead of hidden in the uncertain memories of the leaders, and when these rules could be consulted by those affected.

It was probably in Uruk that writing first established itself; certainly the oldest written inscriptions yet found are in the ruins of that city. The prosperity and power that came with improved trade and commerce as the result of writing must have helped Uruk grow in size and magnificence. It was the most elaborate city the world of 3100 B.C. had yet seen, covering an area of nearly two square miles. It had a temple 260 feet long, 100 feet wide, and 40 feet high, that was probably the largest building in the world of that time.

Sumeria as a whole, blessed with writing, rapidly became the most advanced portion of Mesopotamia. The regions upstream, actually older as far as civilization was concerned, lagged behind and were forced to submit to the political and economic overlordship of the Sumerian kings.

One more consequence of writing is that it enables one to keep long and detailed records of events that can be passed down from generation to generation with little distortion. A listing of the names of kings; of rebellions, battles, and conquests; of natural disasters suffered or surmounted; even of dull statistics of temple stores or tax records — all tell us infinitely more than we can possibly learn from just studying surviving pottery or tools. It is from written records that we get what we call "history." Everything before that is "prehistoric."

With writing, therefore, it could be said that the Sumerians invented history.

THE FLOOD

From 3100 to 2800 B.C., there was the "Proto-literate" (or "early-writing") period, in which Sumeria flourished. One would suppose that since writing now existed we would know a great deal about that period. The truth is that we don't.

This is not because the language is unknown. The Sumerian language was deciphered in the 1930's and 1940's (as a result of a chain of circumstances I will come back to later in the book) by the Russian-American archaeologist, Samuel N. Kramer.

The trouble is that the records prior to 2800 B.C. are poorly preserved. Even the peoples who lived not long after 2800 B.C. seem to have had a dearth of records of the earlier period. At least, later records which describe events before that key date seem wildly legendary in character.

The reason can be put in a single word — flood. Those Sumerian documents which present a legendary view of history always cover the period "before the flood."

The Sumerians were less lucky with respect to river-flooding than the Egyptians. The Egyptian river, the Nile, floods every year, but rarely fluctuates widely in height. It rises among the

great lakes in east central Africa, and these act as a huge water
reservoir which serves to damp down flooding fluctuations.

The Tigris and Euphrates do not rise in lakes but in mountain springs. There is no reservoir, and floods can be disastrously high in years of much snow and sudden spring heat
waves. (Even as late as 1954, Iraq was badly flooded by the
rising rivers.)

Between 1929 and 1934, the English archaeologist, Sir
Charles Leonard Woolley, excavated the mound that marked
the ancient Sumerian city of Ur. This was at the site of an old
mouth of the Euphrates, just ten miles north of Eridu. There
he came across a layer of silt eleven feet thick, with no relics
of any sort in it.

He decided this was sediment laid down by a gigantic flood.
He estimated that flood to have been 25 feet deep and to have
covered a stretch of land 300 miles long and 100 miles wide —
virtually all the land between the rivers.

Things, however, may not have been quite so wildly disastrous. Flood can affect some cities and not others, for one city's
dikes may have just suffered a period of neglect, while another's
may hold, through the heroic and unremitting labor of its citizens. Thus, Eridu has no layer of silt equivalent to that in Ur.
Certain other cities which do have silt layers have them exist-
ing at times that are distinctly different from those of the layer
in Ur.

Nevertheless, there must have been one flood that was worse
than any other. Maybe it was the one that buried Ur, at least
for a time. Even if it did not destroy other cities as badly, the
economic disruption that resulted from the partial destruction
of the land must have sent Sumeria into a short dark age.

This super-flood, or Flood (we can use a capital F for it),
may have taken place about 2800 B.C. It and the disorders that
followed must have virtually wiped out city records and left
later generations helpless to do more than try to reconstruct the
history from what some remembered the records to have been.
Perhaps storytellers eventually seized the opportunity to make
up sagas on the basis of the few names and events remembered,
and thus substitute interesting drama for dull history.

For instance, the kings listed in later records as having reigned "before the Flood" are given absurdly long reigns. Ten of them are listed, and each is supposed to have reigned for tens of thousands of years.

We find traces of this in the Bible, for the early chapters of Genesis seem to have been based, in part, on Mesopotamian legend. Thus, the Bible lists ten patriarchs (from Adam to Noah) as having lived before the Flood. The Biblical writers could not, however, swallow the long reigns ascribed them by the Sumerians (or those who followed them). They restricted the age of these antediluvian patriarchs to less than a single thousand years. The most long-lived man in the Bible was Methusaleh, the eighth of these patriarchs, and he is listed as having lived only 969 years.

A Sumerian legend of the Flood grew up, which is the world's first known epic. Our most complete version dates from a time more than two thousand years after the Flood, but older scraps also survive and much of the epic can be reconstructed.

The hero is Gilgamesh (gil'guh-mesh), who is a king of Uruk, living some time after the Flood. He is a man of heroic bravery and accomplishments. Indeed, the adventures of Gilgamesh cause him to be referred to sometimes as the "Sumerian Hercules." It may even be that the legend (which became very popular in later centuries and must have spread throughout the ancient world) contributed to the Greek myths of Hercules and to some of the incidents in the *Odyssey*.

When a close friend of Gilgamesh died, the hero decided to avoid such a fate and began to seek the secret of eternal life. After a complicated search, enlivened with many incidents, he came upon Ut-napishtim who, at the time of the Flood, had built a large vessel in which he saved himself and his family. (It was he who, after the Flood, set up the sacrifice that pleased the famished gods so much.)

The Flood is here pictured as having been worldwide, which it may have been in effect, since to the Sumerians Mesopotamia was just about all the world that counted.

Ut-napishtim had not only survived the Flood but he had

also received the gift of eternal life. He directed Gilgamesh to
the whereabouts of a certain magic plant. If he ate that plant,
he would regain his youth permanently. Gilgamesh obtained
the plant but, before he could eat it, it was stolen by a serpent.
(Serpents, because of their ability to shed their old, faded skin
and appear in a bright, new one, were thought by many ancients to have the power of rejuvenation, and the Gilgamesh
epic explains this, among other things.)

The tale of Ut-napishtim is so like that of the Biblical tale
of Noah that most historians suspect that the latter was derived from the Gilgamesh epic. It is also possible that the serpent who seduced Adam and Eve and deprived them of eternal life may have been inspired by the serpent who deprived
Gilgamesh of that same gift.

WARFARE

The Flood was not the only kind of disaster Sumeria had to
face. There was also warfare.

There are signs that in the early centuries of Sumerian civilization the cities were separated by stretches of uncultivated
land and did not really impinge upon each other. There may
even have been a certain sympathy among the cities, a feeling
that the great enemy to be conquered was the erratic river, and
that they all faced that enemy together.

However, even before the Flood, the expanding Sumerian
city-states must have eaten up the empty land between them.
The lowest couple of hundred miles of the Euphrates was
packed solid with farmland by then, and population pressure
pushed each city-state to infringe as far as it could upon the
territory of its neighbor.

Under similar conditions, the contemporary Egyptians

formed a united kingdom and lived for centuries in peace under what is called "the Old Kingdom." * The Egyptians, however, were isolated, surrounded by sea, river cataracts, and desert. They had little reason to cultivate the art of war.

The Sumerians, on the other hand, exposed on two sides to the possible ravages of nomads, had to develop armies and did so. Their soldiers marched in ordered ranks and used donkey-drawn carts to carry supplies.

And once an army is developed to fight off nomads, there is the strong temptation to put it to good use during the intervals between nomad raids. Each party to a boundary dispute would therefore back its views with its army.

Perhaps the warfare before the Flood was not yet terribly bloody. Wooden spears with stone tips, and stone-tipped arrows were prime weapons. Stone edges could not be made very sharp nor could they be guarded against chipping and cracking on impact. Leather shields were very likely more than adequate against such weapons, and the usual battle may have had many blows and much sweating but, all things considered, few fatalities.

About 3500 B.C., however, methods were discovered for getting copper out of certain rocks and by 3000 B.C., it had been discovered that if copper is mixed with tin in the proper proportions, an alloy we now call "bronze" is formed. Bronze is a hard metal, which can be worked to a sharp edge and fine point. Furthermore, if blunted, it can easily be beaten sharp again.

Bronze still hadn't become common even at the time of the Flood, but it was enough to shift the balance in the perpetual battle of farmer versus nomad heavily in favor of the farmer. What bronze weapons existed could only be formed by an advanced technology, something well beyond the ability of the unsophisticated nomads. Until such time as nomads could be outfitted with metal weapons of their own, or learned some trick as good or better, the advantage rested with the city folk.

Unfortunately, beginning soon after 3000 B.C., the Sumerian

* See my book *The Egyptians* (Houghton Mifflin, 1967).

city-states used bronze weapons against each other, too, so that
the cost of war escalated (as it has escalated many times since).
All the cities were weakened as a result, for no one city could
permanently defeat its neighbors. If we can judge by the history of other, and better-known, systems of city-states (as, for
instance, those of ancient Greece), the weaker units invariably
allied themselves against any one city which seemed to be coming dangerously close to overall victory.

We might speculate that it was partly because of this chronic
warfare and its drain of the peoples' energy that the system
of dikes and canals was allowed to deteriorate. Perhaps that
was why the Flood was as extensive and damaging as it was.

Still, even through the disorganization that followed the
Flood, weapon superiority in the form of bronze must have
kept Sumeria safe from the nomads. At least, the Sumerians
are still in power in the centuries after the Flood.

Indeed, Sumeria eventually recovered from the Flood and
grew more prosperous than ever. Post-Flood Sumeria contained some thirteen city-states that divided among themselves
a cultivated area of 10,000 square miles — about equal to that
of the state of Vermont.

Yet the cities had not learned their lesson. Once recovery
set in, the dreary round of fighting without end began over
again.

According to what records we have, the most important of
the Sumerian cities immediately after the Flood was Kish,
which lay on the Euphrates some 150 miles upstream from Ur.

While Kish is a city of respectable antiquity, it had made no
unusual mark before the Flood. Its sudden rise to prominence
afterward would make it seem that the great cities downstream
had been temporarily washed out of action.

Kish's supremacy was short-lived, but as the first ruling city
after the Flood (and therefore the first city to rule during the
time of firm historical records) it gained a remarkable prestige.
In later centuries, Sumerian conquering rulers called themselves "King of Kish" to signify they ruled all of Sumeria, even
though Kish had by then become unimportant. (This is similar to the way in which the German kings of the Middle Ages

called themselves "Roman Emperors" even though Rome had long since fallen.)

Kish lost out because the cities downstream did recover at last. They were rebuilt; they collected their strength once more and resumed their customary roles. The Sumerian king-lists we have name the kings of various cities in related groups, which we refer to as "dynasties."

Thus, under the "First Dynasty of Uruk" that city replaced Kish and became preeminent some time after the Flood as it had been before. The fifth king of this First Dynasty was none other than Gilgamesh, who reigned about 2700 B.C., and who supplied the kernel of truth about which the mountain of fantasy in the famous epic was built. By 2650 B.C., Ur took its turn at leadership under its own First Dynasty.

A century later, about 2550 B.C., the name of a conqueror crops up. It is Eannatum, king of Lagash (lay'gash), a city forty miles east of Uruk.

Eannatum defeated the armies of both Uruk and Ur, or at least he claims to have done so on stone pillars he set up and marked with inscriptions. (Such pillars are called by the Greek term "steles.") It is not always possible, of course, to believe such inscriptions entirely, because they are the equivalent of modern "war communiqués" and are often exaggerated out of vainglory or to maintain morale.

The most impressive stele left behind by Eannatum is one that shows a close-ranked phalanx of men, each holding his spear straight forward, each wearing his helmet, and all marching over the prostrate bodies of their foes. Dogs and vultures are shown tearing at the dead, so that the stone relic is called the "Stele of the Vultures."

This stele commemorates a victory of Eannatum over the city of Umma (um'uh), twenty miles west of Lagash. The inscription on the stele claims Umma started the war by taking away certain boundary stones, but then there was never an official account of a war that didn't insist the other side started it, and we don't have Umma's account.

For a century after the reign of Eannatum, Lagash remained the strongest of the Sumerian cities. It grew luxurious, and beautiful metalwork, dating to this period, has been located in its ruins. It may have controlled as much as 1800 square miles of territory (half again as large as the state of Rhode Island), enormous for the time.

The last of the line of this First Dynasty of Lagash was Uru-kagina, who came to the throne about 2415 B.C.

He was an enlightened king concerning whom we can only wish we knew more. He seems to have felt there was, or ought to be, a feeling of kinship among all Sumerians, for an inscription he left behind contrasts the civilized city dwellers with the barbarous tribes outside. Perhaps he longed to set up a United Sumeria that could present an impregnable wall against the nomads, and develop within that wall in prosperity and peace.

Urukagina was a social reformer, too, for he attempted to reduce the power of the priesthood. The invention of writing had placed such power in the hands of the priests as to make them a positive danger to development. So much wealth was controlled by them, that not enough was left for the economic growth of the city.

Unfortunately, Urukagina met the fate of many reformer kings. His motives were good, but the conservative elements held the real power, and even the common people, whom the king tried to help, probably feared the priests and the gods more than they desired their own good.

Moreover, the priests, placing their interests above that of the city, did not hesitate to connive with rulers of other cities who, for a century, had been under the domination of Lagash and who were more than willing to try to gain dominance in their turn.

The city of Umma, which had once been crushed by Eannatum of Lagash, now had its chance for revenge. It was ruled by Lugalzaggesi, a capable warrior who slowly enlarged his power and dominion while Urukagina was embroiled with his attempt to reform Lagash. Lugalzaggesi took Ur and Uruk, and established himself as king of Uruk.

From Uruk as base, about 2400 B.C., Lugalzaggesi struck at

Lagash, defeated its demoralized army, and sacked the city. He was left in complete control of all of Sumeria.

No Sumerian had ever been as successful, militarily, as Lugalzaggesi. According to his own boastful inscriptions, he sent armies far north and west until they reached the Mediterranean. By now, population density in Mesopotamia was ten times what it was in the nonagricultural areas. A number of Sumerian cities, such as Umma and Lagash, had populations of from ten to fifteen thousand.

But the Sumerians had more than themselves to contend with now — militarily, at any rate. Sumerian culture had passed beyond the narrow bounds of Sumer itself and other peoples were ready to show themselves apt pupils.

2

THE AKKADIANS

THE FIRST EMPIRE

Some time before the Flood, a new wave of nomads had entered Mesopotamia. The Sumerians were quite capable of holding the newcomers away from their own main centers of population along the lower Euphrates. The nomads turned northward, therefore, and occupied the territory upstream from that of Sumeria itself. They moved into the area where the Euphrates and Tigris come to within twenty miles of each other, before moving apart again downstream to enclose fertile Sumeria.

The newcomers' point of origin was quite different from that of the Sumerians. Archaeologists could tell that from the languages, once these were deciphered.

The Sumerian language is made up of one-syllable words (like the modern Chinese) and does not resemble any other known language on earth. The language of the new arrivals consisted of polysyllabic words. Its structure was very much like that of a whole family of languages of which the best-known ancient representative was Hebrew and the best-known modern one is Arabic.

The various ancient peoples who spoke this group of languages were described in the Bible as having descended from Shem (or Sem, in the Latin version), one of the sons of Noah. In 1781, therefore, the German historian, August Ludwig von Schlözer suggested that these languages be called "Semitic."

Presumably, all the ancient peoples who spoke Semitic languages were descended from some single group among whom the original parent language ("proto-Semitic") had developed. Then, with time, and with the wanderings and separations of the descendant tribes, proto-Semitic had broken up into various dialects that eventually made up the member languages of the Semitic family. Where the original proto-Semitic may have been spoken is not certain, but the best guess seems to be that the homeland was Arabia.

It was from out of the Arabian fringe to the southwest, then, that the Semitic-speaking invaders entered Mesopotamia in 3000 B.C. as, a thousand years earlier, the Sumerians had entered from the mountainous fringe to the northeast.

(It is important to remember that the term "Semitic" refers only to the language and not to the race. It is extremely common to speak of peoples speaking Semitic languages as "Semites" and I will, on occasion, do so, too, but there is no such thing as a "Semitic race." People change their language easily without changing their physical characteristics. Thus American Negroes speak English and Haitian Negroes speak French, but that doesn't make them any the more racially akin to Europeans.)

The most important of the cities in the territory penetrated by the Semites was Kish. It must have been Sumerian to begin with, but the Semites gradually infiltrated and took it over.

For six centuries, through the Flood and beyond, the Semites remained largely in the background. Their territory was by no means as prosperous as that of Sumeria itself. The full system of Sumerian irrigation technique had not yet been adopted, and the lower level of productivity meant less wealth and power. (The force of Sumerian proficiency becomes apparent when one realizes that Sumerian farms in the time of the greatness of Lagash were fully as intensely productive as modern farms — though at a much greater cost in physical labor, of course.)

However, the Sumerian cities were burning themselves out, while the Semitic cities were slowly improving their own status. What the Semites needed chiefly, now, was some inspiring leader who could unite them and guide them to victory. Even while Lugalzaggesi was making himself supreme in Sumeria, that Semitic leader — the first great Semite in history — had come on the scene.

Eventually, this new leader gave himself the name of Sharrukin, but a later king of the same name is known as Sargon in English versions of the Bible. It is as Sargon (sahr'gon) then that this early Semite is known to us.

Sargon's fame led, in later centuries, to the growth of legends concerning him. One legend, in particular, dealt with the dangers he had to pass through as an infant. He was born (says the legend) to a woman of good birth, but his father was unknown. His mother, out of shame at having an illegitimate child, gave birth to him secretly and then tried to get rid of him before anyone found out.

She made a small boat out of reeds and smeared it with pitch to keep it waterproof. She put the baby in it and set it afloat on the river. He was found by a poor gardener and brought up lovingly, but in poverty. Finally, in adulthood his innate talents led him to leadership, conquest, and supreme power.

The tale of the foundling infant, saved by great and nearly miraculous luck, and growing to become a leader of men, is very common in legendary history, but that of Sargon is the earliest we know. Many followed it. In Greek myths, Oedipus and Perseus were so cast away. In Roman myths, this was true of Romulus and Remus. In Hebrew legends, Moses was so cast away, and his case is very similar to that of Sargon.

It is very possible that the great fame of the Sargon legend may have influenced the later tales, particularly that of Moses.

In adulthood, Sargon entered the service of the king of Kish and, through merit, rose to be the most trusted of all the king's subordinates. This trust, apparently, was misplaced. Where the king is weak and the prime minister strong, it has happened all too often in history that the king is overthrown and the prime minister becomes the new king. So it happened in Sargon's case.

It is very likely that Sargon deliberately adopted his name as a propaganda device when he became king. The name means "legitimate king" which is exactly what he was not. Even ancient men knew, apparently, that no matter how outrageous a lie may be, it will be accepted if stated loudly enough and often enough.

As a usurper, Sargon felt it would be better to establish a new capital which would start fresh with himself than remain in an old one filled with the monuments and memories of an older dynasty. He therefore founded the city of Agade (ah-gah'dee) somewhere in Semitic territory. He made the city famous, and he is known as "Sargon of Agade" in the history books.

The name of the city spread to the entire region, which is known to us as Akkad (ak'ad), an alternate form of Agade. The early Semites of this area are therefore known as Akkadians, and their language is called the Akkadian language.

The Akkadian cities, united under this strong man, could now turn against Sumeria. Lugalzaggesi was still king of Uruk, but he had reigned thirty years now. He was old and tired, and about 2370 b.c. he went down before Sargon. We have no details of the war, of course; only Sargon's proud inscription that he crushed his enemy and took all Sumer to the Persian Gulf.

The whole of Sumeria and Akkad was under a single rule now and indeed the two lands melted together completely. During Sargon's long reign, Akkad was completely Sumerianized. Irrigation technique was used to the full, and Akkad passed Sumerian culture still further upstream. In fact, one speaks of Sumero-Akkadian culture as one speaks of Graeco-Roman culture.

The Akkadians never gave up their own language, but they had no system of writing. This they had to borrow from the Sumerians. They adopted the cuneiform system even though that system, designed for Sumerian monosyllables, did not fit as well with Akkadian polysyllables.

The prestige of Sargon's conquest of Sumeria was such that Akkadian began to increase in importance, and the Sumerian language began a long decline that was to continue even during those periods when the Sumerian cities temporarily regained their political importance.

Sargon was even able to spread his dominion beyond Sumeria and Akkad. Sumerian colonists had penetrated far up the Tigris shortly after the Flood. Indeed, the disasters of the Flood may have driven survivors northward out of the scenes of devastation. There, on the Tigris, some 200 miles north of Akkad, colonists had founded the town of Ashur (ash'er.) It gave its name to the whole region of the upper Tigris, a region we know now by the Greek version of the name, Assyria.

Sargon controlled Assyria, as well as Sumeria and Akkad. All of Mesopotamia was his, and he is even supposed to have stretched his power westward from the upper Euphrates to the Mediterranean. This is not entirely certain, but it is at least more likely to have been true in his case than in that of his predecessor, Lugalzaggesi.

Sargon also absorbed a power center to the east of Sumeria. This was the land just north of the upper tip of the Persian Gulf and east of the Tigris. The Sumerians called the inhabitants of the land the "Elamtu" and the name of the land has entered our language as Elam (ee'lam).

Sargon chose the most subservient and least trouble-making of the Elamite cities and made its ruler his viceroy over the land. The city in question was Shushan, a town about 125 miles northeast of Lagash. This initiated the preeminence of the town which was to remain an important capital for two thousand years. We know it by the Greek version of its name — Susa (soo'zuh).

Elam had early accepted Sumerian culture and the cunei-

form system of writing. Even before the Flood it was quarreling and fighting with the Sumerian cities. It could not stand
before Sargon, however, and became part of his wide-spread-
ing Empire.

Sargon ruled the first true empire in the history of civilization, the first realm of any size to have been established by a
single man ruling over many peoples of diverse background.
At this time there were three other centers of civilization in the
world. These were along three other rivers: the Nile in Egypt,
the Indus in what is now Pakistan, and the Yellow River in
China. These other three civilizations were made up of peoples of homogeneous background and were not empires in the
sense that a single ruling group dominated a number of subject peoples.

An empire usually glows brightly while it exists. A ruling
group has little hesitation in appropriating the painfully gathered wealth of subject peoples. The surplus goods that would
ordinarily have been scattered through a dozen or more Sumerian city-states were gathered up into Sargon's capital. This
attained a size and level of luxury that was unmatched by anything previously. It is by the Imperial Capital that contempo-
raries (and posterity, too) judge an Empire, and its magnificence impresses them mightily and leads them to judge the
Emperor a great man and hero, even though it may all be
based on robbery, and though the provinces of the Empire
may be sunk in misery.

Sargon of Agade died about 2315 B.C., after a successful reign
of over half a century. Sumeria was in revolt when he died but
his older son, who succeeded, quickly suppressed the rising,
and the Akkadian Empire remained intact.

Under Sargon's grandson, Naram-Sin (na-ram'sin), who succeeded about 2290 B.C., the Akkadian Empire reached its peak.
Naram-Sin pushed its influence into Asia Minor, the great peninsula lying to the west of northern Mesopotamia; and
strengthened its hold on Elam, too.

Naram-Sin is best known today for a stele commemorating a
victory of his over a nomad horde in Elamite territory. The

stele shows him storming a mountain fortress, leading his men up the slopes, himself a calm and heroic figure twice life-size — his enemies surrendering and dying.

To our eyes, Naram-Sin's stele seems much superior, artistically, to the Stele of the Vultures, constructed two and a half centuries earlier. The Sumerians consistently depicted themselves as rather squat, plump fellows with round heads, large and staring eyes, and huge noses. They do not seem particularly attractive to us for all their intellectual and inventive prowess. However, it is hard to say how much of this representation is "true-to-life" and how much is merely artistic convention.

In any case, the Akkadian soldiers shown in Naram-Sin's stele are thinner, taller, and much more graceful in appearance (in our eyes at least) than the conventional pictures of the Sumerians.

THE CONQUERING NOMADS

Naram-Sin died about 2255 B.C., and almost at once the Akkadian Empire began to experience grave difficulties. Within a single generation it passed from the peak of its power to destruction, something that was to happen a number of times in later Mesopotamian history.

The ancient Empires, even when they seemed glorious and strong, always carried within themselves a kind of ticking time-bomb.

When a region consists of quarreling city-states, they may waste their wealth and energy in mutual warfare but each city-state has a fighting army and a tradition of patriotism. Often they will unite to fight off a common enemy from outside. Under such circumstances nomad invaders are often beaten.

But when an empire is formed, all strength is centralized at the capital and with the ruling people. The provinces are disarmed and deprived of their armies as far as possible.

One of two alternatives may then be found. The provinces, usually inhabited by subject peoples, remain sullen and unreconciled, and seize every opportunity to rebel against the central government. Such rebellions are usually unsuccessful and are put down harshly while the empire is strong, but every such rebellion, even when crushed, destroys some of the prosperity of the empire and bleeds a little of the strength of the rulers. Far from fighting enemies from without, revolting provincials are very apt to call in nomads, hoping to use their help against the central government.

If, on the other hand, the provinces are cowed into submission, or little by little deprived of their warlike tradition, they are in no position to fight off invaders when these arrive. And, still nourishing resentment against the rulers, they are quite apt to greet these newcomers as liberators rather than as enemies.

It follows that if an Empire declines even slightly from its peak, a vicious cycle sets in of sudden revolts, further weakening, additional revolts, calls for outside help and, very often in a single generation, the Empire is gone.

In the time of the Akkadian Empire, one prominent nomad tribe were the Guti, who lived in the Zagros Mountains, where once the Sumerians had dwelt.

A generation after Naram-Sin's death, the Guti saw their chance. The weak successors of the king were fighting among themselves for the throne, and the various provinces were in revolt and eager for nomad help. The Guti swept down, defeated the demoralized Akkadian army, took Agade and destroyed it about 2215 B.C. The Empire was theirs.

Agade was so thoroughly destroyed that, alone of all the Mesopotamian capitals, its site is still not known. Such a complete destruction bespeaks unusual fury. It makes one wonder if contingents of the subject peoples had not joined the Gutian army, and if it had not been Sumerian and Elamite soldiers who had made certain that not one brick remained on another to remind them of the long oppression.

If so, however, the subject peoples found the Guti a poor substitute. Under their crude rule, prosperity declined. They were too unused to the complexities of civilization to organize matters properly, particularly in connection with the canal network. This was allowed to sink into disrepair, with consequent famine and death resulting. A short "dark age" swept over the ancient Mesopotamian civilization.

Akkad bore the brunt of this, for it was Akkad that had been the center of the Empire and bore the prestige of its tradition, so that it was in Akkad that the Guti established their own center in place of the destroyed Agade.

Some of the Sumerian cities in the south took advantage of the safety of distance and purchased a certain amount of self-government by paying heavy tribute to the new rulers.

Uruk got along under its Fourth Dynasty and Ur under its Second Dynasty. The most remarkable ruler of the Gutian period was, however, the governor of Lagash, Gudea (goo-day'uh). Under him, about 2150 B.C., Lagash had a virtual golden age. The city was no longer the conquering and victorious one of Eannatum's time, three and a half centuries before, but it was all the better for that. Lagash flourished in peace, not dreaming of conquest.

Gudea was a priest as well as a governor, of course, and was particularly interested in temples. He beautified those that already existed and built fifteen new ones. He so impressed his people with his piety that after his death he was deified, and worshiped as a god.

Art flourished under him, and the sculptors of Lagash learned to handle a very hard rock called diorite, obtained from abroad. The figures were brought to a high and beautiful polish. The most famous statue of this sort is one of Gudea himself. It is about a foot and a half high and shows Gudea seated with his hands clasped over his abdomen (a Sumerian artistic convention, denoting pious reverence) and a quiet expression on his handsome, though large-nosed, face.

The statues are covered with inscriptions that are an important source of Sumerian history. Indeed, it was the discovery of the palace of Gudea toward the end of the nineteenth century that first gave modern man the hint that the Sumerians had once existed.

It is rare, though, for nomad rule over a civilized Empire to endure long. The luxuries of civilization are very attractive and seductive to those who have known only the rough life of the nomad. Even if the original conquerors scorn the luxury as decadent, their children will succumb. The nomads cease being nomads.

The crude Gutian warlords quickly became cultivated kings in this way. They probably even strove to become more Akkadian than the Akkadians, for they had a nomad ancestry to live down. Thus, the nomad rule ends by absorption.

Frequently, though, such absorption is not enough. Even though the nomads grow civilized, they must always contend with the dislike of the people they rule. Those who think back on many centuries of civilization resent the nomad ancestry of their rulers. The fact that the nomads are in the driver's seat by right of conquest makes them resented all the more. Consequently, when the nomad dynasty softens and grows lax, and when their army is no longer the hard-fighting group of roughnecks it once was, they get thrown out.

THE CITY OF ABRAHAM

The Guti lasted only about a century. About 2120, they were expelled from Mesopotamia. The actual liberator seems to have been the ruler of Uruk, which was now under its Fifth Dynasty. He may have acted in alliance with Ur but, if so, the ruler of Ur rapidly displaced his ally and was dominant by 2113 B.C.

This ruler of Ur, Ur-Nammu, was the first king of Ur's Third Dynasty, and for a century, the Sumerians showed a last gleam of greatness. Under the Third Dynasty of Ur, all of Mesopotamia was united in an Empire as large as the Akkadian had been, but one that was commercial rather than military.

Ur-Nammu himself was perhaps the greatest of his line. Under him, the laws of the land were reduced to writing. It is very likely that this was done before him; it is hard to suppose, for instance, that Sargon of Agade would not have done it in the course of his long reign. The fact is, though, that nothing survives of such earlier codes; Ur-Nammu's is the oldest we have. What remnants survive are the oldest written laws in history.

Those remnants we have seem rather enlightened, too. Ancient laws tend to punish by mutilation (an eye for an eye and a tooth for a tooth), but Ur-Nammu's code stressed money compensation instead. Perhaps this was a natural view in a commercial society.

Sumerian brickwork reached a peak in the century of Ur's Third Dynasty. Ur built an enormous ziggurat, the largest Sumeria had ever seen. What is left of it has been uncovered in the excavations at the site where once Ur stood, and the remnant is still impressive. It is about 260 feet long by 175 feet wide and its lowermost walls are eight feet thick.

Two stages are left in the ruin with its peak sixty feet high. When intact, though, it is believed there were three stages with an overall height of some 120 feet.

Also found on the site of Ur are literally tens of thousands of clay tablets covered with inscriptions. One might think that such a find would tell us a great deal about the history of the country, but they are not those kinds of records. They are records of bookkeeping items and business transactions. It is as though some civilization of the far-distant future came across stacks and stacks of papers in the ruins of New York and found they were all old receipts and bills of sale.

Of course, this shouldn't be sneered at, either. A great deal about the daily life of a people can be told from such drab records. You can get notions of the kinds of food people ate, the sort of businesses they conducted, the extent of their trade and what they bought and sold. You can even tell the extent of an empire by taking note of the places from whose ruins similar documents are uncovered. When the documents are dated, they are usually dated as a certain year in the reign of a certain king, and from this you can figure out the names of the different kings, the order in which they reigned, and how long each one reigned. When dates stop mentioning the kings of Ur, you can tell that Ur's power had been broken in that particular place.

For its power did break and by 2030 B.C. it came virtually to an end. For a generation it maintained itself as a city-state, at least, but then came the final blow. An Elamite army took advantage of the anarchy of Mesopotamia and of a famine within Ur itself to beat down the proud city's defenses and occupy it in 2006 B.C. They took prisoner the last king of the Third Dynasty, Ibbi-Sin.

Temporarily, Elam, which had been a conquered province of the Akkadian Empire, found itself the strongest power in Mesopotamia. That this was so was partly because the city-states of the region were now quarreling with each other and were back at the game of war.

In what had once been Sumeria, two city-states were of prime importance: Isin and Larsa.

Isin (is'in) was the farther upstream, just south of Nippur. For a century after Ur's fall, Isin was the most important city-state in the south. Toward the end of this period, about 1930 B.C., one of its rulers codified the laws of the city and recorded them in the Sumerian language. Parts of this code survive.

Larsa is farther south, just a dozen miles downstream from Uruk. By 1924 B.C., Larsa, which was under Elamite influence, had defeated Isin, and then experienced its own century of greatness.

Farther north were two other important city-states. There was Ashur and farther downstream on the Tigris, Eshnunna. Fragments of a third code of law put out by a ruler of Eshnunna have also been found.

But these city-states were not really Sumerian in the old fashion. The Sumerians as a ruling class had come to an end with Ur. In the period following 2000 B.C., the ruling classes of

the cities that had once been Sumerian, spoke Akkadian. Mesopotamia became entirely Semitic in language and was to remain so for fifteen centuries.

Sumerian did not die all at once. It persisted for a while in
that most conservative of all institutions, religion. It remained
as a "dead language" used in religious ritual, much like Latin
today.

With their language, the Sumerians themselves faded away.
They were not killed or slaughtered; they just stopped thinking
of themselves as Sumerians. The sense of nationality slowly
vanished and by 1900 B.C., none remained.

For two thousand years, the Sumerians had led the way.
They had invented wheeled transport, astronomy, mathemat-
ics, commercial enterprise, large-scale brickwork, and writing.
They might almost be said to have invented civilization.

Now they were gone. Seven centuries before the Trojan
War, eleven centuries before a tiny village named Rome was
founded, the Sumerians, already hoary with tradition — were
gone. Their very existence was forgotten until the great ar-
chaeological digs of the closing decades of the nineteenth century.

And yet a trace remained. In one great book coming down
from ancient times — the Bible — shadowy traces of the Sumerians are to be found. One passage points specifically to the
period of the Third Dynasty of Ur.

In this last century of Sumerian existence, say about 2000
B.C., the coming death was clear. The loss of empire, the famine, the Elamite occupation were so many deadly blows. Many
enterprising men of Ur must have felt that there was no longer
a future in that once-great city and set out to journey abroad
in search of better fortune elsewhere.

One such journey is mentioned in the Bible: "And Terah
took Abram his son, and Lot . . . and Sarai his daughter-in-
law . . . and they went forth . . . from Ur . . . to go into
the land of Canaan" (Genesis 11:31). They traveled the length
of the Fertile Crescent, northwestward to the peak of the arch,
then southward to the western end. Abram eventually changed

his name to Abraham and, according to the legend, was the ancestor of the Israelites.

The Bible goes on to describe a raid conducted by a Mesopotamian army against the city-states of Canaan, and, in doing so, makes it seem that Abraham's time is that which immediately follows the fall of Ur:

"And it came to pass in the days of Amraphel king of Shinar, Arioch king of Ellasar, Chedorlaomer king of Elam, and Tidal king of nations; that these made war . . ." (Genesis 14:1-2).

It is clear from the prominence given him in the rest of this Biblical passage that Chedorlaomer led the coalition, and it was in this period of its history only — the century following Ur's fall — that Elam was the leading power in a fragmented Mesopotamia. The city of Ellasar, another member of the coalition, is generally taken to represent Larsa, and it was only at this time that Larsa was prominent.

"Tidal king of nations" seems to have been a rather minor princeling, and the great interest in this passage lies in the identity of Amraphel, king of Shinar. Taken literally, it would seem to refer to someone who ruled all the Mesopotamian region (for Shinar is Sumeria), but this does not fit the situation as it would have been then. Indeed, if Amraphel were really the ruler of all Mesopotamia it would be he, not Chedorlaomer, who would head the coalition.

The answer to this puzzle involves a new group of invaders who had entered Mesopotamia and who must now be considered.

3

THE AMORITES

ENTER BABYLON

The new invaders arrived from the west and south, as the Akkadians had done a thousand years before. They spoke a Semitic language very much like Akkadian and soon adopted the Akkadian version of the tongue once they settled down in Mesopotamia. By this kinship of language they made themselves natives in time and did not remain the hated "foreigners" the Guti had.

These Semitic newcomers were called "Amurru" in the Mesopotamian records and there is some dispute as to whether the word means "westerners" or "nomads." In either case, we know them as Amorites.

About 2000 B.C., with the glorious days of Ur over and Sumeria beginning its final decline, the Amorites drifted out of the desert into the Fertile Crescent, east and west.

In the west, they colonized the lands adjoining the Mediterranean Sea, mingling with the inhabitants of Canaan (who also spoke a Semitic language). Indeed, the Canaanites are often referred to as Amorites in the Bible, as when God is described as telling Abraham it is not the time to inherit Canaan "for the iniquity of the Amorites is not yet full" (Genesis 15:16).

In the east the Amorites entered what had been Akkad, and it was they, rather than the fading Sumerians, who were responsible for the vigor of the city-states between 2000 and 1800 B.C. They took over the town of Larsa, for instance, which flourished under Amorite rule.

The Amorites also took over a small Akkadian town named Bab-ilum (Akkadian for "gate of god") and made it their own. In the Hebrew of the Bible, the name of the town becomes Babel (bay'bel).

Babel had not, until then, made much of a mark on the Mesopotamian world. It was located on the Euphrates, just a little to the west of Kish and must have been very much in the shadow of that great city. As Kish declined, however, Babel had a chance to shine more brightly.

The Amorites achieved their most remarkable early success farther north, however. They took over Ashur in 1850 B.C. and found there a rich prize indeed. The northern arch of the Fertile Crescent was now pulsing with civilization, and toward the close of the period of the Third Dynasty of Ur, merchants from Ashur had penetrated deep into Asia Minor. Now with the governing hand of Ur removed, Ashur was left to itself and it grew into a rich trading city of proud merchants.

In 1814 B.C., an Amorite outlaw, possibly a member of the ruling family, made himself ruler of Ashur. His name was Shamshi-Adad I (sham'shee-ah'dahd), and he established a dynasty that, through numerous upheavals, was to last for more than a thousand years. Under Shamshi-Adad I, Ashur controlled the full width of northern Mesopotamia, for the new monarch took the city of Mari, 150 miles southwest on the Euphrates. This was another trade center, newly grown rich, close to the growing towns of the western half of the Fertile

Crescent. The spreading realm of this, Ashur's first period of greatness, was an earnest of things to come, the first appearance of a redoubtable "Assyria" on the world map.

If we return now to the puzzle of "Amraphel king of Shinar" mentioned in the previous chapter, it must be, then, that he was one of the Amorite rulers in Mesopotamia. — But which?

It seems most likely that he was one of the early Amorite chieftains in Babel. He was called "king of Shinar" (that is, king of Mesopotamia) because Babel did eventually rule over all the land and its glory was read backward in time to the earlier ruler.

In 1792 B.C. the sixth of the Amorite line, presumably a descendant of Amraphel, succeeded to the rule in Babel. He was Hammurabi (hahm"oo-rah'bee). The situation, on his succession, did not seem promising for the new monarch, nor did it seem at all likely that the future lay with Babel.

To the north was Shamshi-Adad I, forging a strong Assyria. To the south, the danger seemed even worse. Two years before, in 1794 B.C., Rim-Sin, who had ruled Larsa ever since 1822 B.C., finally managed to inflict a last defeat on the city of Isin and united the lower reaches of the river valley under his rule.

Fortunately for Hammurabi, his enemies were not united, and they were both growing old. Hammurabi was blessed with both military and diplomatic ability and, what's more, he was young and patient, and could afford to wait, while painstakingly allying himself with one power to beat another. Sooner or later, someone would die.

It was Shamshi-Adad I of Ashur who did. He died in 1782 B.C., and under his less forceful successor, the Assyrian power declined. With pressure from the north decreased, Hammurabi turned south. In 1763 B.C. Hammurabi smashed the aged Rim-Sin, and all the south was his. He moved northward and in 1759 B.C. had taken Mari and put it to the sack. Ashur avoided quite so drastic a fate. After some years of resistance, it submitted, in 1755, to serving Hammurabi as tributary. Its ruler retained his throne and the dynasty of Shamshi-Adad survived to be the plague of the rest of Mesopotamia in times to come.

Hammurabi died in 1750 B.C., but for the last five years of his life he ruled an Empire as large as Naram-Sin's had been six centuries before.

The glory of Babel truly began with the reign of Hammurabi, for he kept it his capital and ruled his wide realm from it. It grew to be a mighty metropolis that was to be the greatest city of western Asia for fourteen centuries. We know it best today by the Greek version of its name — Babylon (bab'ih-lon).

The region that had once been Sumeria and Akkad took its name thereafter from its great city, and was called Babyloni? throughout the remaining centuries of ancient times.

THE CHANGING OF THE GODS

The triumph of Babylon on earth was reflected in a similar triumph in the Mesopotamian heaven.

The Sumerians, as was common among ancient peoples, worshiped gods. How else could the caprices of nature be explained? How could the existence of the universe otherwise be accounted for?

Presumably each tribe had some one god felt to be a symbol and representation of the tribe. There would be a close connection between a tribe and its god. Provided the god were properly worshiped with suitable rites, it would care for its people, keep the environment favorable, help defeat the tribe's enemies (and their god).

Once a group of tribes settled down in close proximity, however, and adopted a common culture, there would clearly be numerous such gods. To keep the peace, one might give them all some weight and establish a "pantheon," a group of many gods related to each other. Usually, by the time a people make their way onto the stage of human history in noticeable fashion, such a pantheon already exists.*

With many gods, it was natural to introduce specialization.

* The Israelites, who were soon to enter upon the stage, were unusual among the peoples of the time in refusing to set up such a pantheon. At least, those among them who insisted on but a single God won out in the end.

One god might be in charge of the rain, another in charge of the river, and so on. Storytellers and poets could weave together tales that would describe and explain the universe in allegorical ᵗerms. What we call mythology was thus the ancient attempt at science. We still puzzle over the same problems today — the creation of the universe and the pattern of the weather — but we use different tools and techniques to find the answer.

The simplest and broadest division of labor is to place one god in charge of the land (or underworld), one in charge of the waters (the salt sea or the fresh rivers), and one in charge of the air (or the sky above.) Generally, it was the god of the sky who was the chief god, for the sky encompassed both land and water, and it was from the sky that the rain fell (and the thunderbolt darted).

In the old Greek myths, which involve the pantheon best known to modern westerners, the three sons of Cronos divided the universe among themselves. Zeus took the sky, Poseidon the sea, and Hades the underworld, and it was Zeus who was the chief god. The only explanation we have is the mythological one that it was Zeus who led the rebellion against their father, Cronos. The earthly facts behind that explanation are lost in the prehistory of the Greeks.

Among the Sumerians, there was a similar tripartite division among three major gods. Anu was the god of the sky, Enlil the god of the earth, and Ea the god of the fresh, life-giving water. Anu was, apparently, the chief god among the Sumerians, at least in a later stage of their history.

The mythological reason is found in the Sumerian story of the Creation. This deals (as many such creation myths do) not with the formation of the universe out of nothing, but with the establishment of an ordered universe out of a disordered chaos.

In the Sumerian myth, chaos was represented as a primordial goddess named Tiamat. She, apparently, represented the dark, destructive sea, with its chaotic tumbling waters that seemed so dreadful to a primitive people without a seafaring technology. In order for the universe to be born, she had to be defeated. (Or perhaps this represented the historical fact that the river had to be tamed by way of a canal system.)

In the Sumerian form of the myth, it must have been Anu who finally advanced against Tiamat, defeated her, and out of her body constructed the universe. As reward for this victory, he would naturally be granted rulership over the gods.

Here it is possible to speculate over the historical facts that lay behind the myth. Despite the existence of the pantheon, each Sumerian city retained some favorite god as a special patron. (This was somewhat in the fashion of the Athenians who considered Athena the patron goddess of Athens.)

Enlil was the god particularly worshiped in Nippur, and Ea was the patron god of Eridu. These were the two chief Sumerian cities of the Ubaid period, before the invention of writing, and it was only natural that these two gods therefore became of major importance. Perhaps one or the other was originally the chief god.

At the close of the Ubaid period, however, it was Uruk which advanced to the fore; it was in Uruk that writing was invented; and it was perhaps Uruk which led Sumeria right up to the Flood. Uruk's god was Anu, and it was Anu who was established as chief god firmly enough, thanks to writing, for this to endure even when other cities took their turn at hegemony.

When the Akkadians entered Mesopotamia, they brought their own gods with them — gods that we can identify by the fact that they bear Semitic names. These gods were permitted into the Sumerian pantheon, but in the lower echelons. They included Sin, god of the moon; Shamash, god of the sun; and Ishtar, goddess of the planet Venus (and of love and beauty as well).

In some cases, Sumerian cities adopted one or another of these Akkadian gods, presumably as Akkadian language and influence grew more important following the deeds of Sargon of Agade. Thus, Sin became the chief god of Ur (the name has no connection with our word "sin," by the way), and Ishtar was particularly worshiped in Uruk. The people of Uruk, to account for this innovation, explained that Ishtar was the daughter of Anu, and this relationship entered the official mythology.

It was the custom for the people of Mesopotamia (as well as of other peoples) to incorporate the names of gods in their own names. This served to indicate piety and, possibly, to bring good luck, since the gods were presumably not immune to flattery. Among the historical characters we have mentioned, we find Ea in Eannatum of Lagash, Sin in Naram-Sin of Agade, and Rim-Sin of Larsa. Shamash is to be found in Shamshi-Adad I of Assyria, which also includes the name of Adad, a storm god. These names have meanings, of course (Naram-Sin means "beloved of Sin," and Rim-Sin means "bull of Sin"), though it is not always easy to tell what the meanings are.

(We are not so free with divine names ourselves, but there are examples. From the Latin, we have Amadeus, which means "love of God"; from the Greek, we have Theodore or Dorothy, which means "gift of God"; from German, we have Gottfried, which means "peace of God.")

The Amorites, when they took over Mesopotamia, did not bring in a clutch of gods as the Akkadians had done. Their culture was too similar to the Akkadian, perhaps, and in adopting the Akkadian version of the Semitic language, they adopted the Akkadian version of the names of the gods as well. Their own national god, Amurru (representing the nation in his very name), remained minor.

The Amorite dynasty in control of Babylon, for instance, adopted the patron god of that city as their own. His name was Marduk (mahr'dook) and he was looked upon as a sun god. The town of Borsippa (bawr-sip'uh), just south of Babylon, and early under its domination, had Nabu as its patron god. He, too, was adopted by the dynasty, but in a subordinate position. Nabu was described as the son of Marduk in the myths.

As long as Babylon was an inconsiderable city, Marduk remained an inconsiderable god. However, when Hammurabi made Babylon the greatest city in all of Mesopotamia, a process began in which Marduk had to become the greatest god. Slowly, the priesthood tampered with the legends (they "rewrote history" so to speak) until Marduk emerged as the great hero of the creation myth.

The records we have of that myth are post-Hammurabi and give the later version. In this version, Anu does indeed go forth against Tiamat, but his heart fails him and he backs away.

It is Marduk (pictured as a son of Ea, a concession to the fact that he was a comparative late-comer and was not featured in the earliest myths) who stepped into the breach. Fearlessly, he encountered Tiamat and killed her. He created the universe and he therefore rules it, and became lord over gods and men. He was sometimes called Bel-Marduk or simply Bel, for Bel means "Lord." Second in command was Nabu.

For a thousand years and more, while Babylon remained supreme in the lower valley of the Tigris and Euphrates, Marduk remained supreme in the Babylonian heavens.

Thus, in a passage in the Bible, written some twelve centuries after the time of Hammurabi, when the fall of Babylon is predicted, that fall is given in terms of the gods it still worships: "Bel boweth down, Nebo stoopeth" (Isaiah 46:1). Nebo is, of course, the Hebrew form of Nabu.

Yet Marduk did not rule everywhere in Mesopotamia. In the north, the Assyrians clung grimly to their own national god, Ashur, for whom their chief city was named.

THE PILLAR OF THE LAW

Hammurabi was an efficient and capable ruler and was more than a mere conqueror. He organized his realm carefully, was an arduous worker, and is best known to us today for his careful codification of the laws.

He was by no means the first Mesopotamian to reduce laws to writing. As mentioned earlier, Ur-Nammu of Ur had produced such a written code over two centuries before Hammurabi. Rulers of Eshnunna and of Isin had done likewise. Undoubtedly, written law-codes existed earlier still — which unfortunately do not survive.

What makes Hammurabi's law-code remarkable is that it is the oldest we have almost in entirety.

The Code of Hammurabi was inscribed on an eight-foot-high stele of hard diorite. It was clearly intended to be permanent, and in a sense it was, for we have it today still (in pretty good shape) some three and a half millennia after the time of Hammurabi.

The stele is topped by a relief which showed Hammurabi standing humbly before the sun god, Shamash, who sits on a throne on a mountaintop with his shoulders aflame. (The situation is similar to that in which Moses, five centuries later, is described in the Bible as going up Mr. Sinai to receive the lawcode from God.)

Down along the face of the stele are twenty-one columns of finely written cuneiform, outlining nearly three hundred laws that were to govern men's actions, and guide the king and his officials in dispensing justice. Undoubtedly, the code leaned heavily on the laws worked out by the various Sumerian cities and, as far as possible, represented the customs that had slowly grown up over the centuries.

The stele originally stood in the town of Sippar (sih-pahr′) some thirty miles upstream from Babylon. Its patron god was Shamash, the lawgiver in this case, and the stele was placed in the city's impressive temple to Shamash. It was evidence to all men that this was the law as given by the gods. It could be consulted by anyone, who need not fear that judges, out of faulty memory or hidden bribes, would pervert that law.

The stele containing the Code of Hammurabi was not, however, located in the ruins of Sippar. In the centuries after Hammurabi, the land was to have its share of misfortune and disaster. An invading Elamite army eventually plundered the city and carried away the stele with them as spoil. It remained in Elam's capital, Susa, permanently. It was still there, in Susa's ruins, in 1901, when a French archaeologist, Jacques de Morgan, uncovered it and brought it back to the west.

The Code tells us much of the social system of the time. Freemen were divided into nobles and peasants. There were slaves, too, an institution that was universal throughout ancient times. (The justice of slavery was never questioned in ancient times, not even in the Old or the New Testament.)

The inequality of man held even down to fine details. Thus, there was a greater penalty for harming a noble than a peasant and a greater penalty for harming a peasant than a slave. On the other hand — fair is fair — a nobleman had to pay a heavier punishment than a peasant for committing equal crimes and had to be responsible for heavier payments to the temple.

Slaves were branded on the forehead and were forbidden to hide or mask that brand. On the other hand, wanton cruelty in the treatment of slaves was forbidden, and methods were devised whereby they might buy their freedom. On the whole, slaves were better treated and had more protection in Amorite Babylon than in Roman times, two thousand years later.

The Code is strongly business-oriented, which again shows the commercial basis for Mesopotamian civilization. It upholds the absolute sanctity of contracts, and carefully stipulates the legal manner in which property can be owned, sold, or transferred. It regulates trade, profits, and hiring practices. It guards against short weight, shoddy goods, inferior workmanship, and business frauds generally.

Marriages, too, were treated as a contractual arrangement, and provisions were made for divorce and for the adoption of children. While a man might divorce his wife at will, he had to return the dowry she brought him, when he did so (and that probably kept a number of husbands from divorcing their wives for trivial reasons). In fact, women and children were expressly protected in the Code.

It dealt also with the vital matter of irrigation. Men were responsible for their own part of the dikes and ditches and could be made to pay heavy damages where flooding was traced to their neglect.

The Code also dealt with crimes of passion and of neglect. Mutilations were common as punishment, more common than in the older code of Ur-Nammu and this was a step backward. If a son struck a father, the hand that dealt the blow was cut off. If a carpenter built a house that collapsed and killed the owner, the carpenter was put to death. However, there were allowances for accident. If a murderer could present evidence that the killing was unintentional and the result of accident, he could get off with a fine.

The Code goes into detail with respect to the medical pro-

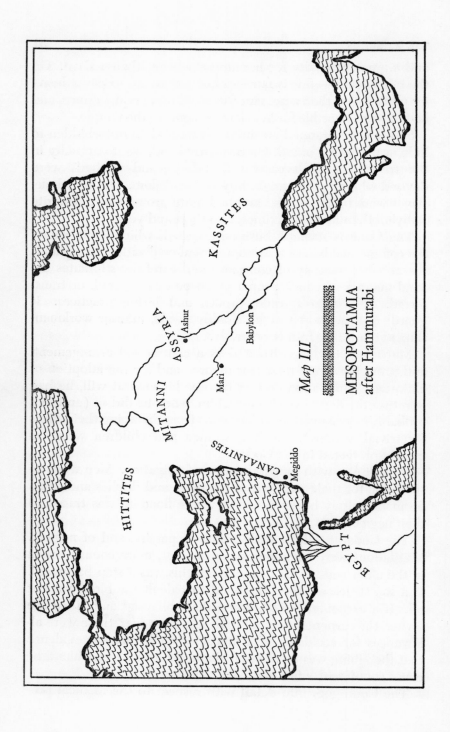

Map III

MESOPOTAMIA
after Hammurabi

KASSITES

ASSYRIA

Ashur

Babylon

MITANNI

Mari

HITTITES

CANAANITES

Megiddo

EGYPT

fession, which seems to have already been highly developed in 1800 B.C. The fees and ethics of physicians and surgeons were regulated. A clumsy surgeon could lose the hand that had guided the knife.

From the Code and from other evidence of the time, it seems clear that personal morality was at least as high in Babylon as among ourselves. The view of Babylon as a particular den of vice stems chiefly from the Bible. The Biblical writers were, of course, enemies of Babylon and can scarcely be expected to present a fair picture.

Aside from religious prejudice, there is also the fact that large cities are almost always morally suspect to inhabitants of less urbanized areas (think of the small-town views of cities like New York and Paris, for instance).

Then, too, Babylon — and virtually all other ancient cultures — participated in fertility rites as part of their organized religion. Ritualized sexual experiences were considered to contribute to the fertility of the soil. The Jews who, virtually alone among ancient peoples, maintained a strictly puritanical view toward sex, failed to recognize the religious motivation behind such rites and viewed it as vile immorality. This view has come down to us and unfairly colors our view of the ancient pagan cultures.

Under Hammurabi's able rule, art and literature flourished. Hundreds of letters remaining from his time show the elaborate administrative network he set up and closely supervised. His work endured. His dynasty did not last long and Babylonia was to feel the weight of foreign rule, but the system set up by the great king survived, with modifications, for fifteen hundred years.

THE COMING OF THE HORSE

By the time of the Amorite take-over in Mesopotamia after 2000 B.C., bronze had been in reasonably common use for a thousand years. It was no longer the decisive factor it had once been. Knowledge concerning it was widespread now over all the Fertile Crescent and beyond. Nomadic tribes could undoubtedly obtain their share of such weapons (as North American Indians were able to obtain rifles even though they could not make them themselves).

The balance of power, which had been in favor of civilization, slowly evened, but still not entirely. Organization counted. The Amorite tribes could penetrate Mesopotamia after the Elamite invasions and had weakened the city-states sufficiently, but the nomadic victory had been comparatively slow. It was a seeping inward, rather than a violent overthrow.

Meanwhile, however, a revolution was taking place somewhere beyond the borders of civilization, possibly in the broad steppes north of the Black Sea and the Caucasus Mountains. A new weapon was in the making that was to revolutionize warfare as sharply as bronze had done, but this time it was to swing the balance far in the direction of the nomad and against the city-dweller.

Until 2000 B.C., the animals that had been used for pulling weights were oxen and donkeys. The ox was easy to yoke by means of its strong horns, but it was lumbering, stupid, and slow. The donkey was more intelligent, but it was small and it could not pull the heavy, solid-wheeled carts rapidly.

Animal transport could not be used in warfare with any great success therefore. Armies consisted of masses of foot soldiers, who lumbered into each other, wielding their spears and swords until one or the other broke and ran. The carts could serve only as a ceremonial means to keep the ruler and other military leaders from walking, or to carry arms and supplies.

Donkey-drawn carts were the best means of long-distance transport available, and this served, but inefficiently, to keep the communications of the Akkadian or Amorite Empires in operation. The short-lived nature of these empires is probably the best evidence of the inefficiency of the communications.

And then, somewhere about 2000 B.C., a fleet beast of the steppes was tamed — the wild horse. It was much larger and stronger than the donkey and it ran like the wind. At first, though, it seemed useless for transport. It had no horns to use in harnessing, and the methods of harness first attempted forced the horse to pull against its windpipe so that he half-throttled himself. At first, therefore, the horse may have been used primarily as a food animal.

Then, some time before 1800 B.C., someone devised a method of using the horse for specialized light traction. A cart was made as light as possible. It became scarcely more than a small platform on two large wheels, a platform just large enough to hold a man. Even the wheels were lightened, without loss of strength, by being made spoked rather than solid.

A horse, or horses, pulling so light a load could run fleetly, much faster than a foot soldier. With only two wheels, the chariot was as maneuverable, almost, as the horse itself, and could skid into a new direction with little trouble.

It was the nomad who learned to use the horse and chariot, and for a good long time it remained strictly a nomad device. The people of the cities lacked the animal in the first place, or the space required for training in this new kind of movement.

The civilized peoples found to their horror that the nomad raids had suddenly multiplied many-fold in effectiveness, for a body of charioteers would come driving in fiercely, striking from here and then from there, impossible to stop or avert. The psychological effect of the plunging horses and their great speed must have broken the spirit of many a band of peasant foot soldiers even before actual contact was made.

The whole Fertile Crescent lay helpless under the thundering hooves of this new kind of army. The first horsemen included a group of tribes known to us now as the Hurrians, who descended upon the northern arch of the Fertile Crescent from the foothills of the Caucasus, in the century following the death of Hammurabi.

The territory that Shamshi-Adad I of Assyria had conquered was torn away by the horsemen and a series of principalities were established there. Slowly, these coalesced, and by 1500 B.C. they made up a unified kingdom called Mitanni (mih-tan'ee) that stretched from the upper Euphrates to the upper Tigris. The very heart of Assyria about the city of Ashur maintained itself under its old dynasty, but it was tributary to

Mitanni, which was now one of the great powers of the civilized world.

The Hurrian invaders made their power felt far beyond the confines of Mitanni. The turmoil that spread at their approach widened in ripples as peoples were uprooted and were hurled along ahead of the charioteers. The western part of the Fertile Crescent seethed, and Hurrian influence was strongly felt in Canaan even before Hammurabi's death.

The Bible refers once or twice to a group of people living in southernmost Canaan — "And the Horites in their Mount Seir unto el-Paran" (Genesis 14:6) — and it is thought now that these Horites, or "Horim" in Hebrew, are the Hurrians.

Hurrian influence passed beyond Canaan, too. A motley group of raiders consisting of Amorites as well as Hurrians burst into Egypt. The Egyptians called them "Hyksos." Since the Egyptians had no horse-drawn vehicles, any more than the Mesopotamians had had, they could not face the newcomers. Their confused armies retreated, and the whole northern half of their kingdom was lost, and remained lost for a century and a half.

Asia Minor, meanwhile, was being penetrated by another group of northerners acquainted with the horse-and-chariot technique. These are termed the Hatti in Mesopotamian records and are apparently the people called Hittites in the Bible. When they first entered Asia Minor, they found its eastern reaches deeply penetrated by Assyrian merchants. The Assyrians retreated, however, as the Hittites advanced. Immediately after Hammurabi's death, the Hittites spread rapidly and by 1700 B.C., they controlled the eastern half of Asia Minor and were at that stage of their history called the "Old Kingdom." They adopted the ways of civilization, accepted the cuneiform writing system, and adapted it to their language.

The Hurrians and Hittites, coming from the north, did not speak the Semitic tongues that had originated in Arabia to the south. The Hurrian language does not have clear relationships to other languages, but the Hittite language has the kind of grammatical structure associated with almost all the languages of modern Europe and of parts of modern Asia, even as far east as India. The whole family of these languages is known, now, as "Indo-European."

At the upper Euphrates, the empires being gouged out by the Hittites and the Mitanni met, and their mutual antagonism prevented either from becoming as powerful as it might have.

The eastern part of the Fertile Crescent was not spared the anarchy that was spreading over the eastern world. Scarcely was Hammurabi in his grave when provincial revolts rocked the Amorite Empire, and the nomad hordes took full advantage of them. A Hittite army swept down out of the north and Hammurabi's son turned it back only with the greatest effort. Meanwhile the Assyrian dependency had been ripped away by the Hurrians, and Babylon quickly fell back to the limited area of control it had held before Hammurabi.

A particular danger, moreover, arose from the Zagros Mountains, where once the Guti, and before them, the Sumerians had dwelt. For some centuries, the nomads of the Zagros had been quiet. They were known as "Koshshi" to the Babylonians and it is they who may be referred to in some places in the Bible as the "Cushites." The later Greeks referred to them as "Kossaioi" (or "Kosseans" in our spelling) and they are most familiarly known to us as the Kassites.

By 1700 B.C., they had picked up the horse-and-chariot technique and they, too, became conquerors. They swept in from the northeast, took Ur, and sacked it savagely. Babylon itself held on desperately for a century, but in 1595 B.C., after it had been badly weakened by a Hittite raid, the great city itself was taken and occupied by the Kassites, scarcely a century and a half after the death of the great Hammurabi.

The Kassites adopted Mesopotamian culture and the Babylonian version of the old Sumerian religion. They rebuilt the Temple of Marduk in Babylon and in 1330 B.C. sponsored the rebuilding of Ur.

But the nomads had introduced the horse into the areas of civilization and once the city-dwellers learned to use the new war weapon, the nomads' advantage was gone.

The resurgence against the nomads made itself felt first in Egypt, the farthest point reached by them. The Egyptian natives still controlled the southern portion of their country and in 1580 B.C. used the horse and chariot to drive the Hyksos out of the northern portion.

Indeed, the Egyptians themselves emerged in force, for the first time in their history, came into western Asia, and began a career of conquest there. In 1479 B.C., the greatest of their Pharaohs, Thutmose III, defeated a league of Canaanite cities at Megiddo. These Canaanite cities were backed by Mitanni, and Thutmose III went on to defeat Mitanni and reduce it to the rule of a tributary. He defeated the Hittites as well, putting an end to the Old Kingdom.

Egypt's strength receded somewhat after Thutmose III, and the northern kingdoms had a chance to revive. It was Mitanni's misfortune that it entered a period of dynastic quarrels, with no one member of the ruling family able to establish undisputed power. The Hittites, on the other hand, under a series of able kings were able to reestablish themselves completely. The Hittites became the most powerful kingdom in the north and by 1375 B.C. had formed the "New Kingdom."

To the east of floundering Mitanni was a revitalized Assyria. In 1365 B.C., a strong monarch, Ashur-uballit, came to the throne and under him the land regained its full independence from Mitanni.

Ashur-uballit's successor sent armies westward to the Euphrates and sacked the Mitanni capital in 1300 B.C. The next Assyrian king completed the job, smashing what remained of Mitanni in 1270 B.C., and that kingdom disappeared from history a little more than five centuries after the coming of the horse and chariot.

4

THE ASSYRIANS

THE GREAT HUNTER

Ashur-uballit initiated what is sometimes called the "First Assyrian Empire." Under his grandson, Sulmanu-asarid I ("Sulmanu is lord"), Assyria, having completed the destruction of Mitanni, became a great power.

Sulmanu-asarid's name was carried also by certain much later Assyrian kings who figure in the Bible. The Hebrew version of the name is given, in English, as Shalmaneser (shal''-muh-nee'zer), and so this king of the First Assyrian Empire is usually called Shalmaneser I. (In this book I will routinely use the Biblical version of Mesopotamian names since these are far more familiar to us, but I will, when possible, mention the actual Assyrian name, too.)

Under Shalmaneser I, Assyria regained the full extent of the territory it had held under Shamshi-Adad I, the founder of the dynasty. It drove westward to the borders of Asia Minor, reaching the limits of the Hittite kingdom which was itself at the peak of its power, then. (The Hittites managed to fight Egypt to a draw in a great battle in Canaan in 1285 B.C.)

The conquests which made Assyria ruler of a realm five hundred miles in width poured booty and slaves into the land. Shalmaneser I used it to beautify the chief Assyrian cities: Ashur itself, and one called Nineveh (nin'uh-veh). The latter was on the Tigris, about 50 miles upstream from Ashur.

Shalmaneser I apparently felt that Assyria's new power deserved a brand-new capital, and he therefore built Calah (kay'-luh) on the Tigris between Ashur and Nineveh.

Shalmaneser I died in 1245 B.C. after a reign of thirty years, and under his successor Tukulti-Ninurta I ("my faith is in Ninurta"), the First Assyrian Empire reached the pinnacle of its power.

Tukulti-Ninurta conducted successful campaigns eastward into the Zagros Mountains, the very homeland of the once-powerful Kassites. Northward, he penetrated the approaches to the lofty Caucasus where groups of Hurrians were founding a new kingdom which was to come to be known as Urartu (oo-rahr'too) — or "Ararat," in the Bible.

The Assyrian conqueror also defeated the Kassites to the south and placed them under tribute. He then invaded and occupied Elam. Under Tukulti-Ninurta I, Assyria for the first time dominated all of Mesopotamia and before his death, he ruled over a realm broader than that of Hammurabi. Even the Hittites, who had successfully withstood Egypt, reeled under the Assyrian hammer blows and were brought low indeed.

The great conqueror ruled nearly forty years before he was finally assassinated by his own son in 1208 B.C. He gained great fame in his lifetime and was the subject of epic poems. He is even more famous than most people suspect, for he may very well be the original of the earliest pagan monarch mentioned in the Bible.

In the book of Genesis, we read: "And Cush begat Nimrod: and he began to be a mighty one in the earth. He was a mighty hunter . . . And the beginning of his kingdom was Babel, and Erech, and Accad . . . in the land of Shinar. Out of that land

went forth Asshur, and builded Nineveh . . . and Calah."
(Genesis 10: 8-11.)

Might not Nimrod be Tukulti-Ninurta I? That monarch
reigned just at the time the Israelites were invading Canaan
and the noise of his great feats must have filled the air then.
The stories told about him descended dimly to the men who
eventually put the Bible in the form we now have some eight
centuries after the time of Tukulti-Ninurta I.

The role of the cities — Babel (Babylon), Erech (Uruk),
and Accad (Agade) — jumbles together the great conquerors
that preceded the Assyrian: Lugalzaggezi of Uruk, Sargon of
Agade, and Hammurabi of Babylon. Then, switching northward to Ashur (Assyria), the growth of Nineveh and the establishment of the new capital at Calah is mentioned.

Even the phrase "And Cush begat Nimrod" fits, for Cush represents the Koshshi, or Kassites. First there was the Kassite
dynasty in Babylon, and then the Assyrians.

As a matter of fact, the city of Calah where Tukulti-Ninurta I
held his court, and which his father had founded, is now the
site of an Arabic town named Nimrud.

But once again, in the endless cycle of growth and decline,
greatness was succeeded by almost instant turmoil and decay.
Even while Tukulti-Ninurta held his great realm together, another great wandering of people was taking place.

We know little about this new group of rovers, but they seem
to have been Indo-Europeans from the northern steppes. This
time they circled the Black Sea to the west rather than to the
east and included sections of the people we now know as
Greeks.

They drove the people ahead of them into the sea, and these
refugees taking to piracy were as destructive and violent as the
original invaders would have been. We see the sea raiders
swarming down first upon the coasts of Egypt. The surprised
Egyptians called them "Peoples of the Sea," and that is the
name they are usually known by in history. Egypt managed to
survive the onslaught, but was so shaken that it had to endure
long centuries of weakness afterward.

The raiders swarmed into Asia Minor also and onto what

is now the Syrian coast. The destruction of the city of Troy
on the northwestern coast of Asia Minor was probably the result of this invasion. (This was magnified by the later Greeks
into the epic tale of a ten-year siege of Troy by a united band
of Greek chieftains.)

All Asia Minor heaved, and the Hittite kingdom, which had
already been brought to the brink of ruin by Assyria, was destroyed. Assyria itself felt the blows almost as soon as Tukulti-
Ninurta I was gone. It survived but its empire was, temporarily,
shattered. It took over a century for it to collect its strength
again.

During the period of Assyrian weakness that followed the ir-
ruption of the Peoples of the Sea, Babylon itself had a chance
to recover, but the process was infinitely painful. For
over half a century, it was virtually in a state of anarchy. Its
feeble Kassite rulers were freed from Assyrian overlordship but
were unable to organize effective resistance against outside onslaught.

The onslaught came from a resurgent Elam, in a copy of what
took place after the decline of Ur over eight centuries before.
Then an Elamite expeditionary force had taken and sacked Ur;
now the Elamites took and sacked Babylon and its neighboring
cities. In 1174 B.C., they carried off two of the great relics of the
already very ancient Mesopotamian civilization. They carried
off the stele of the law-code of Hammurabi, already six centuries
old then; and the stele of Naram-Sin which was over a thousand years old.

In 1124 B.C., a native Babylonian gained power and put a
final end to the Kassite rule, which had by now lasted (with
increasing weakness) for four and a half centuries.

The new ruler's name was Nabu-kudurri-usur ("Nabu
guards the frontier"). A later king of the same name was known
to the Jews by a version of the name that appears in the English-
language Bible as Nebuchadrezzar (neb"yoo-kad-rez'er). In
some passages of the Bible, the name is given, mistakenly, with
an "n" in place of the "r," as Nebuchadnezzar.

Nebuchadrezzar I managed to defeat the Elamites so decisively that it was a long time before Elam dared march west-

ward again. For a time it looked as though the glory of Hammurabi was returning, and Babylon was to remember Nebuchadrezzar I for many centuries. It had to, for it was to be five centuries more before a native Babylonian was supreme in Mesopotamia.

That Nebuchadrezzar I did not do better but remained only a flash in the pan was owing, very largely, to still another sudden change in war technology.

IRON

For fifteen hundred years men had fought with bronze weapons. It had not been easy. Neither copper nor tin, the two metals that go into the making of bronze, were common, and the search for them was hard and precarious. Indeed, the Phoenicians (the name given by the Greeks to the Canaanites who lived on the seacoast) sent their daring seamen out of the Mediterranean altogether, and north to what must have seemed the end of the world, in order to dig into the tin mines of Cornwall in Britain.

Yet something harder than bronze was known. There were pieces of a gray-black metal occasionally found which, when beaten into swords or lance-heads, formed harder and tougher weapons than ever bronze did, and maintained a sharper edge for a longer time. The trouble was that this metal, which we call "iron," was found only very occasionally. (We now know the finds to have been fallen meteorites that were made up of a particularly tough alloy of iron with a related metal, nickel.)

To be sure, it was possible to form iron from rocky ores that contained the metal in chemical combination, but the early metallurgists did so only rarely, and then by accident. What's more, iron so obtained was impure and of poor quality. The trouble was that while copper and tin could be liberated from their ores rather easily in an ordinary fire, it was much harder to release iron. Hotter fires were needed and more intricate techniques.

Even after iron of the proper quality was obtained, it was necessary to work out methods of smelting that would add to it a proper amount of carbon, in order to produce "steel" which was the tough form of iron that could be used for weapons.

Some time about 1300 B.C., the technique for smelting and carbonizing iron was developed in the Caucasian foothills of Urartu. That land was then under the domination of the Hittite kingdom which was at the height of its powers. The Hittite kings carefully maintained a monopoly over the new technique, for they recognized its importance not only as supplying a metal superior to bronze but one which was, potentially, much more common. Only small quantities of iron were available at first, and it was, for some centuries, up to forty times as costly as silver. Before the supply could be increased and made useful to the Hittites, their end came.

The Hittite kingdom was destroyed during the disorders following the movements of the Peoples of the Sea, and their iron monopoly was broken. The knowledge of the technique of iron-smelting spread rapidly and, certainly, to Assyria which bordered on the iron kingdom of Urartu.

Trade in iron restored Assyria's prosperity and the way was clear for a new conqueror. This was Tukulti-pal-Esarra ("my faith is in the son of Esarra," that is, in Ninurta). He came to the throne in 1115 B.C. A later king of the same name is mentioned in the Bible as Tiglath-Pileser (tig'lath-py-lee'zer), and it is as Tiglath-Pileser I that this new Assyrian king is therefore best known.

Tiglath-Pileser I expanded Assyria's realm to what it had been under Tukulti-Ninurta I. Iron was still too rare to use in quantity as a war weapon, but Tiglath-Pileser I must have equipped some of his elite troops with the metal. With these he pushed downstream into Babylonia, and in 1103 B.C., Nebuchadnezzar I had to give way before the iron-tipped lances of Assyria.

But Tiglath-Pileser I had worse dangers to face. The nomad pressures were mounting again.

It may seem like a deadly but dull game, this constant alternation between civilized conqueror and nomadic incursion. Why is it that the nomads always decide to plunge against the cities when the great kings are dead and gone? And why do they come almost immediately after the great king dies?

Actually, these are not coincidences. Nomadic pressure was fairly constant in ancient times (though occasionally rising to overwhelming proportions). As long as civilized areas are under strong kings with well-organized administrations, the nomads are held off, and we hear little about them. As soon as a weaker monarch ascends the throne, and the land falls into laxness or disorder, the nomad raiders who were previously unsuccessful become successful indeed.

In Tiglath-Pileser's time, it was the turn of Arabia again to serve as the breeding-ground of nomad pressure. These nomads were the Arameans, and they pushed against the borders of the Fertile Crescent, east and west, as the Amorites had done eight centuries before.

Under Tiglath-Pileser I, Assyria's well-led army, backed by a well-organized society, beat back the Arameans in many campaigns. The war bulletins left behind by Tiglath-Pileser I contain the earliest known references to the Arameans.* Defeating the nomads was rarely of permanent use, however. Sending armies against them (as long as they clung to their nomadic way of life and didn't settle down) was much like punching water. The nomadic warrior would fade away and return when the armies were gone.

Assyria wore itself out holding off the Arameans, and after the death by assassination of Tiglath-Pileser I in 1093 B.C., his successors lacked the old king's capacity. With Assyria less efficiently governed, and its armies less well led, the Aramean

---

* The ancient kings often left behind official accounts of their campaigns that were incredibly dull, and probably not entirely accurate. Such chronicles, however dull and suspect, are, however, of great importance to chronology — that is, in determining the years in which particular events took place — if in nothing else.

raids became much more effective. Assyria's power contracted and the land went through another century and a half of weakness.

This period of weakness gave the Israelites a chance for expansion. When they had entered Canaan about 1200 B.C., they had found it occupied by the Peoples of the Sea on the seacoast. These, called the Philistines, possessed iron weapons while the Israelites did not, and for a century the Philistines dominated the land.

Then, in 1013 B.C., the gifted Judean leader, David, established his rule not only over his own tribe of Judah, but over all the other Israelite tribes. In the course of a forty-year reign, he defeated the Philistines and established his power throughout the entire western portion of the Fertile Crescent, right up to the upper Euphrates. This could not possibly have happened, if Assyria had, at that time, been under the control of kings like Tukulti-Ninurta I or Tiglath-Pileser I.

As it was, David's empire was not immune to the infiltrations of the Arameans, either. In the reign of David's son, Solomon, the Arameans had established principalities just north of Israel itself. One of these, with its capital at Damascus, became quite strong. The kingdom of Damascus is usually known as Syria (the name given the region by the Greeks centuries later).

The establishment of Syria greatly weakened Israel and contributed to the disorders that led to the splitting of Israel into the two kingdoms of Israel and Judah, following the death of Solomon in 933 B.C.

THE ASSYRIAN HITLER

The apparently endless vitality of Assyria produced another recovery, however. Assyria had revived after the furious pressure of the Hurrians, and then of the Peoples of the Sea. Now it fought back against the Arameans.

In 911 B.C. Adad-nirari II came to the Assyrian throne. He

reorganized the government and began to inflict defeats on the Arameans once more. (The Arameans had settled down in a series of principalities within the Fertile Crescent, and they were now more easily smashed than when they had been wandering nomads.)

One important factor in Assyria's favor was that its iron supplies increased. By 889 B.C., when Adad-nirari's son, Tukulti-Ninurta II, began his brief five-year rule, there was enough iron in the realm to equip the entire army with iron weapons. The Assyrian army was the first to really exploit the new metal in quantity, and it entered a two-century career of conquest that was to make it the terror of the world.

Nor was it only a matter of iron. The Assyrians were the first to make a science of the siege of cities. From very early times, cities had learned that by building walls about themselves they could hold off an enemy most effectively. From the top of the walls it was easy to fire a hail of arrows down upon the enemy, while the enemy in turn could do little damage in shooting arrows up to the tops of the walls.

A siege became an endurance contest, therefore. Those laying siege avoided attempts to fight their way in and take the city "by storm." Instead they were content to isolate the city and prevent food supplies from entering. In this way, the city could be starved into surrender. The city under siege held out as long as possible in the hope that the besieging army would succumb to boredom, attrition, and disease. It was generally a long pull and often, with both sides suffering, some compromise arrangement was made in which the city agreed to pay tribute but preserved itself intact.

The Assyrians, however, at this period of history, began to devise methods for beating down the wall. They built heavy devices that could not be pushed over, placed them on wheels so that they could be moved easily against the wall, armored them to protect the men within, and equipped them with battering rams to beat down the wall. Once a breach was made in the wall and the besieging army poured in, it was usually all over.

This form of siege warfare introduced a new element of hor-

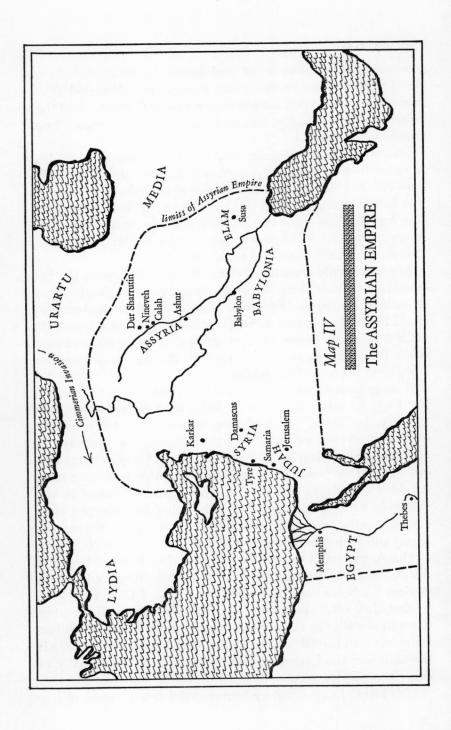

Map IV

The ASSYRIAN EMPIRE

MEDIA

limits of Assyrian Empire

ELAM

Susa

URARTU

Dur Sharrutin
Nineveh
Calah
Ashur

ASSYRIA

Babylon

BABYLONIA

Cimmerian Invasion

Karkar

Damascus

SYRIA

Samaria

Jerusalem

JUDAH

Tyre

LYDIA

Memphis

EGYPT

Thebes

ror. As long as battles were mainly army against army, blood-shed was limited. A defeated army could run away, and even fleeing soldiers could turn and defend themselves. However, when a city was taken by storm, its population was pinned against its own wall and could not flee. It was filled with material goods for looting, and with helpless women and children who might be abused without fear of reprisal. In the fury of war and the excitement of victory, the sack of a city involved cruelties beyond description.

This was shown to be so, in most grisly fashion, in the reign of Ashur-nasir-apli ("Ashur guards the heir"), better known to us as Ashurnasirpal II (ah"shoor-nah'zir-pal) who succeeded Tukulti-Ninurta II in 883 B.C.

He virtually accomplished the destruction of the Aramean principalities, all the way to the Mediterranean, completing the job of his two predecessors. He restored Assyrian prosperity and rebuilt the neglected city of Calah, making it once more the capital of the realm.

Indeed, he constructed a palace for himself in Calah that was one of the first Assyrian structures to have been uncovered by modern archaeologists. (It was uncovered from 1845 to 1851.)

Enough of it remains to show its magnificence. It covers six acres of ground and is decorated with bas-reliefs of extraordinary realism. Many are devoted to showing Ashurnasirpal II (pictured as a man of strong but rather coarse features) hunting lions. Hunting has always been considered a royal sport, but there have been few groups of kings as devoted to it as the Assyrian monarchs. Their addiction to it must have become proverbial so that the Bible describes Nimrod, in the form of a common saying, as "a mighty hunter before the Lord." (Genesis 10: 9.)

The reliefs that show the horses and chariots guided by Ashurnasirpal's strong arm, as he impales lions with arrows, are admirable and even beautiful. Animals seem all muscle and fury and emotion. It is doubtful if anything in the world of art can show animals in more realistic suffering than the Assyrians do when they carve images of wounded lions.

But this displays, somehow, a delight in suffering that reminds one that Ashurnasirpal II is famous, or rather infamous, for something quite different from art. He, more than any other Assyrian, fixed the reputation of that nation in history. He filled his quarter-century reign with cruelties that were unmatched until the days of Hitler.

These cruelties were particularly associated with the new style of siege warfare. Ashurnasirpal II used siege devices with efficiency and thought well enough of them to have them pictured on the inscriptions he left behind. He took the natural tendency of storming armies to commit cruelties and raised it into a deliberate policy of terror, almost unbelievable to any age other than ours, which has witnessed the deeds of Nazi Germany.

When Ashurnasirpal's army captured a city, death by torture was the order of the day. Heads were cut off in quantity and pyramids were built of them. Men were skinned, or impaled, or crucified, or buried alive.

This might have been a deliberate scheme to make Assyria's power more effective. One might imagine the monarch arguing that by such a policy of terror cities would be induced to submit without a siege or, better still, to decide not to revolt in the first place. In the end, Ashurnasirpal might say, the total bloodshed and suffering would be diminished so that the cruelty of war was really kindness. (War hawks have argued in this manner in modern times, too.)

Nevertheless, the fact that Ashurnasirpal II gloatingly detailed his deeds in his inscriptions, with bas-reliefs of the proceedings, and the fact that he apparently enjoyed watching the torture, shows him surely to have been a sadist. He did his vile deeds because he enjoyed them.

In the short run, Ashurnasirpal's policy succeeded. He expanded the Empire and set it upon a firm foundation. He died in peace and, possibly, with the comfortable feeling that he had done well.

In the long run, however, he failed. He had made the Assyrian name hated and detested as no later conqueror was to suc-

ceed in doing till the time of Hitler. The later Assyrian monarchs were by no means as vicious as Ashurnasirpal II; some
were even enlightened and decent human beings. The odor
of sadism clung to all of them, however, thanks to Ashurnasirpal II, and none of them were to know peace. For the rest
of the time allotted to Assyria, its history was to be one long
process of repressing rebellion, for no people would long remain peacefully subject to it.

And when, after two and a half centuries of ceaseless war,
Assyria was finally defeated, it was defeated utterly. Other
nations might go down, survive and revive. Assyria had done
this itself several times before Ashurnasirpal II. When it went
down again, though, after Ashurnasirpal's time, it was completely wiped out, and made to vanish from the face of the
earth.

THE HORSE GROWS LARGER

Ashurnasirpal's son, Shalmaneser III, succeeded in 859 B.C.
and ruled even longer than his father. He set about enlarging
the kingdom further, and his reign saw him continually in the
field.

One Aramean principality had yet survived the Assyrian
resurgence. That was the Damascan kingdom of Syria, which
retained some strength along the western prong of the Fertile
Crescent and was actively engaged in organizing resistance to
Assyria. Its chief ally in this venture was Israel, its neighbor
to the south, which was then ruled by Ahab, a king made famous in the Bible for his idolatry and wickedness (at least according to the views of the Biblical writers).

In 854, the two allies met the Assyrian army at Karkar. This
site is unidentified, but it is thought to be in northern Syria

about thirty miles or so from the Mediterranean shore. The situation was desperate, for the Assyrian army was the best in the world and it outnumbered the allied Syrian-Israelite army by some three to two. Would that we knew the details of what followed, but we don't. All we can say is that against all odds the allies managed to maintain themselves. Somehow they stopped the dreaded Assyrians, winning at least a draw. The Assyrians withdrew, and Syria and Israel gained for themselves another century of life.

Oddly enough, the Bible does not mention the battle (which is one reason we know so little about it); almost as though it does not want to give the credit for this great feat to wicked King Ahab. We know of it from the brief mention in the Assyrian inscriptions which can scarcely be expected to go into much detail concerning a battle that was certainly not a glorious victory for them.

Still, while the allies gained a respite, they were not saved forever. Assyria was too huge and too powerful to be denied altogether. In another campaign after Ahab's death, an Assyrian army devastated Syria and forced it and the other principalities of the west to pay tribute.

Ahab's line was overthrown and wiped out in 843 B.C., eleven years after the great battle, and a new dynasty was established by the Israelite general, Jehu. The tale, as found in the Bible, tends to make Jehu a hero for destroying a wicked dynasty. Assyrian records, however, present a different view of him. A "Black Obelisk" obtained from the ruins of Calah, shows Assyria's subject princes bringing tribute to Shalmaneser. One of these is Jehu of Israel, shown prostrate at the feet of his Assyrian master. Syria and the various Phoenician cities are also placed among the tributaries. And yet, although they were bled by the Assyrian overlords, the little kingdoms retained their self-government and that was due, at least in part, to the great showing they made at Karkar.

A far more dangerous enemy to Assyria was the growing power of Urartu to the north. What had once been a group of competing Hurrian principalities had united themselves into a powerful kingdom about 1000 B.C., when Assyria was beaten down by the Aramean incursions. The Urartian kingdom centered on Lake Van, north of the upper Tigris and 200 miles north of Ashur.

There began, thereafter, a period of constant warfare between Urartu and Assyria; one of long frustration to the latter country. Urartu had no other important enemies and could concentrate its powers against the southern neighbor for several centuries, but Assyria's armies were spread out in every direction. Thus, while Assyria usually won almost every battle, Urartu always managed to recover while Assyria was looking the other way, and soon the northern kingdom was ready to jab again. The duel filled much of Shalmaneser's reign. At one point, the Assyrian armies even took the Urartian capital. But Shalmaneser III could not keep his army sitting there, and when it left, Urartu recovered.

Much the same was true of Assyria's neighbor to the south. In 850 B.C. Shalmaneser III moved downstream to reassert Assyria's power over Babylonia, power that had lapsed since the days of Tiglath-Pileser I a century and a half before. In that interim, a new power had moved into Babylonia; another group of Semitic tribes from Arabia.

These were the Chaldeans (kal-dee'anz), first mentioned in the campaign inscriptions of the demonic Ashurnasirpal II.

Shalmaneser III was never completely victorious over the Chaldeans. Like the Urartians, the Chaldeans absorbed defeats and rose again when the Assyrian armies marched away.

In the reign of Shalmaneser III, the Indo-European peoples were edging forward on the world stage. They had been spreading outward in all directions from their east European homeland since the great horse-and-chariot invasions of the nomads. The first great civilization they contributed to the world, the Hittite kingdom, had faded out three and a half centuries before Shalmaneser's time, but there were other tribes elsewhere; tribes that had skirted the Semitic world of Arabia and the Fertile Crescent far to either side.

Some Indo-Europeans had moved west of the Black Sea and

into Europe proper. Those who moved south into the eastern-most of Europe's three southern peninsulas are known to us as the Greeks.

Other tribes moved east of the Black Sea and passed through the hilly lands of what is now modern Iran. They migrated southward as far as what is now Pakistan as early as 1500 B.C. These eastern tribes called themselves "Aryas" meaning "noble."

Because these tribes spoke an Indo-European language, nineteenth-century historians often spoke of that group of languages as "Aryan," even though they were also spoken by many groups, such as the Greeks and Hittites among others, who were not members of these eastern tribes. With even less justification, people who spoke Indo-European languages were called "Aryans." This term was thrown into complete disrepute by Hitler and his Nazis, who used it in formulating their nonsensical race theories. In this book, I will call the language family "Indo-European."

A form of the term "Aryan" survives, legitimately, in the name of the nation of Iran, which was indeed settled by those tribes three thousand years ago and more. The land has been known by a number of other names (of which the most familiar is "Persia"), and these will be used, when applicable, in this book. The land has been dominated by a number of tribes, closely related in language and culture, but bearing a variety of names. We can lump them all together as "Iranians."

The first of the Iranian tribes to make their mark in Meso-potamian history are the Medes (meedz). Having come down from the north they made their home in the region south of the Caspian Sea and east of the main ranges of the Zagros. This region came to be known as Media (mee'dee-uh). The Medes are first mentioned in the chronicles of Shalmaneser III, who campaigned there in 836 B.C.

The Medes made an important contribution to the history of warfare, and again the horse was involved. The horse and chariot was a remarkable weapon of war which, nevertheless, had its limitations. It could only be used on reasonably flat land. Unexpected hillocks and ditches would overturn the chariot and possibly seriously hurt the charioteer.

It would have been much better if the charioteer could have ridden the horse directly. Even without a stirrup to make his seat firm (the metal stirrup was not invented till a thousand years later), a rider might have developed the skill to remain with his horse, even while that animal was galloping and leaping, and make use of a long-distance weapon such as the bow and arrow. (Any attempt to wield a spear at close distance would have risked having himself knocked off this horse by a returning spear jab.)

The chief difficulty was that the horses available in the first millennium of their use in warfare were rather small. To our eyes, they would have seemed like fleet and hardy ponies, capable of enduring much but simply not the huge animals of today. Such a pony could drag a chariot; or, if one pony had trouble, then two, harnessed side by side, could manage. A horse of this type could not, however, bear the full, direct weight of a man — especially of an armored man — and carry him fleetly in battle for any length of time. Nor could a man ease the situation by riding two horses.

It was the Medes, apparently, who first bred large horses capable of carrying men on their backs, and the Iranian peoples remained the most skillful horsemen in the world throughout ancient times.

The Assyrians obtained heavy horses from the Medes, probably as spoils of war, and in this way added still another specialized arm to their war machine — the mounted archer. The Assyrian horsemen could now cover any kind of ground that a horse could cover and could pursue fleeing infantry across the broken areas that had previously given the defeated army security from chariot-pursuit.

The large horse meant something additional, too. The kings' messengers and couriers could now travel faster and over longer distances, for the large horses did not tire rapidly. The postal service, first set up by the Sumerians, was vastly improved and extended by the Assyrians, and because communications improved, the Assyrians could better organize a large empire than previous conquering peoples had been able to. Larger concentrations of population could be fed, too, and large cities, like Babylon or Calah had populations of as much as thirty thousand.

THE QUEEN THAT WASN'T

Shalmaneser's war-filled reign badly exhausted Assyria and did not, in the end, achieve the necessary goal of putting its enemies completely out of action. Shalmaneser III had won victories in every direction: against Syria and Israel in the west, against Urartu in the north, against Media in the east, against Babylonia (or Chaldea, as it might now be called) in the south. In every case, though, the victories were not decisive and the enemies remained with plenty of fight still left in them.

Furthermore, the king's last years were filled with dynastic troubles. This was routine in the ancient monarchies. The closer the period to our own time, and the more detailed our knowledge in consequence, the better we can see the perennial fighting between father and son, and between brother and brother.

One trouble was that in the ancient monarchies there was no clear-cut line of succession. In general, it was sufficient that someone from the royal family rule, but it did not necessarily have to be the oldest surviving son of the king. There was some reason to this. If the succession went automatically to the nearest relative, some incompetent might become king. A free choice being allowed, the best man would, in theory, succeed.

But who was the best man? In polygamous royal families there were often many grown sons, each of whom considered himself the best man. There might be many different parties waiting for the old king to die and each hoping for some particular relative to succeed.

If the old king died suddenly and unexpectedly, a civil war might be set off. If the old king waited too long, an impatient son might arrange to seize the throne by force (and, if possible, to arrange the assassination of his father as well).

In Shalmaneser's last year, his oldest son rebelled, and the king died in 824 B.C. before that matter was settled. Shalmaneser's younger son fought in his father's name and succeeded in crushing the rebellion. He was not a strong king, however, and Assyrian power ebbed in his reign as the worn-out land sought repose.

When the new king died in 810 B.C., he left an infant son behind and his widow Sammu-rammat took over the actual role. The vision of a woman ruling the great and powerful and, in fact, terrifying kingdom of Assyria, seems to have impressed surrounding lands. At this time the Greeks were just emerging from the dark age that followed the disorders of the Peoples of the Sea. Even in their peninsula, 1,100 miles west of Calah, they must have received dim word of such a queen. At least, their legends, as later given in the works of their literary men, describe a curiously foreshortened history of Assyria that centers about such a queen.

The first Assyrian king, according to Greek legend, was Ninus, and he founded Nineveh. (The capital of Assyria in later times was Nineveh, and the Greeks may have reasoned that the city would have to be named after its founder. It is also possible that Ninus is a dim memory of Tukulti-Ninurta I, in which case the Greek-legendary Ninus and the Hebrew-legendary Nimrod would be one and the same.)

Ninus was supposed to have conquered all of western Asia in a series of lightning campaigns (the telescoped work of a dozen Assyrian conquerors) and married a beautiful woman named Semiramis (seh-mir'uh-mis). It seems clear that Semiramis is a memory of Sammu-rammat.

After Ninus died, the legend goes on, Semiramis succeeded to the throne. She was supposed to have reigned forty-two years and to have founded the city of Babylon. She was consistently successful in all she did until finally she attempted to conquer India and failed.

There are many romantic and colorful details to the story, and the later Greeks attributed to Semiramis every remarkable structure or monument they came across in western Asia. Yet it is all out of whole cloth; all born of galloping imagination; inspired by the simple fact that a woman for a short time ruled over Assyria.

The original Sammu-rammat ruled only eight years, not forty-two; nor was she particularly successful or victorious. Indeed, following the reign of her son, Assyria entered a period of stagnancy, while a series of incompetent rulers followed one another on the throne. So fierce was Assyria's reputation, however, that she remained intact, in her homeland at least, even if her empire crept back at the fringes. None of her neighbors dared prod her too sharply.

But those neighbors flourished in their own homeland in this interval of Assyrian dormancy. Urartu, in particular, reached its period of greatest glory. From 778 to 750 B.C., it was under the rule of Argistis I, who united all of northernmost Mesopotamia under himself and forged a realm which for a while was as large and as strong as the then-weakened Assyria.

Israel, too, had its moment of prosperity. Syria had been badly damaged by Shalmaneser III and could no longer compete. In 785 B.C., Jeroboam II succeeded to the throne of Israel. He extended his rule to the Euphrates, and both Syria and Judah were subservient to him. For the forty years he reigned, it was almost as though the kingdom of David had been restored.

But, alas for Urartu and Israel, and for all of western Asia, Assyria was not dead, she was only sleeping.

THE POLICY OF EXILE

The general failure of the kings of Assyria to shake the kingdom out of the doldrums and their inability to deal effectively with Urartu ruined the prestige of the royal family. It had

ruled Assyria steadily now for just over a thousand years, ever
since the time when Shamshi-Adad I had set himself on the
throne of Ashur as an Amorite usurper, and when Hammurabi
was still but a Babylonian princeling. The dynasty was decaying now and the army was restless.

There was a military uprising in the capital in 745 B.C., and
when the confusion cleared the old dynasty was gone. In its
place was a new king, someone not of the royal family.

He took, however, the name of a famous old Assyrian conqueror in an effort to assure continuity and to indicate a return to the "good old days" of victory and strength. He called
himself Tiglath-Pileser III.

He began by reorganizing the empire. Matters had grown
lax in the half-century of slipshod rule that had preceded him.
He therefore tightened administrative procedures, making all
officials responsible directly to him. He improved finances and
established a professional army of hired soldiers ("mercenaries"), many of whom were non-Assyrians. In this way, there
need be no time lost in calling together peasant levies at every
emergency, or losses due to the fact that soldiers might be in-
sufficiently trained. Instead, the army could now be kept on a
perpetual war footing and on a high pitch of efficiency. This
was expensive, but the money could always be obtained from
the tributaries, and more than ever Assyria had to loot its vic-
tims dry and add further to their desperate hatred.

After all that, the new king went about settling accounts with
enemies outside.

For one thing, there was the matter of the nomads. The
Medes had been growing impudent and had been raiding
Assyrian outposts. Tiglath-Pileser III had no intention of waiting for them to grow bolder still. He went out after them, chasing them tirelessly, smashing them when he caught them. It
was still impossible to defeat nomads thoroughly, but the Medes
got the idea. They stayed independent to be sure, but they
paid tribute and remained respectful.

A quick campaign to the west terrorized the small nations
there also. Jeroboam II had died in the very year in which
Tiglath-Pileser III had come to the throne, and his feckless suc-

cessors were unable to keep Israel from falling apart. Israel had to agree quickly to pay tribute to Assyria, and the last lightning flash of Israelite prosperity was over.

Tiglath-Pileser turned northward toward the greater enemy, Urartu, whose diplomacy was supporting disaffection and rebellion against Assyria wherever it could be found. Tiglath-Pileser smashed hard. He could not drive the Urartu forces out of all their strongholds, but he managed to close his fist over the southern half of the country. Urartu was mortally wounded. It declined and was never to regain its full strength.

Back to the west, then, where another attempt at an anti-Assyrian alliance (as in the great days of Ahab a century before) was being attempted. Tiglath-Pileser took Damascus, and put an end to the kingdom of Syria after its two centuries of life. Israel subsided again.

Tiglath-Pileser III initiated a new Assyrian policy for the handling of defeated nations. The old system of terror without end was abandoned. Instead, Tiglath-Pileser adopted the far subtler practice of removing the leaders of a nation, carting them off to some far-off portion of the kingdom, and replacing them with people from another part.

There was shrewd psychology to this. It was universally felt at the time that every god was tied to the soil; that a god could properly be worshiped only in one given place. If people were deported from their homeland, they were deported also from the place of their gods. They were hurled into a new land that was not only without their old language and customs, but even without their old gods. With that the exile's feelings of identity vanished, what we would today call his sense of "nationalism" was smashed.

The end result was a general weakening of parts of the non-Assyrian portion of the empire, to the benefit of the Assyrian ruling party.

The deportations had another important and utterly unlooked for effect; this was on the language of Mesopotamia. Ever since the days of Sargon of Agade, Akkadian had been the language of the area, no matter what new conquerors came in. Assyrians and Chaldeans alike adopted and spoke the Akkadian language, and in the time of Tiglath-Pileser III it had been dominant for some fifteen centuries.

In the western portion of the Fertile Crescent, however, other Semitic dialects were in use — Hebrew, Phoenician, Aramean. These made use of an alphabet (a Phoenician invention of about 1500 B.C.) which made them very easy to learn to write. In matters of international trade it became very tempting, then, to use a west-Semitic language rather than Akkadian. This was true even in the Assyrian homeland, for it was far easier for an Assyrian merchant to learn to read and write Aramean, with its two dozen letters, than for a Syrian to learn to read and write Akkadian, with its thousands of separate symbols.

The Arameans were the great merchants of the Assyrian period, and they spread their language all over the western half of the Fertile Crescent. In time, for instance, it replaced Hebrew among the Jews. The very latest books of the Bible were written partly in Aramean, and the language of the common people of Judea in the time of Jesus was Aramean. It was the language Jesus himself spoke (probably the only language he spoke aside from Hebrew itself).

When Tiglath-Pileser III scattered the Arameans into exile in Mesopotamia and elsewhere, he also spread the Aramean language. Akkadian, with all its difficulties, had held on till then as a sheer matter of conservative tradition. Now, however, it began to break down in the face of the alphabetic script of Aramean. The language became Assyria's second official tongue, and slowly it began to replace Akkadian, as Akkadian had once replaced Sumerian.

Tiglath-Pileser III also turned his attention to Chaldea. For nearly four centuries, Babylon and southern Mesopotamia generally had acknowledged the supremacy of Assyria in theory, but had kept its own kings and customs and had remained a bothersome problem to Assyria. Whenever Assyria grew weak, Babylon's independence grew more marked.

Tiglath-Pileser III determined to put an end to the troubles that arose out of the lax bond that held together Assyria and Chaldea. When the Chaldean ruler of Babylon died and a dispute arose as to his successor, the Assyrian king settled matters in 729 B.C. by marching into Babylon and making himself monarch of the land, under the name Pulu (which was, perhaps, his real name). For the first time since the rise of Assyria, the same ruler ruled directly over both Calah and Babylon. This was reflected by the fact that Assyria's patron god, Ashur, took over the leadership of the gods, replacing old Marduk.

Nevertheless, neither the old dynasty nor the old religion of Babylon was utterly crushed. They sank low, but sullenly waited for the chance to return.

THE LAST DYNASTY

In 727 B.C., Tiglath-Pileser III died, and his son Shalmaneser V came to the throne. This period when one king succeeds another is always a critical moment in the lives of the ancient empires. The new king may be incompetent, or he may have a rival for the throne; therefore, it is the time of succession when a subject nation must seize the opportunity to rebel.

So when the redoubtable Tiglath-Pileser III was laid in his grave, Hoshea of Israel took a chance that there would be a return to the incompetence that had marked the Assyrian monarchy for generations before — and refused tribute.

It is hard to tell whether Shalmaneser V was really to prove competent or not. He didn't stay king long enough. He moved decisively, to be sure, and placed Samaria, Israel's capital, under siege in 725 B.C., but that siege was not a great success. Three years passed and the Assyrian army still sat outside Samaria's walls. We may well suppose there was unrest within that army in consequence.

At least, there was a mutiny and, in 722 B.C., Shalmaneser V was gone. A new king suddenly made his appearance, a king whose background is unknown, though he must have been a general. Where Assyria's first dynasty had lasted a thousand years, its second lasted only twenty-three years, and it included only two kings. With the new usurper, Assyria began its third and last dynasty, sometimes called the "Sargonids."

The usurper chose a famous name, as usurpers often do, to hide the reality of their low birth under a surface glitter. This time it was Sargon ("legitimate king" which is exactly what he was not), and he is usually called Sargon II. Often, the statement is made that the new king was deliberately modeling himself on Sargon of Agade and that that is why he is Sargon II. This is not so. Assyria had a Sargon I as king in the days before Hammurabi, some six centuries after Sargon of Agade, and the reference is to that.

If the mutiny was caused by the soldiers' discontent over the failure to take Samaria, it was unjustified, for Samaria fell almost immediately after the coup, and would probably have fallen even if Shalmaneser had remained king. Indeed, one might wonder whether Samaria fell before or after Sargon became king. Sargon claimed the fall to his own credit, but no one compels an absolute king to be absolutely honest. The Bible never mentions Sargon as conqueror of Samaria; it gives the credit to Shalmaneser. One can only wonder.

Once Samaria fell, the policy of deportations initiated by Tiglath-Pileser III was followed. In fact, this was the most famous instance of that policy. The Israelite leaders who were removed from the land represent the "ten lost tribes." These were never found again and for many centuries, legend located them in one place or another and fancied they had multiplied into a prosperous and powerful kingdom. The truth of the matter is that they were simply assimilated by the population in northwestern Mesopotamia where they were placed. Within a century or two of the end of the Kingdom of Israel, their descendants had lost all consciousness of their national identity.

The entire western end of the Fertile Crescent was now reasonably quiet, for it had been incorporated wholesale into the Assyrian realm. The small kingdom of Judah, the only scrap of David's empire which still existed (and which was still ruled by a descendant of that king) paid tribute. The various nations of Asia Minor paid tribute. Even the island of Cyprus, a hundred miles out to sea, must have felt the touch of Sargon's power, for his viceroys set up steles there.

But if the west was quiet, the north was thunderous with danger. North of the Black Sea, where once the primitive Indo-European tribes had dwelt, there were tribes known to the Greeks as Cimmerians (sih-mee'ree-anz). They may have been living peacefully on their steppes for centuries, but in the eighth century B.C., a new group of tribes, called the Scythians (sith'ee-anz), were pouring westward out of central Asia.

The Cimmerians fled before them and forced their way southward through the Caucasus. They were following the routes the Hurrians, Hittites, and Aryans had taken a thousand years before, but the Cimmerians were less fortunate. Unlike the earlier nomadic invaders, they had to contend with a great empire at the height of its power.

To be sure, the Cimmerians collided first with Urartu. Urartu, having been badly damaged by Tiglath-Pileser III, found it hard to oppose the new hordes. They didn't even get a fair chance to try, for Sargon saw the chance to settle matters with the old enemy. While the Cimmerian nomads raided Urartu's northern frontiers, the Assyrian army marched against them from the south.

Urartu, thus caught in a cruel vise, had to choose quickly which enemy to submit to. It chose the Assyrians, for the Assyrian force was overwhelming. Indeed, Sargon's methods in the north were typically Assyrian. He did not hesitate to break the Urartian spirit of resistance by destroying the land itself. He deliberately wrecked the canal systems of cities who resisted too strenuously. Such wrecking, which could be carried through in days, could take years, or even generations, to repair. In the end, such a policy was self-defeating, for the prosperity of the land, once destroyed, was lost to the conquerors as well as to the natives.

Yet Sargon was not without a touch of the progressive as well. The Urartian irrigation system included underground ditches which carried water with very little loss through evaporation. Though Sargon destroyed the system, he admired the principle, and brought the notion back to Assyria, from which it spread over the ancient world generally.

The Urartians met final defeat at Assyrian hands in 714 B.C. and accepted Sargon's domination, though the native kings retained a nominal power over a small portion of their old territory. Together, Urartu and Assyria then withstood the Cimmerians and kept them out of the Fertile Crescent itself.

Sargon also had trouble in Babylonia. There, the ruling Chaldeans chose the moment between kings to make their move. Even as Sargon II came to the throne, a Chaldean chieftain seized Babylon and proclaimed himself king. His name was Marduk-apla-iddina II, and in the Bible he is referred to as Merodach-Baladan. For ten years, he held power while Sargon was occupied to the west and north. It was only after the Cimmerian pressure had been temporarily held off that the Assyrian could turn southward. When he did so, Merodach-Baladan had to give way, and was driven into exile in 711 B.C.

Meanwhile, Sargon's consciousness of his own lack of legitimate claim to the throne must have forced him to leave Calah, with its strong associations with past kings of other dynasties. He aspired to build a capital all his own, one that would be associated only with himself.

He selected a site just north of Nineveh and began building the new capital in 717 B.C. By using hordes of prisoners of war and driving them ruthlessly, he completed the city in ten years and called it Dur-Sharrukin ("Fort Sargon").

It had been empty land before that, except for some farms, and Sargon was able to work with lots of space. It was thoroughly planned in a very geometric manner. The city was a perfect square, with its sides just over a mile long, and its corners facing due north, south, east, and west. The city contained a seven-stage ziggurat, numerous temples, and a palace for Sargon himself that covered 25 acres. Sargon planned a library, too, and by collecting the cuneiform-covered bricks that held the ancient literature of Mesopotamia, he started a fashion that reached an important peak some seventy years later.

But alas for human vanity. When the new capital was done, it remained standing there virtually empty, for Sargon found himself fully occupied in a new war. The Cimmerians, having pounded against an impenetrable wall of Assyrian shields just south of the Caucasus, slipped off westward and invaded Asia Minor. The damage they did there was beyond the power of the local principalities to handle, and Sargon himself had to mount a campaign into the peninsula. There, in 705 B.C., he died, apparently in battle against the nomads.

Sargon's successor never made use of the city Sargon had been building. It died before it was truly born and, indeed, Sargon's main palace was never quite finished.

Yet the city and palace served a purpose. In 1842, the French archaeologist Paul Emile Botta, digging in the mound upon that ancient site, uncovered Sargon's palace. It was the first Assyrian structure to be restored to the light of day and it was the first hint of the mighty empire that till then had been hidden from mankind under the mists of the distorting legends of the Greeks.

FRUSTRATION AND FURY

Sargon's successor was Sin-akhe-eriba ("Sin has increased the brothers"). Apparently, he was a younger son and his mother was grateful to the moon god, Sin, for the number of boys she bore the king. We know the new ruler by the form of the name that appears in the Bible — Sennacherib (seh-nak′er-ib).

Like so many other Assyrian kings, Sennacherib felt it necessary to have a capital of his own. The magnificent capital that had been freshly built by his father did not suit him. Perhaps it bore too much the stamp of his father, and Sennacherib wanted something on which he could more easily make his own mark.

Whatever the reason, he chose Nineveh for his capital. It was an old city that had been in existence as a northern outpost from quite early Sumerian times. It had always been a prominent city of the Assyrian heartland, yet it had never before served as capital.

Sennacherib rebuilt it from the ground up, and made it a great metropolis. To bring it fresh water, for instance, he built a special stone-rimmed canal that led southward from the hills miles to the north. It was seventy-five feet wide in spots, and water was led across a valley over a stone aqueduct, in a style that anticipated the later Romans.

The king built a large eighty-room palace, 600 feet by 630. He flanked its doorways by that most characteristic piece of Assyrian sculpture — strong, winged bulls of stone, twenty tons or so in weight, each bearing the head of a bearded monarch. Apparently, they represented some sort of powerful spirit who protected the entrance to the palace and, therefore, the king who lived in it. (This notion of guarding doors is common. The Egyptians used sphinxes, lions with human heads. We ourselves tend to use ordinary lions, as at the New York Public Library.)

These winged bulls are seen so often in connection with writings on Assyria that they have become almost as representative of the land as an eagle is of the United States, or a bear is of Russia. Indeed, the fame of Nineveh must have spread the notion of these winged creatures to all parts of the empire. It seems almost certain, for instance, that the mysterious "cherubs" mentioned in the Bible are these winged bulls or something very close to them. It is a powerful cherub with a sword of fire that bars the way to any return to the garden of Eden. Six-winged cherubs guard the Divine Throne in Isaiah's vision, and two cherubs (undescribed) are on top of the Ark of the Covenant.

For various reasons, the cherubs stopped being fearsome, supernatural man-headed beasts, and became, first, angels, and then baby angels. Nowadays, we are quite ready to call a cute little baby "cherubic" but wouldn't dream of using that adjective where it belongs by applying it to the majestic monsters that guarded the entrance to Sennacherib's massive palace.

Nineveh remained the Assyrian capital for the remainder of the life of the Empire. That was less than a century, but it was in this period that a number of Judean prophets flourished, and their denunciations of the Assyrian capital gave Nineveh a notoriety that has remained ever since and that has wiped out any thought of earlier capitals from the mind of most people.

The Judeans had good reason to execrate Nineveh, for the king who made it his capital visited devastation upon Judah.

Sennacherib, you see, had to face the usual problem of an incoming despot of any empire, let alone one as hated as the Assyrian. The fires his father had extinguished broke out again.

Nor were these new fires entirely spontaneous. On the rim of the empire were independent nations who strove continuously to encourage rebellion within the Assyrian realm. Only by keeping the dreaded Assyrian army perpetually busy with rebels could the outsiders be certain that they themselves would not be marked out for conquest.

On the western fringe of the Assyrian Empire was Egypt, which intrigued constantly with Judah and the other small states in the west. Egypt offered money and promised military aid if they would take strong anti-Assyrian action. On the southeastern fringe of the Empire was Elam, and its specialty was that of keeping the Chaldeans of Babylonia constantly active, through the political refugees it sheltered.

Elam encouraged Merodach-Baladan, the Chaldean, to try to seize control of Babylon, as soon as Sargon died. Sennacherib had to dash downstream and defeat the Chaldean again. Then he turned westward to meet another threat.

Succumbing to the Egyptian blandishments, Hezekiah, king of Judah, refused to pay the agreed-upon tribute to Assyria. This amounted to a formal declaration of rebellion. Sennacherib swept through Judah and surrounding territories, devastating everything with a coldly efficient savagery, and settled down for a siege of Jerusalem in 701 B.C.

Jerusalem was in a naturally strong, almost impregnable, position, and Hezekiah had prepared well, laying in ample stores. Yet, impartial observers, judging on past performance, would likely have felt that Jerusalem's fate was settled, and that in the long run the Assyrian army would have to take the city either by starvation or assault.

The Assyrian army did not. Jerusalem remained intact, and the jubilation at the result rings in the Bible. According to the Biblical story, a sudden plague struck the Assyrian army in the night and the broken remnant of the forces had to lift the siege and retreat.

Herodotus, the Greek historian, also tells of a mysterious defeat of Sennacherib's army. His tale has nothing to do with Jerusalem apparently (in all his nine books, Herodotus never mentions the Jews once), but he tells of a plague of mice that nibbled the Assyrian bowstrings, left the host insecurely armed, and forced them to retreat.

Undoubtedly, Sennacherib did retreat with Jerusalem untaken, but the reasons may be more prosaic than either the Bible or Herodotus make them seem. Egypt was very weak at the time, but she had to make *some* effort to relieve Jerusalem. After all, she could scarcely afford an Assyrian victory. Sennacherib must have known of Egyptian intrigues and, if Jerusalem fell, the way would be clear for him to drive across the Sinai peninsula and wreak his vengeance on the land of the Nile. Anyone knowing Sennacherib would know that the vengeance would not be a mild one.

Consequently, an Egyptian army marched to the relief of Jerusalem, and Sennacherib had to fight it. The Assyrians won, but in the process, they were inevitably weakened and that reduced their chances of taking Jerusalem. On top of that, Sennacherib's viceroys in Babylonia must have been sending him messages that the area would be in flames again soon, and to the Assyrian monarch, the great metropolis of Babylon would seem more important than the little hill town of Jerusalem.

So, in frustration, the Assyrian army had to retreat. But it

was only a slight Assyrian setback; for except for retaining its
own king and customs, Judah could have had very little to
celebrate. The land was devastated and Hezekiah had to pay
a perfectly enormous indemnity and, moreover, return to paying tribute.

Judah continued to pay tribute for the remainder of Assyria's
history and was so badly drained of strength that she never
rebelled against that nation again. Hezekiah's son, Manasseh, who reigned for half a century, found no safety in any
course of action other than that of being an abject Assyrian
puppet. He did his best to suppress the nationalistic Prophetic
party which kept up a steady drumfire of anti-Assyrian propaganda that might at any time provoke the final disaster of a
new invasion and siege. As a result, Manasseh is execrated by
the Biblical writers.

Babylonia did indeed burst into flames again, and Sennacherib saw clearly that Babylon would never be quiet as
long as Elamite help was at its service. He therefore determined to mount an offensive directly against Elam, and to
do so not by fighting his way through Babylon and reaching
Elam with dangerously weakened forces but by mounting an
unexpected attack from the sea.

He built ships in the north and west to keep Elam's spies
from learning too soon of what he planned. Since Assyrians had
no sea experience, Sennacherib employed Phoenicians to man
his ships. He may have had the services of some Greek sail-
ors as well. (It may have been now that Greece and Assyria
made contact in this relatively peaceful way. Some of the
Greeks returned home eventually with tales of the great city
of Nineveh, and it may have been these that served as source
material for Greek legends of Ninus and Semiramis.)

Finally, the fleet was ready. It sailed swiftly and quietly
down the Euphrates, passing Babylon and leaving it un-
touched, then reaching the Persian Gulf at last. The Assyrian
expeditionary force landed on the Elamite shore and drove inland.

If the Elamites had faced him and fought, Sennacherib might
have won a great victory, but the Elamites countered the un-

expected Assyrian move with a move of their own that was equally unexpected. They left their nation guarded by a skeleton force and sent their main army into Babylonia, uniting with the rebels there and facing Sennacherib with the danger of being cut off from his base. Sennacherib had to retreat, all his cunning plans having gone for nothing.

This was a frustration that far outweighed anything he might have felt in connection with Jerusalem, and it drove Sennacherib into a veritable transport of fury.

Until then, Babylon had been safe, thanks to the glory of its history. It was the greatest, richest, and most cultivated city of the west with already a thousand years of history behind it. It maintained the age-old Sumerian religion and was the home of the chief god of its version of that religion, Marduk (who had been promoted to that position far back in Hammurabi's time).

To be sure, Babylon was under the thumb of Assyria but that could scarcely affect the Babylonian sense of superiority. The Babylonians must have viewed the Assyrians very much as, five centuries later, the Greeks were to view the Romans. The Assyrians (like the Romans) were good at making war, but at nothing else. For everything that counted in life — religion, language, culture — Assyria had to come to Babylon.

Assyria itself must have felt this and unwillingly paid Babylon an almost superstitious reverence. It was as though even the Assyrian kings dared not face the execration of posterity if they damaged Babylon. (Much this feeling protected such later cities of famous cultural history as Athens, Florence, and Paris.)

But Sennacherib, turned mad with frustration, could be held back no longer by any consideration of Babylon's greatness. It would have to be taught a lesson, a horrible one. The world in general would see that not even Babylon could withstand the Assyrian fury, and perhaps once it witnessed the Assyrian revenge, there would be no further troubles.

Sennacherib, in 689 B.C., forced his way into Babylon, and set about the complete destruction of that city. He destroyed its canal system, breaching the dikes, and filling in the ditches

with the mud of houses which he washed down by diverting
the current of the Euphrates. He destroyed even the temples
and carried off to Assyria the statue of Marduk itself. His
aim was to make the city a level area of empty devastation.

He didn't quite succeed. The city survived, very miserably
at first, but it survived.

Sennacherib himself, however, came to a bad end. In 681
B.C., while engaged in religious devotions, he was killed as a
result of a conspiracy engineered by his two eldest sons.

AT THE PEAK

We know no details of the plot against Sennacherib, but
somehow it must have miscarried, for the son-assassins had to
flee hastily northward into Urartu and place themselves beyond the immediate reach of the Assyrian army. There they
attempted to raise forces of their own.

A younger son of Sennacherib meanwhile claimed the throne,
and the nation's leaders rallied around him. This younger
son, the third of the Sargonids, was Ashur-akh-iddina ("Ashur
has given a brother"), known to us by his Biblical name of
Esarhaddon (ee"sahr-had'n).

Esarhaddon quickly defeated the army of his brothers and
put an end to their threat. He was most unusual for an Assyrian monarch in that he avoided war whenever possible.

Thus, he attempted to win over Babylonia by kindness rather
than wrath. He undertook to restore historic Babylon (perhaps
he even felt remorse at his father's merciless treatment of that
great city). It was an enormous task that took him something
like a dozen years, but finally in 669 B.C. Babylon was rededicated, a great city once more. What's more, Esarhaddon labored to restore all the temples that had been broken down and
desecrated in the previous reign.

He even maintained a kind of wary policy of coexistence
with Elam, leaving it strictly in peace provided only Elam
ceased its interference in Babylonia. A new Elamite king es-

tablished a pro-Assyrian policy and for a score of years things worked out well.

In the west, tiny Judah was left to itself provided its king, Manasseh, maintained the necessary tribute-payments, which he did.

In the north, Esarhaddon took the necessary measures against the nomads. The Cimmerians had killed Sargon a generation before, but that had been in the course of a smashing Assyrian victory, and they had remained quiet during Sennacherib's reign. However, the Scythian pressure on their own rear was becoming ever stronger and the Cimmerians found themselves forced deeper and deeper into Asia Minor, while the Scythians themselves were now occupying Urartu.

Esarhaddon marched against them and defeated them in 679 B.C., insuring a period of further quiet. Nor did he neglect to use the arts of peaceful persuasion as well. He established a kind of kinship with the Scythians by taking one of their high-born damsels into his harem. (It always seemed to please and honor barbaric tribes to have one of their princesses vanish into an Imperial harem.)

Only in the far west did Esarhaddon launch an old-fashioned campaign of conquest. Egypt's part in the embarrassing failure to take Jerusalem had not been forgotten; and no doubt Egypt had been busily stirring the pot of rebellion ever since.

Twice Esarhaddon launched offensives against Egypt. A preliminary advance in 673 B.C. underestimated the effectiveness of Egypt's desperation. Egyptians fought with the courage of despair and threw back the Assyrians.

Esarhaddon shrugged and drew back to do the job properly. With a larger and better-equipped army he drove forward again in 671 B.C., and this time, he took the Nile Delta and sacked Memphis, the great twenty-five-century-old metropolis of northern Egypt. For a while, Egypt was placed under Assyrian viceroys.

At that moment, the Assyrian Empire stood at the peak of its power. Esarhaddon held all the Fertile Crescent firmly. The powers that rimmed it and maintained a certain self-government were tributary and quiet: Asia Minor, Urartu, Media,

Elam, Egypt. Even the nomads in the north were under control.

Indeed, it must have seemed to Esarhaddon that only internal troubles could now upset matters. He labored therefore to settle the succession in his own lifetime, wishing for no assassination attempts on himself and no civil war after his death.

He had two grown sons with reasonable claims to the throne and he made arrangements to see that both were well settled. He made arrangements to have the nation's leaders swear allegiance to the younger of the two sons as the next king. This was Ashur-ban-aplu ("Ashur creates the son"), or Ashurbanipal (ah"shoor-bah'nee-pal) as he is better known to us.

Esarhaddon arranged to have the older son, Shamash-shum-ukin (shah'mahsh-shoom-oo'keen) rule in Babylon as his younger brother's viceroy. Why Esarhaddon chose his younger son for the top job is uncertain. Presumably, he recognized him as the more capable of the two (and, if so, he was right).

It might have seemed that, with even the internal succession arranged, Assyria had never been so secure in its history. If so, that was an illusion. As long as Assyria maintained its position by pure might, and took from its subjects in loot far more than it gave back in terms of security and prosperity, so long would those subjects wait their chance to rebel. And as soon as a weakling mounted the Assyrian throne, all would tumble.

Indeed, even a strong king could not avoid rebellion. Egypt had not been long under the Assyrian thumb before it rebelled, and Esarhaddon was marching westward on his third Egyptian campaign, in 669 B.C., when he died.

THE ROYAL LIBRARIAN

The succession, however, took place without trouble, and in exactly the manner Esarhaddon had planned. Ashurbanipal reigned in Nineveh as the fourth Sargonid, and the fourth successive capable king of that line. Under him, Nineveh reached its peak, and its population may have climbed to a hundred thousand. Its trade caravans reached as far as India.

Ashurbanipal was, in some ways, the most remarkable of all the Assyrian rulers.

Like all the great kings of that realm, he was a capable and tireless general and never shirked the unending task of defending the ever-heaving Empire. But, in addition, he was a scholar. He was thoroughly educated and he was fascinated by Mesopotamia's ancient history. (It was already 2,500 years since writing had been invented.)

Ashurbanipal made it his task to collect a copy of every worthwhile cuneiform-covered tablet in Babylonia. (He could read and write cuneiform himself and did not have to depend upon a lowly scribe.) In this way, he built an enormous library in his palace, one that was carefully catalogued and in which every tablet was inscribed with his name.

It was the greatest library ever gathered up to that time, and was to prove of enormous use thousands of years after the death of the royal librarian.

In the mid-nineteenth century, Ashurbanipal's palace and library were uncovered. In 1872, an English archaeologist, George Smith, located among the remnants being carefully uncovered and deciphered, nothing less than the epic of Gilgamesh told on a dozen tablets. The Babylonian tale of the Flood was deciphered, and the similarity to the Biblical tale was apparent. Scholars suddenly found themselves thinking of sources for the early books of the Bible that were other than Divine inspiration. Ashurbanipal's library held enormous quantities of other information, too. It is shattering to think how little we might know of ancient Mesopotamian history without Ashurbanipal's scholarly enthusiasm twenty-six centuries ago.

Ashurbanipal elaborated, enriched, and beautified his palace and his capital, and under him royal luxury reached a new high. Undoubtedly, anyone observing him in his palace, surrounded by all this luxury and (far worse in the eyes of the rude warriors of the time) engaged in scholarly pursuits, would have thought him an effeminate man, unfit to be ruler of the most militaristic empire the world had yet seen.

In fact, the Greeks later told their own legendary version of a king of Assyria, whom they called Sardanapalus (sahr"duh-nuh-pay'lus). He was, they said, a complete effeminate who dressed in women's clothes and never moved out of his harem. In the end, when his subjects rebelled and it looked as though his palace were sure to be captured, he dumped everything he owned into one pile, together with his wives, his slaves, and himself, set fire to it all and went out in a blaze — though not exactly of glory.

Even the Greeks had to admit, though, that Sardanapalus, before he gave in, did shake off his sloth, don a warrior's armor, and lead his hosts bravely against the foe.

It has long been supposed that Sardanapalus was the Greek version of Ashurbanipal and, undoubtedly, Ashurbanipal's scribbling in cuneiform and his habit of reading scholarly books aloud to his wives (who must have hated it) helped give rise to the legend. However, Ashurbanipal was fated to die in peace and with his Empire almost intact. It was someone else, as we shall see,who died in the Sardanapalian manner.

Far from being a harem-bound effeminate, Ashurbanipal had to fight almost constantly. Egypt was in rebellion at the time of Esarhaddon's death, and Ashurbanipal led two assaults against that land. In the second, he marched up the Nile to Thebes, the great capital of southern Egypt, and sacked it. It was the farthest any Assyrian army had ever marched, or ever was to march.

Yet it didn't help. In 655 B.C., after the sack of Thebes, Egypt revolted again. A native Egyptian who had begun his career as an Assyrian vassal managed to make himself independent and proclaimed himself as King, ruling as Psamtik I (sam'tik).

Undoubtedly, Ashurbanipal, unwearied, would have returned to Egypt a third time, but even he couldn't be in two places at once and, as a matter of fact, he was needed in three places.

For one thing, the Cimmerians were making trouble again,

and Ashurbanipal now had to ignore Egypt (which maintained its newfound independence for more than a century) to face the enemy in Asia Minor.

There, at least, Assyria was not alone. The small kingdoms of Asia Minor were fighting off the Cimmerians desperately. Indeed, a general called Gyges (jy'jeez) was founding a new kingdom in western Asia Minor, which was called Lydia, and he proved particularly effective against the nomads. Ashurbanipal helped him generously and between them, the Cimmerian menace was finally put to an end. In the process, however, Gyges died in battle in 652 B.C.

Ashurbanipal next had to turn southward. Ashurbanipal's preoccupation with Egypt and Asia Minor had not gone unnoticed in Elam, which had been quiet long enough. Perhaps now was the golden moment to wreck and inherit the Assyrian Empire.

The tool it needed seemed to be at hand. Surely, while the younger brother enjoyed supreme power, the older brother in Babylon must have grown restless. Elamite agents could not have failed to point out to Shamash-shum-ukin that if he rebelled against his younger brother he could count on Elamite help; and possibly on Egyptian help as well.

Shamash-shum-ukin allowed himself to be persuaded and in 652 B.C., he revolted. Civil war began at once and for four years Ashurbanipal bore down remorselessly on Babylonia. In 648 B.C., Shamash-shum-ukin was faced with final defeat and he knew exactly what to expect if he were taken. He therefore dumped everything he owned into one pile, together with his wives, his slaves, and himself, set fire to it all and went out in a blaze — though not exactly of glory.

Does this sound familiar? It is. This is the end of Saradanapalus, and the Greek legend was clearly inspired by Ashurbanipal's older brother, not by Ashurbanipal himself.

But Ashurbanipal wasn't through. Babylonia, he saw, would never cool down as long as Elam was in existence. As Esarhaddon had struck at Egypt, the western source of disaffection, so Ashurbanipal determined to strike at the eastern source.

The Elamite war took ten years and Ashurbanipal won it all

the way. He took Susa in 639 B.C. and destroyed it. He carried off the chief Elamites into exile. All of Elam he turned into a wasteland, and the kingdom, which had existed in Sumer's time, and been a power in Mesopotamia in the days of Abraham, now came to a final end. It ceased to exist and its name vanished from the face of the earth.

5

THE CHALDEANS

THE END OF NINEVEH

The last fourteen years of Ashurbanipal's reign are a blank. We know almost nothing of them.

By the time of the destruction of Elam, Ashurbanipal had reigned thirty hard years and had probably reached his late fifties. Undoubtedly, he was tired. Undoubtedly, he longed for a period of peace in which he could remain in his palace and be with his beloved antiquities. After all, the Empire was quiet and — except for Egypt — it was even intact.

We can imagine him deciding with sullen obstinacy that he had earned his rest and that Egypt could go to the devil. So he disappeared inside his palace and it may be this period of his life that helped inspire that portion of the Greek legend of Sardanapalus that refers to his remaining hidden in his harem.

But if peace seemed to rest over the Empire, that was an

illusion. It was not peace, but rather an approaching death. The endless wars had finally worn out the Assyrians. The Cimmerian devastations of Asia Minor, and Ashurbanipal's own destruction of Elam had upset the trade routes, and prosperity must have declined drastically.

Ashurbanipal's torpor toward the end made things worse. The Assyrian army rusted with disuse and the subject peoples gathered courage. Egypt set them a resounding example, for it had rebelled and had made its rebellion stick.

The lesson was taken to heart most clearly in Babylonia, where the Chaldeans, who had resisted Sargon, Sennacherib, and Ashurbanipal, still dreamed of independence despite their threefold defeat. Ashurbanipal's viceroy, established in Babylon after the self-immolation of Shamash-shum-ukin, died in 627 B.C., and for a while there was a tug-of-war between various contenders for local control. The winner was a Chaldean, Nabu-apal-usur ("Nabu guards the prince"), better known to us by the slurred version of that name — Nabopolassar (nab″oh-poh-las′er).

It was clear that Nabopolassar planned to go his own way, and if Assyria had been what it had once been, he would never have been allowed to come to power. But Ashurbanipal lay dying and Assyria lay frozen.

In 625 B.C. Ashurbanipal died, having reigned forty-three years. His death was the cue for disaster, for he had no strong successor. The Sargonids had turned up four unusual men of strength and ability, and that is perhaps already more than one might expect. A fifth did not come along.

Ashurbanipal was succeeded first by one son, who reigned five years, then by another. Neither seems to emerge as an individual from the shadowy mist that hides Assyrian history after Ashurbanipal's destruction of Elam.

Almost as soon as the old king died, Nabopolassar, gauging the strength of the new king, declared his independence of Assyria.

This meant war, of course. However weakened Assyria had grown, however incompetently it might be led, it knew only one way of life, that of fighting. For ten years, an inconclusive war continued between Nineveh and Babylon, while other parts of the Empire seized their own chance to throw off Assyrian oppression.

Slowly, Assyria sank under the burden, but fought every inch of the way with a resolution one can scarcely help admire. Nabopolassar and his Chaldeans drove far upstream and into the Assyrian heartland, but at a tremendous cost. The Chaldean leader had to look about worriedly for help, lest a slight turn in the fortune of war lose him everything he had gained.

He found his allies among the nomads to the north and east. During Ashurbanipal's reign, the Medes and Scythians had been fighting each other. This had well served Assyrian purposes. Nevertheless, there had been a slow but steady drive toward unity among the tribes. In Ashurbanipal's last years, a Median chieftain, known to us by the Greek version of his name, Cyaxares (sy-ak'suh-reez), succeeded in establishing his rule over a number of tribes, Scythian as well as Median. By 625 B.C., he emerged as king of an independent Media, stretching out over much of modern Iran.

It was to Cyaxares that Nabopolassar turned. In 616 B.C., when Assyria was fighting with its back to the wall, defending the ancient cities of its heartland, Nabopolassar formed a treaty of alliance with the Medes. The treaty was sealed by a matrimonial arrangement. Nabopolassar's son (of whom we shall hear more) married Cyaxares' daughter.

With that, Cyaxares plunged into the attack on Assyria and took Ashur, Assyria's ancient capital. That was really the end. Assyria might fight both enemies with undiminished resolution, but victory had become impossible.

Such was Assyria's position, in fact, that she was forced to seek a counter-alliance with Egypt. What else could dramatize Assyrian desperation so completely? Only forty years before, Assyria had marched the length of the Nile in the pride of power, and now she had to come humbly to ask help of a Pharaoh who had once been an Assyrian puppet.

Egypt agreed; not out of a spirit of forgive-and-forget, but out of careful self-interest. Egypt did not want a one-sided victory in either direction. A weak Assyria was good, but a destroyed one was bad. If Nabopolassar won too completely, he would represent a new danger.

But Egyptian help was far too little and far too late. In 612 B.C. Nabopolassar and Cyaxares mounted a joint siege of Nineveh, and took it, as a howl of joy went up from the subject peoples who had so long lain under the dread of Assyria's heavy, armored hand.

The Judean prophet, Nahum, calls out, "Woe to the bloody city!" (Nahum 3:1) and ends with a remorseless, "All that hear the bruit of thee [the news of Nineveh's destruction] shall clap the hands over thee: for upon whom hath not thy wickedness passed continuously" (Nahum 3:19).

Nineveh was destroyed with a completeness that testifies well to the hate in which it was held. Nor did its conquerors allow it ever to be rebuilt. It passed from history and from the very consciousness of man. Two centuries later, a Greek army passed that way and had to ask what that large mound of earth might be. It was all that was left of the great capital, and all that remained left until the nineteenth century.

Only the accident that the Jews incorporated the hated name in their Biblical writings kept it alive in the memory of western mankind.

THE DIVISION OF THE SPOILS

But even after Nineveh fell, the Assyrians did not give up. Fragments of the Assyrian army remained and while they remained, they fought.

They retreated to the last city left of all the wide dominion over which Assyria had ruled as briefly as a dozen years before. This was Harran (hah-rahn′), 130 miles west of Nineveh and 60 miles east of the Euphrates. It was located just at the northern peak of the Fertile Crescent.

There, the Assyrian last stand held out under Ashur-uballit, a general who may fairly be called the "last of the Assyrians." Sometimes he is called Ashur-uballit II, since a ruler of that name had restored Assyrian power after its near-extinction by the Hurrians. Perhaps the general deliberately adopted the name to symbolize the fact that Assyria would rise again, as it had once done. If so, the symbol proved false.

Two armies moved toward Harran, one to try to destroy Ashur-uballit, and one to try to save him. The former was a Chaldean army, of course, led by Nabopolassar. The latter was an Egyptian army, hurrying to keep the Chaldeans from gaining overwhelming power.

A new king, Necho II (nee'koh), had mounted the Egyptian throne in 609 B.C., and it was he who led the rescue army. To accomplish his purpose, however, he had to pass through Judah, and Judah did not wish that.

With Assyria's fall, Judah had regained a moment of independence and she wanted to keep it. Her king was Josiah, the grandson of the Manasseh who had been an Assyrian puppet. Under Josiah, Judah had undergone a religious reform in which its God, Yahweh, was recognized as the only God of the land, to be worshiped only at the Temple in Jerusalem. Safeguarding land and creed, Josiah stepped forward to stop Necho.

In 608 B.C., at Megiddo in northern Israel, a battle was fought and Egypt won the victory. Josiah was killed and his body was brought back to a lamenting Jerusalem, while one of his sons assumed the throne under Egyptian sponsorship.

The delay caused by the battle, even though this had ended in an Egyptian victory, was fatal for Necho's plans. While Necho was busy fighting off Josiah, Nabopolassar had taken Harran, and Ashur-uballit had to retreat to the Euphrates. There he joined forces with Necho and, for a while, the two attempted to mount a counterattack that would take Harran. It failed, and Ashur-uballit disappears from the stage of history. How he died, or what happened to him, no one knows.

And so, in 605 B.C., disappeared the last trace of Assyria, twelve centuries after the time of its first conquering king, Shamshi-Adad.

Even while Assyria was vanishing under the blows of the Chaldeans, the same fate was befalling Assyria's old rival, Urartu, under the blows of the Medes. Only a century and

a half before, Urartu had almost matched Assyria in power,
but a chain of disasters had wrecked it. Defeat by the Assyrians, Cimmerians, and Scythians had left it all but power-
less, and the Medes put an end to the last of its shadowy kings
and, by 600, had absorbed its territory. Urartu, like Assyria, disappeared from history.

But even with the last Assyrian gone, Necho was still there
on the Euphrates. Nabopolassar was ill and returned to Babylon, but he left his son in his place. This son (who had
earlier married Cyaxares' daughter) was named Nebuchadrezzar. He is usually listed as Nebuchadrezzar II in formal histories, because of the earlier ruler of that name who had governed
Babylon five centuries before.

Nebuchadrezzar met Necho at Carchemish (kahr'kuh-
mish), a city on the upper Euphrates, west of Harran. There,
Necho's army was smashed as thoroughly as three years earlier
it had smashed that of Judah. Hastily, Necho had to evacuate
the western half of the Fertile Crescent, dashing back pell-
mell to the dubious safety of the Nile. Nebuchadrezzar might
well have followed, but almost at the moment of victory, he
received the news that his father had died. He had to return
to Babylon, therefore, to make sure that he was safely invested
with the crown.

Now there was time to breathe. Assyria was dead and Egypt
was quiet. Nebuchadrezzar and Cyaxares made a peaceful
division of the Assyrian spoils. Cyaxares had added to his vast
dominions in Iran, Urartu and the eastern portion of Asia Minor. His empire looked enormous on the map, but it consisted
largely of undeveloped lands, and Media was to remain reasonably peaceful for its half-century of existence.

The entire Fertile Crescent, much smaller in area than Media,
but making up by far the most civilized and richest portion of
the western world (leaving Egypt out of consideration) was in
Nebuchadrezzar's firm grip.

Nebuchadrezzar's dominion is sometimes called the "New
Babylonian Empire" or the "Neo-Babylonian Empire," but I believe the best name for it is "Chaldean Empire."

Nebuchadrezzar's career was remarkably like that of his

Assyrian predecessor, Ashurbanipal. Both ruled for over forty years; both were largely successful in warfare, though with important failures; both spent their last years in tired obscurity; and the greatness of their empires died with their own deaths in each case.

The chief field of Nebuchadrezzar's military efforts was in the west where independent Egypt was still indefatigably stirring up trouble. Egyptian intrigue kept the small land of Judah at odds with Nebuchadrezzar, despite the pro-Babylonian activity of the Jewish prophet Jeremiah.

Twice Judah tried to revolt and twice Nebuchadrezzar had to react strongly. Both times, he laid siege to Jerusalem and forced Judean submission. The first time, in 598 B.C., he carried off some of the leaders in a continuation of the Assyrian policy of deportation, but left Judah a king, a Temple and self-rule.

The second time, in 587 B.C., he lost patience completely. This time he destroyed Jerusalem and its Temple. The Davidic dynasty was ended after having reigned in Jerusalem for over four centuries, and another large supply of leading citizens were carried off into exile in Babylonia.

Nebuchadrezzar then went on to attempt to chastise those who had assisted Judah, but his plans met an unexpected obstacle because of Tyre, a city on the Mediterranean coast about a hundred miles north of Jerusalem. It was one of the coastal cities inhabited by people known to the Greeks (and therefore to ourselves) as Phoenicians.

The Tyrians were known for their daring seamanship. Their vessels plowed the full length of the Mediterranean, founding colonies on the African coast, in Spain, and even outside the Mediterranean. Spanish minerals brought them wealth and power; Sennacherib had hired them to man his fleet against Elam, and Necho had hired them to attempt the circumnavigation of Africa.

Tyre's core was a rocky island just offshore. In fact, the name "Tyre" stems from a west-Semitic word for "rock." With the Tyrian force concentrated on that island, and with food and other supplies brought to it from all over the world by its efficient fleet, it could easily stand against the largest land army

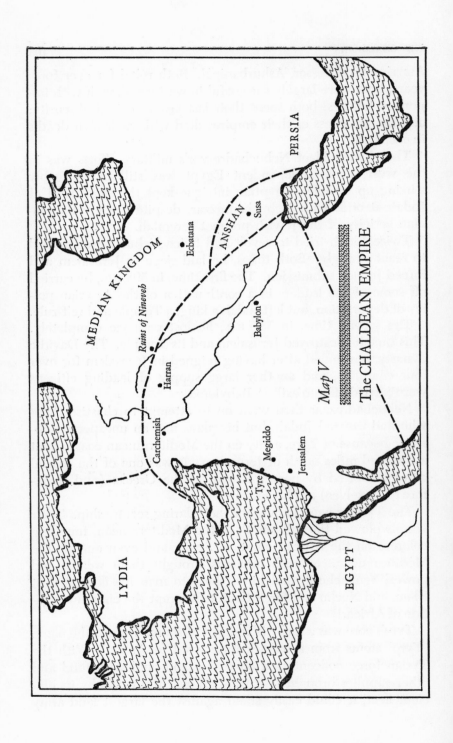

MEDIAN KINGDOM

PERSIA

Ecbatana

ANSHAN

Susa

Ruins of Nineveh

Babylon

Harran

Carchemish

LYDIA

Megiddo

Tyre

Jerusalem

EGYPT

Map V

The CHALDEAN EMPIRE

anyone could bring against it, if that land army were led without military genius, or if a superior fleet failed to sail against it simultaneously.

The other Phoenician cities had yielded to Nebuchadrezzar, but Tyre remained defiant and, in 585 B.C., right after the fall of Jerusalem, Nebuchadrezzar's armies clicked into position on the shore opposite the island.

They might as well have saved their time. The Tyrians were not in the least perturbed. While they had their fleet, the world was theirs, and each year merely saw Nebuchadrezzar's prestige dwindle. For thirteen years, the stubborn, useless siege continued until both parties were heartily weary of the trouble of it all. Nebuchadrezzar raised the siege at last, with Tyre unconquered and unpunished, but Tyre had to pay a healthy tribute to save itself future trouble.

The uselessness of it all may have broken Nebuchadrezzar's spirit. He sent a long-threatened expedition against Egypt, but Egypt had been preparing for such an eventuality since the battle of Carchemish. The details aren't known to us, but Egypt survived and retained its independence. We can conclude then that Nebuchadrezzar's Egyptian campaign, like that of his alter ego, Ashurbanipal, was, in the end, a failure.

BABYLON IN ITS GLORY

In the second half of his reign, Nebuchadrezzar confined himself to Babylon, which he beautified, much as Ashurbanipal had beautified Nineveh.

Nebuchadrezzar surpassed the deeds of his predecessor, however, and it was in his time, not before, that Babylon truly became the Babylon of legend, the huge and wealthy metropolis.

In Nebuchadrezzar's time, Babylon was undoubtedly the

greatest city of the western world. Thebes in southern Egypt may have been more impressive in its prime, with its colossal temples and monuments, but that city was in decay now, as was its northern twin, Memphis. The Greek cities of the time were little more than unimpressive towns clustered about a small temple or two, and Rome was a faraway Italian village no one had yet heard of.

A century after Nebuchadrezzar, the Greek historian Herodotus visited Babylon and could speak of it only in breathless awe. He claimed that it covered a square plot of ground, fourteen miles on each side (which would make it a considerable city in size even by modern standards) and that its walls were 300 feet high and 80 feet wide.

This is very likely an exaggeration that results from Herodotus' too-ready acceptance of the vainglorious statistics offered him by the Babylonian priesthood. Our own present-day excavations don't show Babylon to have been nearly that large nor its walls to have been nearly that size. Still, the reality must have been impressive enough.

At its peak, Babylon was supposed to have a population of a million. This, too, is very likely an exaggeration, even after one lumps in the people of the various suburbs. If the figure is accepted, however, Babylon would be the first million-person city in the history of the western world, and there was not to be a second until Imperial Rome six centuries later.

One of the gates leading through the city's wall, is the so-called "Ishtar Gate." It has been uncovered by archaeologists and is seen to be decorated with blue enamel bricks bearing red and white reliefs of bulls and dragons. On passing through the gate, one finds oneself on what is left of the straight main street of the city, lined on either side with walls bearing brick lions in relief, along with other decorations.

The complex of buildings that made up Nebuchadrezzar's palace covered 13 acres of ground and the largest room in it — the throne room where foreign delegations were received — was about 200 feet long and nearly that in width. Its walls, too, were decorated with glazed brick lions.

The palace stood on an eminence overlooking the city and

there are signs that Nebuchadrezzar built structures which
were then covered with earth and planted with shrubs and
flowers. According to legend, he did this to please his Median
wife who detested the flat land of Babylonia and longed for
the hills of her home. Nebuchadrezzar therefore built these
artificial hills.

Viewed from a distance, the gardens seemed suspended in
air, and these are the famous "Hanging Gardens of Babylon"
which the admiring Greeks counted among the "Seven Won-
ders of the World."

Nebuchadrezzar beautified and enlarged the temples, of
which there were over eleven hundred in Babylon. He paid
special honor to Marduk, and completed a great ziggurat in
Marduk's honor that had long remained unfinished because of
the continuous furore of the wars with Assyria. Once finished,
it was the largest Babylonian temple of all time, 300 feet on
each side and with seven successively smaller stages (one, it is
thought, for each planet) rising skyward.

Babylon was a trade center, and men of all nations jostled
each other there. It was also the intellectual leader of the world,
for all the accumulated science and technology that dated back
to the Sumerians through three thousand years was available
in its halls of learning.

The Greeks, in particular, came to learn. Greek science had
its beginnings with a man named Thales (thay'leez), who lived
in the city of Miletus (my-lee'tus) on the Aegean coast of Asia
Minor at just the time that Nebuchadrezzar was ruling in Babylon. Legend has it that he traveled to Babylon for his education. So, according to legend, did almost all the early Greek
philosophers that followed Thales; Pythagoras (pih-thag'
oh-ras), for instance.

Undoubtedly, the beginnings of Greek science in Nebuchadrezzar's time can be attributed in part to the Babylonian
learning brought back (and improved upon) by the early
Greek philosophers.

Thales brought back and improved on certain aspects of
Babylonian mathematics. It was now that the old Sumerian
habit of reckoning by sixties entered the west, so that we still

have 60 minutes to the hour and 360 degrees to a circumference of a circle.

Pythagoras must have brought back the accumulated astronomical lore of the Babylonians. Astronomy was, indeed, a specialty of the learned men of Babylon during this time of the city's peak. So much did other men marvel at Babylonian astronomical lore, that the very word "Chaldean" came to mean astronomer. And since the chief purpose of astronomy at the time was to work out the influence of the planets and stars on events upon the earth, the word came also to mean "astrologer" and "magician."

Thus, the Greeks had originally thought that the evening star and morning star were two separate planets, which they called Hesperos ("west") and Phosphoros ("light-bringer") respectively. Pythagoras, however, having visited Babylon, was able to argue that they were really a single planet, which was present on one side of the sun on some occasions and on the other side on other occasions.

Furthermore, the Babylonian habit of naming the planets in the honor of gods was adopted by the Greeks, too. The Babylonians called the evening star and morning star combination, Ishtar, after their goddess of beauty and love — a fitting name for this most beautiful and brightest of planets. When the Greeks abandoned the names of Hesperos and Phosphoros, they, too, adopted such a name and called the planet after their own goddess of beauty and love, Aphrodite. The Romans named it Venus, and it is that name that remains with us.

Venus is only visible in the evening and the morning, but another planet, nearly as bright, can be visible throughout the night. It seemed natural to name that one after the chief god. The Babylonians called it Marduk, the Greeks called it Zeus, and the Romans (and we) called it Jupiter. Similarly, a red planet, the color of blood and therefore reminiscent of war, was named after the war god: Nergal to the Babylonians, Ares to the Greeks, and Mars to the Romans and ourselves.

By Nebuchadrezzar's time, the Babylonians had worked out a careful calendar based on the phases of the moon. Each new moon began a new month. Unfortunately, there were 354 days in 12 such lunar months, while in the full cycle of the seasons (the solar year) there were 365¼ days. In order to keep the months even with the seasons, it was necessary to have 13 months in some years. The Babylonians worked out a 19-year cycle in which there were 12 years with 12 months each and 7 years with 13 months each in a fixed pattern that kept the moon and the sun even.

This calendar was adopted by the Greeks, and nothing better came along for five centuries, until Julius Caesar of Rome ordered worked out what is essentially our modern calendar, based on an Egyptian original.

THE JEWS IN EXILE

Nebuchadrezzar's reign was a most remarkable one for the Jews; the turning point, in fact, of their history. It might have seemed at first glance that the destruction of their independence, their monarchy, their capital, and their Temple would have meant the complete and utter end of Jewish history. Yet they survived.

Partly this was the result of the cosmopolitan atmosphere of Babylonia, and its religious tolerance. The Jews in exile were not oppressed. Rather, they could buy land, engage in business, and even prosper. Indeed when, eventually, some of them made ready to return to Jerusalem, those who remained behind were prosperous enough to help them considerably:

"And all they that were about them strengthened their hands with vessels of silver, with gold, with goods, and with beasts, and with precious things" (Ezra 1:6).

Furthermore, the Jews retained a full measure of religious liberty. No effort at all was made to force them to worship Marduk.

To be sure, in the Biblical book of Daniel, there are tales of the persecution of Daniel and of three other Jews (Shadrach, Meshach, and Abednego) by Nebuchadrezzar, who threw them in fiery furnaces and into lions' dens, but these are fictional tales. The book of Daniel was written four centuries after the Babylonian captivity at a time when the Jews were being persecuted by a Greek-speaking king, Antiochus IV. The book of Daniel, by talking of earlier persecutions, was serving to hearten the Jews for resistance against Antiochus.

It was because of the book of Daniel that Babylon came to be looked upon as the very epitome of the pagan, persecuting power. In later centuries, its name was used to stand for Rome, and it was pictured as the very sink of sin (as in the book of Revelation, for instance). Because of the various Biblical references, we still tend to think of Babylon as having been a particularly wicked city, and that is quite unfair, for it was no more wicked than any other large city.

Indeed, the Jews were so well treated in Babylon that there is no sign of their having made any trouble for the authorities. During the period of the Exile, the chief Jewish prophet of the time was Ezekiel, and he sounds like a completely patriotic Babylonian. He inveighs bitterly against all the enemies of Nebuchadrezzar, predicting the destruction of Tyre and Egypt (which didn't come to pass) and never predicting evil for Babylon itself. Even the destruction of Jerusalem, he blamed not on Nebuchadrezzar, but rather on the evil practices of the Jews themselves.

It was through Ezekiel that a very remarkable thing happened, something that was unprecedented in history and that explains — even more than the Babylonian tolerance — the Jewish survival. Throughout ancient times, it had remained taken for granted that when a people were defeated, its gods were defeated, too; and when a people were deported, lost their sense of national identity, and died as a nation, their gods died, too. This had happened to the Israelites who had been deported by Sargon two centuries before.

It did not happen with the Jews. Their land was gone, their Temple was gone — yet Ezekiel maintained firmly that this was not because their God had been weak or had been defeated. He had merely been displeased, and was punishing the Jews. When the punishment was over, the Jews would be restored; and meanwhile the Jews had better learn to be good.

Under Ezekiel's guidance, learned men among the Jewish exiles (the scribes) began to put Jewish legends and historical records into written and organized form in a way designed to fit the scheme of history that Ezekiel and the others thought was correct. Thus was born the present form of the early books of the Bible.

The Jews in Babylon were attracted to Babylonian culture, of course, as were all the people who entered Mesopotamia after the Sumerians had founded that culture. They could not resist adopting some Babylonian lore, therefore.

Their own records went back to their entry into Canaan, with dim legends of Moses and, before him, of the ancestral patriarchs, Abraham, Isaac, and Jacob.

For the time before Abraham, however, they depended on the Babylonian legends, and the first ten books of Genesis contain these legends after their polytheism and idolatry have been removed. The great tale of the Creation, given in the first chapter of Genesis, is probably inspired by Babylon. The monster of chaos, Tiamat, has become "Tehom" ("the deep") over which the spirit of God brooded.

The list of ten patriarchs before the Flood, and the Flood itself, seem to have come straight from the old Sumerian records as preserved by the Babylonian priesthood of Nebuchadrezzar's day.

The tower of Babel (see Genesis 11:1-9) is a version of the ziggurat, and the tale of its having been left unfinished was probably inspired by the unfinished state of the ziggurat to Marduk in Babylon at the time the Jews were first taken into exile.

Jacob's dream of seeing a ladder stretching from earth to heaven (Genesis 28:12) with angels ascending and descending may also have been inspired by the ziggurats with their external stairways rising from one stage to the next, stairways up and down which solemn processionals of priests moved.

The story of Abram (Abraham), the primal figure from whom all Jews reverently claimed descent, was also tied in with Babylonia. The Biblical story tells that Abram reached Canaan from

Harran (where the Assyrians many centuries later were to make their last stand), and that his family remained there. It was to Harran that he sent for a wife for his son, Isaac, and in Harran that Jacob found four wives.

This sounds quite reasonable, for Harran, in patriarchal times, was a Hurrian center and many connections have been found between the ways of the patriarchs, as described in the Bible, and Hurrian customs.

In the story as we have it in Genesis now, however, it is related that Abram and his family arrived at Harran from "Ur of the Chaldees." It is possible, perhaps, that this legend may reflect an actual emigration from Sumeria to Canaan. But it is also possible that the scribes who were polishing and editing the Jewish legends could not resist tracing Jewish origins back to the lofty Babylonian civilization and making themselves the equal in descent and ancientness of their conqueror.

Ur was still in existence in Nebuchadrezzar's time, a decaying village that was nearly dead but that had an awesome record of greatness in dim and ancient times. Ur may have been chosen for this very dim antiquity that breathed upon it. It is called by the anachronistic title of "Ur of the Chaldees," for although the Chaldeans ruled there in Nebuchadrezzar's time, they certainly did not in the time of Abraham, nearly fifteen centuries earlier.

All these legends, the Jews made peculiarly their own. They took the calendar of the Babylonians and made that their own, too, and have kept it indeed for two thousand years after Babylonian civilization came to an end. Even today, the Jewish religious calendar is still Babylonian down to the very names of the months.

The Jews also adopted the Babylonian seven-day week, but made the seventh day, their distinctively Jewish Sabbath, a day peculiarly dedicated to God. The "Law of Moses" made up much of the early books of the Bible and, undoubtedly, it owed much to the inspiration of the law codes descended from those of Hammurabi and his predecessors.

There was no danger thereafter of the Jews losing national consciousness. Even with land and Temple gone, they now had their Bible, their Law, and their Sabbath, and had marked themselves off from others, given themselves an identity, and insured their survival. Even if they hadn't returned to Jerusalem, they would have preserved their identity. The proof of that is that they have done so for all the twenty-five centuries that have elapsed since Ezekiel's time, despite an intensified exile far longer and far harder than anything visited upon them by Nebuchadrezzar. It is with good reason that Ezekiel, the prophet who lived in Babylon, is known as the "father of Judaism."

Nor is that all. A generation after Ezekiel, at the time the Babylonian Exile was drawing to an end, another prophet arose, perhaps the greatest of all the Jewish poets. We know nothing about him except his writing, however; not even his name.

His work was attributed to an earlier prophet, Isaiah, who lived at the time of Sennacherib's siege of Jerusalem, two centuries before, and is included in the Biblical book of Isaiah, as chapters 40 to 55 inclusive. Modern commentators refer to him as the Second Isaiah.

It was the Second Isaiah who first clearly had the vision of Yahveh as not merely the God of the Jews. He saw him as the God of all the Universe. It is with the Second Isaiah that a true monotheism begins. The universality of God was recognized by later Jews generally, no matter how nationalistic they might be. It was this view which made it possible for Judaism to give birth to its daughter religions of Christianity and Islam, which spread through vast areas and teeming populations which Judaism itself never touched.

And that concept, too, had arisen in Babylon.

THE ROYAL ANTIQUARIAN

Nebuchadrezzar died in 562 B.C., and when his strong hand was removed, a time of troubles began at once. His son, Amel-Marduk, succeeded. He is known to us chiefly through a casual

mention in the Bible, where his name is distorted to "Evil-Merodach" (ee'vil-meh-roh'dak). The Bible notes that in Evil-
Merodach's time, the exiled king of Judah was treated with
greater leniency, having by then been imprisoned for just a
quarter of a century.

Evil-Merodach did not remain king for long. Within two
years, he had fallen to a palace conspiracy, and the husband
of his sister (and, therefore, Nebuchadrezzar's son-in-law) ascended the throne in 560 B.C. This was Nergal-shar-usur, better known by the Greek version of his name, Neriglissar.

Neriglissar died in his turn in 556 B.C., and his son (Nebuchadrezzar's grandson) was quickly set aside and assassinated.
Thus did the dynasty of Nabopolassar come to an end after
seventy years. Out of several parties contending for the throne,
the one that came out ahead placed Nabu-naid ("Nabu
is exalted") on the throne. He is better known to us by the
Greek version of his name — Nabonidus (nab"oh-ny'dus).

It was a disastrous choice, for though Nabonidus seems to
have been a fine human being, he was a remarkably poor king.
Indeed, the kingship scarcely interested him in itself. He was
an antiquarian, a student of ancient relics, and for him being
king meant merely that he now had an opportunity to delve
into the past with all the resources of the state at his call.

He dug up ancient cuneiform tablets with enthusiastic zeal
and carefully restored them. While he did little for Babylon
itself, he was rapidly interested in restoring the temples in old,
old towns such as Ur and Larsa.

Such activity did not, however, please the powerful priesthood of Babylonia. Nebuchadrezzar had increased the power
of the priesthood of Marduk until they felt the other gods to be
of little account. But Nabonidus was not a native of Babylon, having been born in Harran which was then under Median
control. Indeed, he had been the son of a priestess of Sin, the
moon god, and was particularly interested in that god, and
the cities, such as Harran and Ur, which it patronized. The
priests of Marduk were jealous and that was to prove a factor
in disaster.

Nabonidus' interest in scholarship led to a decay in Babylonian defenses, for war and conquest were the last concerns of the studious king. He placed his son, Bel-shar-ushur, in charge of the national defense and washed his hands of that part of the business. The son is better known by the Biblical version of his name, Belshazzar (bel-shaz'er).

(The Biblical book of Daniel, written four centuries after the fact, shows little acquaintance with Babylonian history. In it, Belshazzar appears as the king of Babylon and as the son and successor of Nebuchadrezzar, all of which is incorrect.)

Somehow, one feels that Nabonidus deserves to have lived out his life in peace, since it is always pleasant to find a king who prefers scholarship to war. In fact, when Nabonidus succeeded to the throne in 556 B.C., there was a peculiar air of peace about the entire western world. Besides Babylonia, there were three great powers: Media, Lydia, and Egypt. All were prosperous and peaceful, almost sleeping, under kindly and gentle monarchs.

It doesn't seem fair, but within a generation all four kingdoms were destroyed.

The agent of destruction was already at hand. He was a man named Kurush, better known to us by the Greek version of his name (in Latin spelling) — Cyrus.

6

THE PERSIANS

THE GENTLE CONQUEROR

Because Cyrus was the founder of a great empire, his life was dramatized by later legend-makers after the fashion of that of Sargon of Agade, some seventeen centuries earlier.

Cyrus was supposed to have been the son of a daughter of Astyages (as-ty'uh-jeez) the king of Media. Astyages was told by an oracle that this grandson was destined to be his death, so he had him abandoned in the mountains to die of exposure. A female dog found him, however, and cared for him, till a shepherd found the baby and brought him up. Naturally, when Cyrus grew up, the oracle was fulfilled, and he was the death of his grandfather.

This can be dismissed. There are so many legends of this sort, and all are so alike, that little value can be placed upon them. Their purpose is usually to convince the populace that a usurping king is really a member of the old royal family, at least on his mother's side.

Actually, Cyrus began his career as a chieftain of the principality of Anshan, a land just on the southern border of what had once been Elam. He was Cyrus II of Anshan and he traced his rule from an ancestor named Hakhamani who may have ruled a century and a half before his time. To the Greeks this name became Achaemenes and his descendants, including Cyrus, are therefore referred to as the Achaemenids (uh-kem'ih-nidz).

In the time of Cyaxares, the tribes of Anshan were absorbed into the Median Empire, although they retained considerable self-government under their own chieftains. The larger region of which Anshan was a part stretched along the northern shores of the Persian Gulf, and was called Fars by the natives. It is better known to us by the Greek version of the name, Persis. This is changed to Persia in English, and the Iranian tribes inhabiting Fars are therefore known as Persians, and the body of water to the south becomes the Persian Gulf.

It is important to remember that the Medes and the Persians are both members of the Iranian group of tribes. Their languages are the same, as are their customs and culture. When Persian strove against Mede, it was but a civil war, and if a Persian replaced a Mede on the throne, it was really nothing more than the establishment of a new dynasty.

In 559 B.C. Cyrus declared Anshan independent of Media. Astyages, who had reigned for a quarter of a century in peace, was reluctant to bestir himself and did so ineffectively at last. A halfhearted expedition sent into Persia was easily defeated by Cyrus, who then built the city Pasargadae (puh-sahr'guh-dee) — "the fortress of Persia" — on the site of the victory. This city, deep in Persia, about 130 miles from the Persian Gulf, served as his new capital.

Nabonidus of Chaldea was delighted at this development. Although Chaldea and Media had lived at peace ever since the fall of Assyria, Media was still Chaldea's large neighbor to the north and east, and it represented a potential enemy for the future. Nabonidus encouraged Cyrus, feeling that in this way he was helping to bring about a long and indecisive civil war that would bleed Media and keep it weak. He even seized the

opportunity for a little personal profit. In 553 B.C., he snatched
Harran, his native town and an important site of Sin-worship,
from the preoccupied Astyages.

However, Nabonidus had miscalculated. The civil war was
neither bloody, nor terribly long. Cyrus gradually gained the
allegiance of the other Persian tribes, winning more and more
of the empire to himself by diplomacy rather than war. Finally
in 550 B.C., he marched on the Median capital at Ecbatana (ek-
bat'uh-nuh) about 300 miles north of Anshan. Astyages was
easily beaten, and Cyrus moved his capital into Ecbatana. He
was now the undisputed ruler of Media which is henceforth
known as the Persian Empire.

Down went Media, the first of the four great powers which
had divided the civilized west when Nabonidus became king.
Nabonidus must have been taken aback by Cyrus' complete
and fairly bloodless victory. Yet perhaps he consoled himself
with the thought that Cyrus had now sated his ambitions; that
on the Median throne he would be no more avid for further
conquest than the Median kings themselves had been. He
seems to have acted on this theory, for in the years after Media's fall, Nabonidus engaged himself on some mysterious er-
rand in the desert regions southwest of Chaldea. Perhaps he
was on an antiquarian expedition.

But if Nabonidus counted on Cyrus' pacifism, he counted
wrong.

Next in line was Lydia, then under the rule of Croesus
(kree'sus), whose wealth has made him legendary. Croesus
actually played into Cyrus' hands by declaring war on the
Persian. According to the tale, Croesus was encouraged to
do so by word from an oracle to the effect that if he launched
an attack, a great empire would fall. And one did; his own.
By 547 B.C., all of Asia Minor was Persian, and Cyrus ruled
over the greatest empire (in point of area) that the west had
yet seen.

Once Lydia was under attack, Nabonidus knew his calculations had led him astray. He tried to join with Egypt in aid-
ing Lydia, but such aid was ineffective. Indeed, it was worse

than useless, for it gave Cyrus all the excuse he needed to turn against Chaldea.

In 539 B.C. came the final scene. Nabonidus, incapable of active war, left the defense of the city to his son, Belshazzar, but there was no defense worth mentioning. Cyrus was a master of psychological warfare and had made arrangements with the priests of Marduk, whose discontent with Nabonidus led them easily into treason.

Cyrus thus had a powerful fifth column inside the city which surrendered virtually without a blow. The Biblical book of Daniel tells that Belshazzar was feasting even as the Persians were preparing to storm the city, but this tale does the poor general an injustice. He led his armies as best he could and died fighting at some point outside the city. Nabonidus was exiled far to the east, and the Chaldean Empire came to an end only eighty years after it had been established.

Cyrus held to his end of the bargain. As soon as he entered Babylon, he restored the priests of Marduk to what they considered their proper place. What's more, he himself deliberately took on the usual priestly functions of a Babylonian king and presented himself as the humble servant of Marduk. The result was that the priests praised Cyrus lavishly and kept the city from rebelling after he had left.

Cyrus was one conqueror who saw the virtue of gentleness as opposed to terror. By treating the conquered kindly and with consideration, he won them over, and was able to seat himself more firmly on a less bloody throne, and rule over a larger area than any earlier conqueror had been able to do. It is amazing that it took so long for anyone to dare make the experiment, and even more amazing that so few conquerors have learned this apparently perfectly plain lesson.

The new conqueror won immortal fame by another simple act of kindness. He offered to allow the exiles in Babylon to return to their native lands. This included the Jews, parties of whom at once returned to Jerusalem. The Second Isaiah praised Cyrus to the skies for this deed, and the Biblical delight in the gentle conqueror has fixed a favorable opinion of

him in the minds of hundreds of millions since his time, who
otherwise might never have heard of him. (Was there any way
he could possibly have guessed this would be the result of his
action?)

Only a small part of Babylonian Jewry returned to Jerusalem. The majority stayed in a city and region which, by now,
they considered their home and in which they were comfortable. And, for fifteen centuries afterward, the Jewish colony in
Mesopotamia remained an important center of Jewish learning.

The Persian conquest of Babylonia marked an important
turning point in Mesopotamian history. After nearly two thousand years of domination by various peoples speaking Semitic
languages, the land was controlled by a people speaking an
Indo-European tongue. It meant that the new masters, with
a culture and background widely separated from that of the
Mesopotamian peoples, were that much harder to absorb.

To be sure, the Persians felt the attraction of the age-old
Mesopotamian civilization. They adopted cuneiform writing
and showed themselves sympathetic to the religion of Marduk.
However, they could not accept Akkadian and its complicated
set of cuneiform symbols. They encouraged, instead, the region's second language, Aramean. This was Semitic also but
at least it had an alphabetic base. Under Persian rule, Aramean became the principal language of Mesopotamia, and Akkadian was restricted to the religious liturgy. Even here, it
faded, and the last Akkadian inscription we can find dates back
to about 270 B.C., two and a half centuries after the Persian conquest. After that, the language was extinct, two thousand years
after Sargon of Agade had raised it to supremacy over Sumerian.

Then, too, the Persian kings made their capitals outside
Mesopotamia, so that for the first time in history, the people
of that region acknowledged a master from without. This
meant that the Persian kings felt the Mesopotamian influence
only from a distance and were never completely assimilated
to that ancient culture. Indeed, the Persian rulers fell under
the influence, more and more, of a new way of thought, with
disastrous results for Mesopotamia.

THE WAR OF LIGHT AND DARK

The Persian Empire continued to expand after its conquest of Chaldea. Cyrus himself vanished into the east, extending Persian influence far into central Asia where no Assyrian had ever ventured. There he died in battle in 530 B.C. When he died, the only one of the four great powers that had been in existence a quarter-century before, that was still independent, was Egypt. For his conquests, and for his enlightened treatment of those conquered, Cyrus is sometimes known as "Cyrus the Great."

His eldest son was Kanbujiya, known to us by the Greek version of the name, Cambyses (kam-by'seez). Babylon knew this son well. In 538 B.C., it had been he who had performed the ritual duties of a Babylonian king at the new year festival while his father was off with the army. Then, in 530 B.C., when Cyrus left for his last campaign, Cambyses was appointed regent and made his capital in Babylon.

He succeeded to the throne without trouble and his relatively short reign is marked by his completion of the Persian conquest of the Oriental kingdoms. In 525 B.C. he marched into Egypt, which fell without much of a fight and now all the great powers were Persian. The new empire made up a realm that was enormous in area even by modern standards, and there was no power outside its borders that could threaten it.

Does this mean that it was to experience no troubles? Not at all. Even when a power is too strong to be disturbed from without, it can always be disturbed from within. If it can't find trouble in the natural course of events, in other words, it concocts some.

In the case of Persia, it came about this way — if we follow the official story that was issued later.

When Cambyses left for Egypt, he was anxious that there be no prince of the royal house about whom a dissident group might gather. Such a group might well spread a false rumor about his death in Egypt and seize power. The result might be a civil war that would bring death and misery to many thousands. Cambyses therefore had his brother, Bardiya, executed. This strikes us as a terrible crime but, under the standards of the time, it might have been viewed as a necessary piece of statesmanship. Herodotus calls the brother, Smerdis (smurdis), and that is the name by which he is better known to us.

In the absence of modern means of communications, however, people are scarcely to be expected to know what a dead prince looks like or even if he is truly dead. If someone suddenly claims to be the prince in question, many would follow him. Even noblemen, who might know the claimant was not actually the prince, might seize the opportunity to use him as a tool with which to fight the legitimate king and to gain for themselves additional privileges once the claimant became king in his turn.

While Cambyses was in Egypt, then, a Median priest named Gaumata (gow-mah'tuh) claimed to be Smerdis and, in 522 B.C., was declared king by some of the nobles. He is known to history as the "False Smerdis." (The priests of the Iranian tribes were, by the way, called Magi. Since priests generally are thought to have occult and arcane powers by the common people, "Magi," like "Chaldean," came to signify a wizard or magician. Indeed, our terms "magic" and "magician" are derived from "Magi.")

There is probably more to this tale than the mere attempt of a priest and certain backers to gain the throne. Nationalistic and even religious motives may have been involved, motives that don't show up in the sources of information we have.

For instance, Gaumata was a Mede, and it is quite possible that behind the intrigue were the Median nobles who had been all-powerful before the coming of Cyrus and who had been supplanted by Persian families since. They may well have been striking for a return to their previous positions.

Cambyses was returning from Egypt when the news reached him. He insisted the real Smerdis was dead, but he died himself before he could do much more than that. The cause of his death is not clear and it is at least possible to expect foul play.

With Cambyses, however, was a young man named Dara-yavaush, better known to us by the Greek form of his name, Darius (duh-ry'us). He was a third cousin of Cambyses, a member of a younger branch of the Achaemenid family.

He took over the leadership of the Persian party on the death of Cambyses and hastened to Media. There, in a lightning and most daring stroke, he succeeded in seizing the false Smerdis and killing him out of hand. He then proclaimed himself king and a seven-month interval of uncertainty over the succession was over.

It was Darius, then, who spread the official story of how he came to be king, and Herodotus accepted and passed on this official story. But is there any truth to it? There may be, of course, and Darius may be telling everything exactly as it happened. On the other hand, it may be one of those cases where a great lie has been foisted on history. Can it possibly be that Darius himself engineered the assassination of Cambyses? Can it be, then, that when Cambyses' younger brother (his real younger brother, still alive) tried to take the throne, Darius had him killed, too, and spread the news of a "false Smerdis"?

What would be his motive in doing all this? Simple lust for power? Or was there more? Was it a question of religion?

It seems that some time between 600 and 550 B.C., in the time of the Median Empire, a religious reformer lived in the area south of the Aral Sea, just beyond the northeastern borders of that empire. (According to later legend, he was a Mede who had fled beyond the empire's borders to escape persecution. Yet he might also have been a native of that faraway region.) His name was Zarathustra, but he is better known to us by the Greek form of that name, Zoroaster (zoh''roh-as'ter). Zoroaster's teaching approached monotheism more closely than did any other religion of the time, except for Judaism. Zoroaster preached Ahura Mazda as the great god of the universe, the god of light and of good.

To account for the existence of evil, Zoroaster supposed that another entity existed, Ahriman, who represented darkness and evil. The two, Ahura Mazda and Ahriman, were roughly equal in power and the universe was rent in the war between them. All humanity lined up in this struggle on one side or the other. Those who chose to adhere to high ethical principles placed themselves on the side of Ahura Mazda who would, of course, eventually win.

This doctrine of a war between good and evil had the great virtue of explaining the existence of evil in the world and why it was that good men sometimes suffered and whole peoples were cast into misery despite the existence of a good and merciful God.

After Zoroaster's death, his teaching gradually spread throughout the Persian Empire. It made its influence strongly felt upon Judaism. It was only after exposure to Zoroastrian thought, that the Jews began to work up the doctrine of Satan as the eternal opposer of God. To be sure, the Jews never accepted the thought that Satan might be God's equal or even near-equal, as Ahriman was the equal or near-equal of Ahura Mazda.

The whole system of angels and demons which gradually entered Jewish theology after the return from the Babylonian Exile was probably also derived, at least in part, from Zoroastrianism. The Zoroastrians developed elaborate theories of the afterlife and this, too, Judaism adopted. Before then, the Jews spoke only of a shadowy existence in Sheol, which was much like the Greek Hades.

Zoroastrianism could not have spread entirely without resistance, and in the first decades of the Persian Empire there must have been considerable internal friction between those who accepted and those who rejected the teachings of Zoroaster.

Zoroastrianism, like Judaism, was an intolerant religion. It not only preached what it considered the right way, but stated definitely that other religions were the wrong way. Like the Jews, the Zoroastrians considered that those who worshiped other gods really worshiped demons and that this was the deadly sin of idolatry.

One might suspect that Cyrus and Cambyses were not Zoroastrians, for they consented to worship Marduk in their role as Babylonian kings. Darius, however, was most certainly a Zoroastrian, for in his inscriptions he calls most devoutly upon Ahura Mazda. Can it be then that Darius, in a holy passion for Zoroastrianism, intrigued and killed to gain supreme power in order to establish his religion?

Possibly, but it is doubtful that one can ever definitely prove or disprove this theory.

In any case, Darius' accession must have come as a thunderbolt to Babylonia. Cyrus and Cambyses had treated the Babylonians well, and had bowed down to Marduk. Darius, they could be sure, would do no such thing. Indeed, they may well have felt that the new monarch would make every attempt to suppress their religion. They searched wildly for someone to lead them in a revolt and, of course, they found a leader.

A man of imposing appearance and a ready eloquence announced himself to be the son of Nabonidus, and called himself Nebuchadrezzar III. Men flocked to him and in no time at all he had an army. He threw up defenses along the Tigris and made ready to dispute the crossing when Darius came marching from the east.

Darius chose not to risk a major battle. In modern terms, he infiltrated the front instead, sending his men across the river in small contingents at widely separated points. He then gathered them quickly in the usurper's rear, defeated him, and marched on Babylon in pursuit of the remnant of the opposition. In 519 B.C., he took Babylon, just twenty years after Cyrus had taken it. His treatment of it was more severe than Cyrus's had been, and Babylon sullenly submitted to superior force.

In connection with Darius' sacking of Babylon, Herodotus tells a story that has always served as a tale of unbelievable patriotism. According to the Greek historian, Babylon resisted with such fortitude that the Persians despaired of taking it. A Persian nobleman, Zopyrus, conceived the plan, therefore, of having his ears and nose cut off and of having himself lashed into bloody welts. He then presented himself to the Babylo-

nians as a refugee from Darius' cruelty. One could scarcely
argue with the sight of scars and mutilation, so the Babylonians took him in, rejoicing at the propaganda victory Zopyrus'
defection offered them.

Then, after Zopyrus had remained with them long enough to
gain their confidence entirely, he opened Babylon's gates to
the Persian army.

But the tale can't be accepted. It is one of those embroider-
ies that make history dramatic, but inaccurate. It seems certain that Babylon was in no condition to resist Darius with
such resolution as to make a ruse like that of Zopyrus necessary.

THE ORGANIZER

Darius was a capable man, and, despite the possibly dubious methods by which he came to the throne, he was the best
ruler the Persian Empire was to see. What's more, he had the
very valuable ability of learning moderation. He did not allow
his enthusiastic Zoroastrianism to cloud his judgment of what
was expedient. Once Babylon was battered down, he avoided
driving it to desperation, and allowed the Babylonians the
right to worship after their own fashion. He did the same for
the Egyptians, who considered him a great and a good king
in consequence.

He even helped the Jews. These people had been striving
for more than twenty years to rebuild the Temple at Jerusalem
against the opposition of the local population. The Persian
governors of the region had been persuaded by the anti-Jewish elements to prevent the construction. An order from Darius reversed that situation, and by 516 B.C., the Temple had
been rebuilt and rededicated.

Furthermore, where Cyrus and Cambyses had been conquerors, there remained little for Darius to do in that direc-

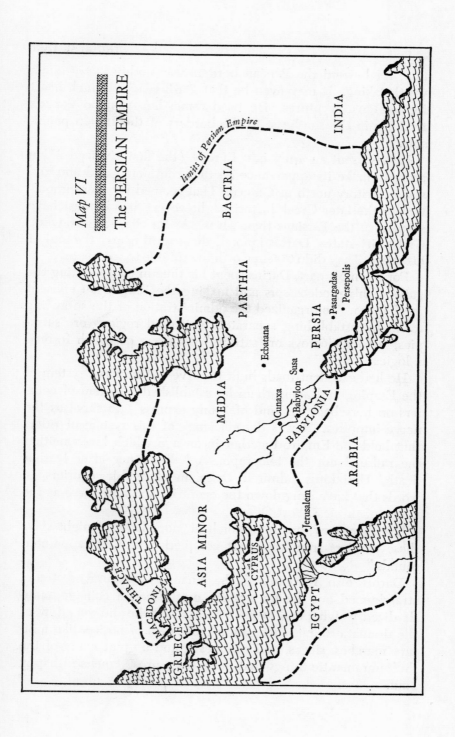

Map VI

The PERSIAN EMPIRE

limits of Persian Empire

INDIA

BACTRIA

PARTHIA

PERSIA

Pasargadae
Persepolis

MEDIA

Ecbatana

Susa
Babylon
Cunaxa

BABYLONIA

ARABIA

ASIA MINOR

THRACE
MACEDONIA
GREECE

CYPRUS

Jerusalem

EGYPT

tion, for beyond the Persian borders was nothing very much worth taking. It may even be that Darius lacked much heart for foreign adventures. He tried some; he extended Persia's territory in the southeast to the borders of the Indian peninsula.

He also sent an army into Europe (the first civilized Asian army to make its appearance on that continent) and annexed some territory north of Greece. That seemed far more important to the later Greek historians, however, than it must have seemed to the Persians themselves. As for the little brawling Greek city-states, Darius ignored them until nearly the end of his reign. They didn't seem worth the trouble to scoop up.

For the most part, Darius spent his time in consolidating the gains of his predecessors and making the Empire an efficient mechanism. He organized the administration of the sprawling realm by establishing separately governed regions or "satrapies," under viceroys or "satraps," each one of which formed a logical unit.

He had excellent roads built to serve as the nerve system of the Empire, and along them he established a system of couriers on horseback (a kind of "pony express") to serve as the nerve impulses. It was the efficiency of this system of riders that held the Empire together in an age which knew neither the railroad nor the telegraph. A half-century after Darius' death, Herodotus admired these indefatigable couriers in words that have rung down the centuries and now serve as the motto of the U.S. Post Office:

"Neither snow, nor rain, nor heat, nor gloom of night stays these couriers from the swift completion of their appointed rounds."

Darius also reorganized the finances, encouraged trade, straightened out the tax system, established a coinage, standardized weights and measures. In short, he did very few of the dramatic things that gain a great deal of notice, like military marches, sieges, and conquests; and a great many of the dull, unromantic things that make for a prosperous and happy land.

Western Asia, including Mesopotamia, was rarely so efficiently and mildly run, either before or after, as it was between 521 B.C. and 486 B.C., the more than forty years in which Darius reigned.

At the very start of his reign, Darius established his winter capital at Susa, the ancient capital of Elam (though he still spent his summers in the cooler climes of Ecbatana). Susa was a most judicious choice. It was part neither of Media proper nor of Persia proper, so that neither of the two chief ruling groups could feel hurt. Also it was almost at the midpoint of the triangle made by the three cities of Ecbatana, Pasargadae, and Babylon, the hearts of Media, Persia, and Mesopotamia respectively, so that the capital was centrally located. With the establishment of Darius' capital in Susa, the region — once Elam — became completely Persian and was thereafter known as "Susiana."

But Darius didn't completely forget he was a Persian, either. He began work on a new and magnificent capital for the Persian homeland about 30 miles south of Pasargadae. This he named Parsa, but it is better known by the Greek name of Persepolis (per-sep'oh-lis) or "city of the Persians."

In a practical sense, Persepolis was a failure, for it never became a real city but remained nothing more than a royal residence, or even more accurately, a royal mausoleum. It contained magnificent palaces, impressive in their ruins, even today. Whereas Cyrus and, possibly, Cambyses were buried in Pasargadae, Darius I and his successors were buried at Persepolis.

Yet Darius' most important work in the long run was nothing more than a propaganda inscription, which he had carved into the side of a cliff near the present village of Bisitun. This is about 75 miles southwest of Ecbatana, on the main road between that old Median capital and the still older Babylon.

The inscription was deliberately placed high up in an almost inaccessible spot where the carvers must have done their work only at great personal risk. (The reason for doing this was undoubtedly Darius' determination to keep the inscription from being erased or altered by successors who might be out of sympathy with him. Rulers often rewrote past history in this fashion, and Darius was not going to have that.)

Men saw the inscription from afar in the centuries that followed, and a Greek traveler, Diodorus Siculus, reported its existence five centuries after it was carved. He attributed it to the legendary queen, Semiramis, since everything ancient and monumental in Asia was attributed to her by the Greeks. The large human figure on the rock face, which was Darius, of course, was considered by Diodorus to be Semiramis, despite the fact that it was thickly bearded.

In modern times, however, the inscription took on new meaning and turned out to be the invaluable key to the history of western Asia. The inscription told of how Darius killed the false Smerdis and came to the throne. It is our source for this story and undoubtedly tells it the way Darius wanted it told. The same story was given in the same words in three different languages, so that as many as possible of Darius's diversely tongued subjects might be subjected to the official version of the tale. These languages were Old Persian, Elamite, and Akkadian.

In 1833, the inscription attracted the attention of an English army officer, Henry Creswicke Rawlinson, who was stationed in Persia. He managed to copy the inscription and for many years worked on the Old Persian, using modern Persian as a guide. When that language had been deciphered, the meaning of the inscription was known. Using that meaning, one had a clue with which to decipher Elamite and Akkadian. With the help of others, Rawlinson plugged away at that task.

By 1850, enough was done to make it possible to begin to interpret ancient Babylonian records. It was only through Darius' inscription and his unwitting donation to the future world of a sort of dictionary, that the remains of the library of Ashurbanipal could be read. Otherwise, that library would have remained nothing more than a collection of bricks covered with chicken tracks.

Then, eventually, with the help of Akkadian, Sumerian, too, could be deciphered.

THE END OF MARDUK

Darius died in 486 B.C. and, in some respects, the greatness of Persia began to die as well. He was succeeded by one of his sons, Khshayarsha, whom we know far better than Xerxes 1 (zurk'seez), the Greek version of his name.

Xerxes was a son of Darius by Atossa, a daughter of Cyrus the Great. Darius had married her after he became king, apparently in order to strengthen his own position and make himself seem less a usurper. He had had sons by previous marriages, but Xerxes was a grandson of Cyrus, and that made him the logical choice for the throne.

It might have been better if some other sort of logic had been used, for Xerxes was far inferior to his father as a ruler.

To be sure, he began his reign under handicaps. Toward the end of Darius' life, in 499 B.C., certain Greek cities on the Aegean coast of Asia Minor had revolted, and the city of Athens, in Greece itself, had helped them. Darius crushed the revolt and then sent an expedition to Greece to mete out punishment to Athens. Surprisingly, that expeditionary force was defeated in 490 B.C.* and while Darius was preparing a larger expedition, he died. It was left for Xerxes to vindicate Persian "honor."

Xerxes was prevented from doing this at once by a revolt in Egypt. There was the usual temptation on the part of a subject people to revolt at the end of a reign, and Egypt succumbed to that temptation. In this, she was probably encouraged by Athenian agents who were terribly anxious to involve the Persian Empire in civil broils before its full strength could be turned on Greece. The rebellion was also the result of Xerxes' religious beliefs. He was considerably more intensely Zoroastrian than his father, and the Egyptian priests may well have anticipated trouble.

---

* This was the famous Battle of Marathon. Details concerning it and other facets of Greek history may be found in my book *The Greeks* (Houghton Mifflin, 1965).

The revolt, of course, merely confirmed Xerxes' dislike for those of his subjects who were of other religions. Xerxes put everything else to one side, including the Greek expedition, and dealt first of all with the Egyptians. (This was exactly what the Athenians had wanted and, in all probability, it saved Greece.)

The Egyptian revolt was crushed, though it took three years to do so, and Xerxes then turned against other non-Zoroastrians in the Empire. The Biblical book of Esther deals with events that supposedly took place in his reign. (Xerxes is called Ahasuerus in that book.) Stern anti-Jewish measures are described as having been narrowly averted through the influence of his Jewish queen, Esther. However, this book is almost certainly a historical romance written three centuries after Xerxes' time and cannot be taken as literally true.

What is historically certain is the fact that Xerxes' fury overflowed onto the Babylonians where nationalist leaders could not resist rising in imitation of the Egyptian effort.

In 484 B.C. Xerxes' armies fought their way into Babylon, and the monarch then deliberately destroyed that city's religious life. Xerxes ordered taken away the golden statue of Marduk, which Cyrus and Cambyses had carefully venerated. A priest who tried to stop those soldiers who were dismantling the temple and laying impious hands on the statue was callously killed by men who lacked any feeling of fear or reverence for the great god.

What had now happened was far worse than what had happened two centuries before when Sennacherib the Assyrian had taken away Marduk, even though Sennacherib had utterly destroyed Babylon and Xerxes had not. Sennacherib had at least been a believer. He was punishing Babylon, but he revered the age-old gods of Mesopotamia. There was hope, then, that through piety another king might yet restore the city and Sennacherib's son, Esarhaddon, did so.

But now Marduk was carried off with ribald disrespect by men of different ways and utterly different gods. It was as though the Babylonians knew they had finally crossed some dividing mark — that Marduk would never be restored and that the old gods were dying at last. The spirit went out of the old culture that had stemmed from the long-dead Sumerians and the final decline began.

Perhaps the Babylonian priesthood experienced a grim pleasure, however, in what happened to Xerxes thereafter. He led a great expedition into Greece in 480 B.C., one that was large enough, it seemed, to overwhelm the Greeks by sheer weight. Yet, unaccountably, it failed, and Xerxes was forced to come back in shamed frustration.

He retired to his harem, remained in stubborn seclusion, and idled away his time in useless projects such as those aiming at enlarging and making more magnificent the palaces at Persepolis. Finally, he was assassinated, in 465 B.C., as a result of a palace intrigue.

But that did not restore Babylon. The city and its people remained frozen in torpor, mere spectators of the great events that were to swirl about them.

Thus, when Egypt rebelled again upon the death of Xerxes and maintained a desperate six-year resistance against the new Persian monarch, Artaxerxes I (ahr″tuh-zurk′seez), Babylon never stirred.

The center of interest of the civilized world seemed, in fact, to be switching away from the ancient river cultures on the Tigris-Euphrates and on the Nile, and shifting to the brawling cities of the Greeks. These Johnny-come-latelies to the scene of civilization were sprouting remarkably. The completely unexpected success of the Greeks against Xerxes' lumbering expedition seemed to have fired them with an almost superhuman energy and a nearly godlike self-confidence. Their science was outstripping the venerable lore of the ancients. Their restless travelers and traders were everywhere, poking curiously into the dust-laden customs of antiquity. Their soldiers were fighting as mercenaries all along the rim of the Persian Empire, and no non-Greek seemed to be able to stand against their heavy armor and their tough *élan*.

Indeed for half a century after the failure of Xerxes' expedition against the Greeks, Greek ships and men had been harassing the Persian coastline, encouraging Egyptian rebels, and generally making nuisances of themselves to the giant empire. Persia seemed for all the world like an undignified giant slapping away at the cloud of Greek mosquitoes that bit it here, there, and everywhere.

THE BATTLE OF THE BROTHERS

The Greeks, Persia realized, might be annoying, but they could never seriously hurt Persia, as long as they remained divided among themselves and fought each other incessantly. Persia learned therefore to keep those fights going and she spent money freely with that end in view.

By the time Artaxerxes I died in 424 B.C., Persia had the satisfaction of seeing the Greek cities lining up in a kind of miniature World War. The whole Greek world flung itself behind the two chief cities, Athens and Sparta, who proceeded to fight each other to the death.

The new Persian monarch, Darius II, did his best to encourage that fighting. Of the two chief cities, Sparta seemed the less ambitious and the more likely to confine its activities to Greece itself. Therefore, Persia threw its weight more and more on the side of Sparta. In the year of the death of Darius II, 404 B.C., Persian policy won out and Sparta crushed Athens.

That would seem well for Persia, and yet it wasn't entirely well, for that very victory had set off a Persian dynastic squabble that was to have fatal consequences for Persia. This came about as follows:

Darius II left behind two sons. The elder succeeded to the throne as Artaxerxes II. The younger son, however, was a man of talent and he did not wish to be overlooked. His name was Cyrus and he is usually called "Cyrus the Younger" to distinguish him from the founder of the Persian Empire. Even as a teen-age boy, he had been handling Persia's relations with the

Greeks and had shown himself to be a shrewd judge of men and events.

It seemed to Cyrus that he had done enough for Sparta to expect something in return, and what he wanted was a contingent of Greek soldiers. With a Persian army and a Greek contingent as a cutting edge, he could make his way to Susa and place himself on the Persian throne.

The Spartans were too cautious to help him officially (after all, he might lose) but the end of the great war between Athens and Sparta had left many soldiers at loose ends and ready for hire. An exiled Spartan, Clearchus (klee-ahr′kus), supervised the hiring of these mercenaries and took charge of them. Eventually, nearly 13,000 Greeks were collected, and in 401 B.C. off they marched with Cyrus' army.

Across Asia Minor, they marched, until finally they reached the upper Euphrates at Thapsachus (thap′suh-kus), 75 miles south of Harran. For the first time in history a large body of Greek soldiers entered the storied land of the two rivers. They crossed the Euphrates and marched downstream for 350 miles. The Greeks were now some eleven hundred miles from home.

Meanwhile, though, Artaxerxes II finally got it through his head that his younger brother was not merely marching to greet and congratulate him — but to kill him. He gathered a large force of his own, including such Greek mercenaries as he could scrape up, and advanced to head off Cyrus.

The two armies met at Cunaxa (kyoo-nak′suh), a village near the Euphrates about 90 miles northwest of Babylon. Only twenty miles from Cunaxa was Sippar which, nearly two thousand years before, had been one of the royal seats of Sargon of Agade.

The two sides made ready, and for the first time in Mesopotamian history, a major battle was to be fought in the land without significant participation by the inhabitants. They were merely spectators while Persians and Greeks fought.

The Greeks drew up their line facing downstream in such a way that their right flank rested on the river. Clearchus, a stupid and unimaginative Spartan, had placed his Greeks on that right flank because in the usual battle between Greek armies, the right flank was the post of honor. Soldiers on the right flank were expected to carry the brunt of the battle.

Opposite them, facing upstream, was the imperial Persian army. Artaxerxes II was in command, and he took the Persian post of honor in the center. Actually, the imperial army was considerably larger than Cyrus' army so that it extended farther out from the river. Its center was opposite Cyrus' left.

Cyrus saw and understood the situation. The imperial army counted for nothing. Only Artaxerxes II, the king, counted. If he died, then Cyrus became the legitimate king, and all the Persian soldiers on both sides would rally to him at once. It was unnecessary, therefore, to mangle the Persian army; it was only necessary to kill the king.

Cyrus therefore asked Clearchus to order the right wing forward obliquely to the left, so as to aim it at the imperial center. Clearchus, however, pointed out that this meant his right flank would be unhinged from the river and be exposed to an attack from the side. Cyrus must then have pointed out that the imperial forces opposing Clearchus were lightly armed troops which could do little against him even if his flank were exposed. Besides, before they could do even that much, Artaxerxes II would be dead or in flight and the battle would be over.

Clearchus, however, refused. He was going to fight the battle by the book. He was going to march straight forward and protect his flank.

He did. Thirteen thousand Greek soldiers marched straight forward, pushing the light forces opposed to them out of the way like so much drapery. Artaxerxes had allowed for that. His main effort was on his own right which was enveloping Cyrus' shorter left and was destroying it while Clearchus and his men were accomplishing nothing.

Cyrus, driven mad with frustration, gathered as many horsemen about him as possible — six hundred — and charged straight at the imperial center, straight at his brother, with only one thought in mind — to kill him and end the battle.

But Artaxerxes was well guarded by ten times as many horsemen as Cyrus could command. He let Cyrus come; his horsemen swallowed up the small charging force, and in the short skirmish that followed, Cyrus was struck down and killed, and the battle was over.

Artaxerxes II had won, and Clearchus found himself with his Greeks, alone and deserted by the rest of Cyrus' army. What did one do now?

It was a problem for Artaxerxes, too. There were too many of those heavily armed Greeks to handle easily, for they had suffered hardly any casualties in the battle. He had enough men to crush them, perhaps, but only at terrific cost to himself, a cost he was not willing to pay if he could think of some other way out.

Since the Greeks would not surrender, Artaxerxes' spokesman offered to supply them with provisions and usher them out of the country. The Persians explained there was a short cut to the sea if the Greeks would allow themselves to be led up the Tigris.

There seemed nothing else for the Greeks to do, but after they had gone some 150 miles upstream, they grew uneasy. Where did the Tigris really go? What were the Persians' real intentions?

Clearchus demanded reassurance. The Persian commander suggested that Clearchus and the other Greek leaders meet with him in his tent in a private and friendly conference. Clearchus, like the fool he was, agreed. As soon as the Greek generals were behind the tent flaps, they were killed.

The Persians were pleased. It seemed to them that without its leaders, the Greek army would now be a headless trunk and would have no choice but surrender and be disarmed. They could then be separated into small groups and pressed into Persian service. Those that refused could be killed.

The Greeks, however, did not do as the Persians confidently expected. They chose a soldier of the ranks, an Athenian named Xenophon (zen'oh-fon), as their leader. They clung together and would not surrender; they had grown another head as soon as the first had been removed. And, in fact, the new head was far more capable than the old.

The Greeks continued to move northward, with the Persians now hostile and watchful, but avoiding battle.

A hundred miles farther upstream, the Greeks passed a huge mound. What was that, they wanted to know? It was all that was left of Nineveh, Assyria's mighty capital, whose very name, after two hundred years, had just about vanished from the earth.

Beyond that they left the river and plunged into the mountains of what had once been Urartu. The Persians were content to let them do this, hoping they might be killed by the fierce and hardy natives of those regions, or simply blunder their way, through gradual attrition, to death.

The Greeks, however, continued to cling together, meeting every emergency with skill, fighting off tribesmen, and managing to keep themselves in provisions. Finally, they crossed the thickness of eastern Asia Minor and came pouring down out of the mountains onto the startled Greek city of Trapezus (trap'uh-zus). It lay on the shore of the Black Sea, and the soldiers as they ran, cried in rapture, "The sea! The sea!"

The Ten Thousand (as they were called in later writings, although there were more than that to begin with) had survived. Xenophon also survived to write the tale of the epic march in a book that still exists and has made good reading, now, for more than two thousand years.

THE MACEDONIANS

UNION AGAINST PERSIA

The short civil war between Cyrus and Artaxerxes II was a
catastrophe for the Persian Empire, for it revealed the weakness of the realm for all to see. The Egyptians had taken advantage of the confusion into which Cyrus the Younger had
plunged the Empire to revolt yet again. This time they succeeded, establishing a precarious independence they were to
maintain for half a century. (Yet Babylonia did not as much
as flicker an eyelid. Marduk was gone and the people mourned
in paralysis.)

Worse than the Egyptian feat was the march that had followed the Battle of Cunaxa. The Ten Thousand had marched
their way through the heart of the Empire and not all the
might of Persia had dared touch them.

Until then, the Greeks had lived in constant fear of Persia, had constantly imagined that they might be crushed if they didn't play their cards just right. Now they suddenly realized that Persia was a paper tiger; that for all its size and wealth and "image," it was quite hollow inside.

Cyrus' wild ambition and his striving for the throne would have brought this about, perhaps, even if he had won at Cunaxa. The Greeks might have come to realize that if a few thousand Greeks could win an empire for a Persian, they might just as easily do so for a Greek.

For the next eighty years, then, there were not wanting voices in Greece to argue that the Greek cities ought to unite and march against Persia. One Greek orator, Isocrates (eye-sok'ruh-teez), openly argued that a Persian invasion was necessary to stop the Greeks from fighting each other. It was the kind of effort that would cause them to unite.

But the Greek cities never did unite of their own accord, even with the tempting Persian bait dangling before them. And Persia therefore managed to cling to life and power.

In 358 B.C., Artaxerxes III came to the throne. He was a cruel but forceful monarch, and under him Persia even showed some strength. Artaxerxes III forced the too independent satraps to come to heel, and then sent armies into Egypt that put an end to that land's fifty years of independence.

Artaxerxes was assassinated in 338 B.C., however, and after a couple of years of near anarchy, a mild and unwarlike member of the royal family, who took the name of Darius III, came to the throne in 336 B.C. The new Darius was very much like old Nabonidus of two centuries earlier, and he was just about the very worst possible king Persia could have had at just that time, for the Greek-speaking kingdom of Macedonia was experiencing a sudden, startling rise.

Macedonia lay north of Greece and until then had been of no importance at all. In 359 B.C., a remarkable man, Philip II, gained control of the kingdom. He reorganized its army and finances, welded the whole land into a keen instrument of aggression, expanded its power at the expense of the Greek cities, and by 338 B.C. had got them to unite — not by persuasion as Isocrates the orator had tried to do, but by force.

Philip was now ready to try to invade Persia. He had even had the Greek cities appoint him head of a united expeditionary force for the purpose. Then, in 336 B.C., just as he was preparing to push off into Asia, he was assassinated.

Succeeding to the throne, however, was Philip's son, who proved himself to be the most remarkable warrior of all time. He was Alexander III, who came to be known universally as Alexander the Great. After spending some time reuniting the Greek cities (which had rebelled at once when the news of Philip's death reached them), he made ready to put Philip's great plan into action.

In 334 B.C., Alexander the Great and his army crossed into Asia Minor. He fought and won a battle almost at once against an overconfident Persian satrap. He won another battle, a much larger one, at Issus in southeastern Asia Minor, against the main Persian army under Darius III.

Alexander then marched through Syria and Judea, taking Tyre after a nine-month siege (showing himself to be a far more ingenious warrior than Nebuchadrezzar had been two and a quarter centuries before). Judea and Egypt submitted to Alexander without a fight.

Finally, in August, 331 B.C., Alexander stood at Thapsacus, exactly where the Ten Thousand had stood just seventy years before. The Greeks at Thapsacus were not under a Persian prince this time, but under a Macedonian who was Greek in language and culture. They were not intending to put one Persian on the throne in place of another. They were intending to take the entire vast realm for themselves.

Alexander, with the Macedonian core of his army, and his Greek auxiliaries, planned nothing less than to find Darius III and take him. In order to do that he crossed the Euphrates, marched over the land that had once been Assyria, reached the Tigris and began to move downstream. His destination was the Persian heartland.

DAVID BEATS GOLIATH

Darius III was waiting for him.

So far, Persia had been unable to stop this ferocious Macedonian, but Darius had only tried once really, and that had
been at Issus two years before. Alexander had won then, but
it seemed to Darius that that was only because the choice of
battlefield had been a poor one for the Persians.

Alexander's chief weapon was his phalanx, a tightly knit,
long-speared band of soldiers trained to march and maneuver
almost like precision dancers. The phalanx was a bristling por-
cupine of spearheads that could break any army it marched
into and resist any that tried to attack. Cleverly supported by
light-armed troops and by cavalry, well supplied, and led by
a man of supremely versatile genius, nothing could defeat it,
and nothing in Alexander's lifetime did.

Darius' chief weapon was numbers. He could call upon the
mighty resources of the largest Empire in the history of the
western world up to that time, and Alexander's band was puny
in comparison. At Issus, the difference in numbers was mini-
mized by the fact that the battle was fought between the
mountains and the sea in a narrow pass where the phalanx
could maneuver properly, but where the Persian numbers were
choked down. Darius had had to leave the scene of battle hur-
riedly to avoid being captured.

Darius was determined not to make the same mistake again.
Having learned that Alexander was moving down the Tigris,
he planned to meet him on a field designed to give his own
numbers the best possible chance. He carefully chose a large
flat region and had the minor unevennesses stamped down.
He hoped there would be absolutely nothing to impede the
sweep of his cavalry, which, he felt, would simply push the opposing horse from the field and then chew away at the edges
of the phalanx till it fell apart to be swallowed up piecemeal

by his enormous army. (He did not, apparently, realize that he was playing into Alexander's hands to a certain extent, for the Macedonian phalanx worked best on absolutely level ground.)

The place Darius chose was near a village named Gaugamela (go″guh-mee′luh), just 18 miles northeast of the haunted ruin of old Nineveh. No battle ever fought near Nineveh or anywhere in Assyria was to be so enormous or dramatic as the battle about to be fought over its grave after it had lain three centuries dead.

The later Greek historians said that Alexander's army numbered 40,000 footmen and 7,000 cavalry, and this may have been very near the truth. The Persian army gathered by Darius, those same historians insisted, was made up of 1,000,000 men and 40,000 cavalry. This is ridiculously exaggerated, for it is doubtful if an army of that size could have been properly provisioned or directed, or if it could have fought as anything but an armed and mindless mob.

Nevertheless, even if the Persian numbers are deflated as much as is likely, it is certain that they still far outnumbered Alexander's force, and that the battle was one of the most remarkable David-and-Goliath affairs in the history of warfare.

If the two sides had been led with equally inspired generalship, the Persians would have had to win, but the generalship was quite uneven. On one side was Alexander; on the other, Darius. Numbers might almost be ignored in view of the great disproportion in the leadership.

When the battle opened on October 1, 331 B.C., the Persian line far overlapped the Macedonian on both right and left. One might have supposed it could just have folded in on both flanks and swallowed Alexander's small force. Alexander had so disposed his men, however, as to allow them to turn and fight any flanking movement. Besides Alexander had one climactic move in mind, and till he had the chance to work it out properly he was content to stay on the defensive.

The sway of the battle was edging Alexander off the section of carefully flattened ground, and this Darius viewed with dismay. He lacked the resolution to hold his hand to the proper moment and he therefore threw in his "secret weapon" prematurely.

This secret weapon consisted of chariots. Chariots had been passé in warfare for some four centuries, ever since the large Median horse had come into use and warriors had climbed onto the horse's back. Darius' chariots, however, had something new added. They were equipped with sharp knives emerging wickedly from the hubs on either side.

These knives, glinting savagely in the sunlight and drawn with all the fury of the charging horses, would neatly slice the legs off any man they encountered. Nor would it be so much the actual number of men so sliced, as the absolute confusion into which the enemy would be thrown (it was hoped) as they panicked at the sight of those hurtling knives or desperately tried to avoid the stroke when overtaken.

Darius sent a hundred scythed-chariots screeching toward the Macedonians, but Alexander was not caught unaware. The charioteers were attacked with arrows as they raced across the open land toward the Macedonians, and the soldiers themselves moved neatly to one side or another to let the chariots pass when they did reach the lines. The crucial danger of panic was averted, and the charge was a complete failure.

Now it was time for Alexander to make his move and it was a simple one. He remembered Darius fleeing at Issus, and he knew he was dealing with a coward. His phalanx was in place and it began to move remorselessly forward like an animated forest of spears, precisely for the spot in the center of the line where Darius III was cowering.

Darius III held out as long as he dared, but that wasn't long. He was a kindly man and a gentle one and would have made a good king if he had had a very capable and ruthless prime minister. But he was on his own and he was a coward. The phalanx was bearing down upon him, and he turned and dashed off the field as fast as his horses could carry him.

What followed was precisely what Alexander counted upon. The heart went out of the Persian host and they gave up. Alexander was the victor. That David-and-Goliath battle near dead Nineveh was really the end of the Persian Empire two centuries after Cyrus had founded it. Persia had died quite near the spot where Assyria had died.

Now Alexander could move on to Babylon where there was no resistance. The people of Babylon were overjoyed and the gates were thrown open to him.

The Babylon into which Alexander and his men marched was by no means the Babylon of Nebuchadrezzar. It was not even the Babylon of Darius. The destruction Xerxes had visited on the temples a century and a half before was largely unrepaired. In particular, the great temple of Marduk remained a ruin.

But Alexander adopted Cyrus' policy with respect to the ways of those he conquered. He allowed them liberty and was only too glad to go through whatever ritual would make them happy. Passing through Judea, he showed the utmost respect to the High-priest of the Temple in Jerusalem so that Alexander remained a hero in Jewish legend thereafter. In Egypt, he showed similar respect to the ancient temples and even visited the Temple of Ammon far out in the desert.

In Babylon, Alexander declared himself the defender of the old ways against the oppression of the Zoroastrians. He ordered all the temples to be rebuilt and, in particular, that the temple of Marduk be restored in all magnificence.

Unfortunately for Babylon, Alexander could not remain to see his order carried out. He had to seize what remained of the empire, and when he left to do so, the viceroys he left behind were not as enthusiastic in the cause of Babylonian recovery as Alexander was.

Alexander passed on to Susa, then to Persepolis where, the story goes, he burned the Persian palaces in revenge for the burning of Athens in the days of Xerxes' great expedition to Greece a century and a half before.

Alexander then turned north to Pasargadae, where he viewed Cyrus' tomb, then doubled back to Ecbatana where Darius III had sought refuge. Darius III would not wait for him but fled eastward. Finally, his courtiers tired of the weakling and in 330 B.C., he was assassinated.

Alexander spent four years then in the far east of the empire, battling with the hardy barbarians and winning every battle (yet not easily, for there were no more coward kings to face). Eventually, he worked his way down the Indus River (in modern Pakistan) beyond the point where even the Persian forces had penetrated. There he won another great battle against an Indian king. He was set to continue across India but now, finally, his troops rebelled. They had had enough, and Alexander was forced to turn back.

By 324 B.C., Alexander was in Babylon again, and there he remained. For a while, Babylon was once again the center and capital of the greatest power on earth, as it had been under Nebuchadrezzar, two and a half centuries before. It was this not because of its strength or magnificence, or because of anything at all in itself. It was so only because it contained Alexander. The smallest village would have been capital of the world under those same conditions at that time.

Alexander chose Babylon as his capital for a purpose. It was his dream to rule over a united mankind. He attempted to be more than king of the Macedonians or general of the Greeks. He tried to enforce a kind of brotherhood of man. He made his Macedonians take Persian wives; he adopted Persian modes of dress and behavior. He hoped to lower all bars to service by Persians or any other nationality in his army. He even hoped to transplant populations.

In this respect, he was far ahead of his time and he was bound to fail in this assault on the stubborn hardheartedness of man. His Macedonians grumbled at every mark of favor he showed Asians. What was the use of conquering, they thought, if they did not end as masters — ignoring the fact that to be master was merely to invite the subject to strive someday to be master in his turn, and thus continue the sorry farce of turn and turnabout forever.

Babylon fitted into Alexander's plans. It was neither Greek nor Persian and it was midway between the two extremes of his empire, 1500 miles from the western boundary and 1500 miles from the eastern.

It lay conveniently to the Persian Gulf, too, and Alexander

dreamed of conquering the lands that flanked that body of water — India to the east and Arabia to the west.

Perhaps even if Alexander had lived out a full life and remained in Babylon and actually carried through his plan of restoring its temples, it might still have remained dead. The cult of Marduk and of the other gods stretching back to Sumerian times had probably decayed too far for revival.

But any revival at all was out of the question, for Alexander had only been in Babylon for some months when, in the early summer of 323 B.C., he fell ill. On June 13, he was dead.

It is hard to believe that after all he had done and accomplished, he managed to die when he was yet but thirty-three.

EXIT BABYLON

Alexander's unexpected death, while still a young man, ruined his lifework in a moment. He had no feasible relative to serve as a successor. There was only a Persian wife, an unborn child, a termagant mother, and a half-wit half-brother.

The logical choice would have to be a general, one of those who had been associated with Alexander in his great work. But if those of Alexander's family were too few and too weak, his generals were too many and too strong. None could seize control from all the others; none was willing to give way peaceably.

The generals held a council in Babylon after Alexander's death. One of them, Perdiccas (pur-dik'as), led the group that took up the legitimist view — that the rule must be kept in the old Macedonian royal family. He himself proposed to remain in charge till Alexander's child was born.

Some of the other generals weren't having that at all. To them it seemed merely a device that would serve to make Perdiccas universal and absolute ruler. One of them, in particular, was Ptolemy (tol'uh-mee). He had made himself governor of Egypt immediately upon Alexander's death, and he decided at once to have no higher ambitions. Nevertheless, no one else, he was determined, was to rule in Egypt. When Perdiccas marched against him to change his mind for him, Ptolemy resisted. Perdiccas' maneuvers failed; he grew unpopular with his associates and, in 321 B.C., he was assassinated by a group of officers led by another of Alexander's generals, Seleucus (see-lyoo'kus).

As reward for his part in killing Perdiccas, the quarreling generals let Seleucus have Babylonia. The fortunes of war forced Seleucus out for a while, but by 312 B.C. he entered Babylon permanently.

In a way, this was a booby prize. Throughout the centuries during which the Macedonian generals and their successors quarreled over the slowly dwindling remnants of Alexander's Empire, it was always the portions nearest Greece that counted the most. It was Greek culture that was admired and desired; all else was barbarian.

Ptolemy held on to Egypt and made the city of Alexandria (which had been founded by Alexander the Great and had been named for him) his capital. He turned it into a little Greek world in which he might live isolated from the Egyptians. Other generals fought wearily and drearily for Asia Minor, Macedonia, and Greece itself. Few even bothered with Babylonia, let alone the great Persian provinces beyond.

In Asia Minor, Alexander's general, Antigonus (an-tig'ohnus) still dreamed of uniting the entire empire under himself. He was the ablest of the generals and was strongly supported by an equally able son, but almost all the other generals combined against this dangerous and ambitious old man, and he could never quite muster the strength to beat them all.

By 306 B.C., Antigonus could wait no longer. He still hadn't won supreme power, but he was about seventy-five years old and he had to hurry. He therefore assumed the title of king, taking the name if he could not have the fact.

At once the remaining generals (quite a few had died by

then) did the same. Ptolemy became king of Egypt, and Seleucus assumed the title of king in Babylon.

Little by little, Seleucus extended his rule over the Iranian provinces, and eventually he controlled not only Babylonia but everything to the east. There is no neat name for this portion of Alexander's Empire, particularly since its boundaries changed and shifted with the decades. It is usually called the "Seleucid Empire" after its founder, and Seleucus dated its founding from 312 B.C. when he made his final entry into Babylon.

Seleucus inherited, to a certain extent, Alexander's dream of a united mankind. He encouraged Greek colonization of the Babylonian and Persian world, yet at the same time was not a nationalist. He was the only general who kept the Persian wife he had been forced, by Alexander, to marry. He was sympathetic with his Babylonian subjects and was popular with them.

In fact, he and his successors did their best to shore up the rapidly sinking Babylonian culture, if only to oppose it to the Iranian culture which remained strong and vital east of Mesopotamia and continued to be the great adversary to the Greeks and Macedonians. As a result, the ancient city of Uruk, for instance, continued to be a center of culture throughout the Seleucid period. The old priesthood could count on state support, and the Aramaic language was encouraged. Zoroastrianism, on the other hand, was frowned upon and went into a decline.

Unfortunately, no amount of artificial transfusions could bring the corpse back to life. The Greeks themselves made that the more certain by the very character of their culture. For the first time, conquerors had entered Mesopotamia without feeling the attraction of the ancient culture that had been brought to life by the Sumerians.

It was the Babylonians rather who, for the first time, felt the lure of the alien. Greek became a language of increasing popularity among the upper classes. The Greek system of writing on papyrus or parchment made the old brick writing obsolete, and cuneiform — the first of all language systems

— began to fade and die. By the end of the Seleucid period, it was virtually extinct.

Babylon itself, the great Babylon, withered.

Seleucus, it seemed, wanted a capital of his own. This is a natural desire for any king, especially one who is first of his line and doesn't want to be surrounded by memories of a past in which he plays no part. Ptolemy had his Alexandria, and Seleucus may well have wanted to match his fellow general-king in this respect.

In 312 B.C., therefore, the year in which he made his final entry into Babylon, Seleucus began the building of a new city on the Tigris, only 40 miles north of Babylon. He named it, in his own honor, Seleucia (see-lyoo'shee-uh) and planned it to be a city of Greek culture for himself and his successors, while Babylon was to remain the native capital.

Unfortunately, Babylon was a corpse and Seleucia was too close. As Seleucia grew, Babylon declined. The very structures of the old city were dismantled to help build those of the new. The entry of Seleucus into Babylon was therefore the last event of note for that city, the last mark it made in the history books. After that it was nothing more than a slowly dwindling town, then a slowly decaying village, then — nothing.

One last breath of life Babylon managed to exhale before the end. In Seleucus' time, a priest of Marduk in Babylon was persuaded to write a Babylonian history in Greek. His name may have been Bel-usur ("the lord protects") but he is known by the Greek version of that name, Berossus (beh-ros'us).

His book, in three volumes, would be priceless to us now, but it is lost, probably forever. The chance of unexpectedly coming across a copy somewhere is virtually nil. Nevertheless, our knowledge of it isn't zero. Parts of his history were quoted by Greek historians whose works do survive, and every scrap of such quotations have been lovingly studied and compared with original material scrabbled from among the digs of Babylonia. Whenever a scrap of Berossus can be compared with a scrap of other material, there seems to be a reasonable tally.

But, despite Berossus, the dead is dead. From the time of the establishment of the Seleucid Empire, it is no longer quite fair to speak of Babylonia. I will now go back to the more general term, Mesopotamia.

THE PULL OF THE WEST

It would have been better for Seleucus, and for the Seleucid Empire, if he had been quite satisfied with his eastern realm. Even Seleucus, however, could not entirely dismiss the Greek west from his mind.

To begin with, he had to oppose the insatiable drive of Antigonus for supreme rule. Seleucus was one of the leading spirits in an allied drive that finally defeated and killed the old man in 301 B.C. at Ipsus in central Asia Minor.

In reward, Seleucus received the province of Syria, so that his realm finally reached the Mediterranean. He did not quite have the entire Fertile Crescent. Ptolemy of Egypt retained the southern portion of the western half, including Judea.

Seleucus celebrated his acquisition of Syria by founding, in 300 B.C., a city which he named Antiochea (in honor of his father, who was Antiochus). We know it as Antioch (an'tee-ok). It is located in northern Syria, just ten miles from the sea. It served as the western capital of the Seleucid Empire and as its window on the Greek world.

This western success sharpened Seleucus' appetite for more. In 281 B.C. he defeated and killed the eighty-year-old general, Lysimachus (ly-sim'uh-kus), who had once fought with Alexander. Seleucus took over all of Asia Minor and gloried in the knowledge that he was the last one alive of all Alexander's generals. At seventy-seven, only he remained of all those generals who had been with Alexander a half-century before in his epic march of conquest across western Asia.

He crossed into Macedonia to take over that as well, and there in 280 B.C., he met his death by assassination.

He set a bad example for his successors (the "Seleucids"). Had they tended to their knitting, had they labored to strengthen their heterogeneous empire, they might have lasted many centuries, and Greek culture and knowledge ("Hellenism" after Hellas, the Greek name for their own country) might have taken permanent root in western Asia.

Nor must we think of this (with our western prejudices) as serving only for Asia's benefit. In the generations after Alexander, Europe received a great deal from Asia. Putting loot, and even knowledge, to one side, there were material objects till then unknown to Europe that were of great benefit. Europe received a delightful article of food they called the "Persikon melon" ("the Persian fruit"), and the first word underwent a series of changes until we have it now as our well-known and well-loved fruit, the peach. Europe also discovered the citron, the cherry, alfalfa, and cotton. Undoubtedly, had European influence held more firmly in Asia, both continents would have profited enormously.

But the trouble was that the Seleucids always faced west and let the vast east take only a secondary place in their calculations. The victories of Seleucus I in his last years were a deadly precedent. The Seleucids began a long-running quarrel with the Ptolemies of Egypt that continued for a century after the deaths of Seleucus I and Ptolemy I. Everything was thrown into this seesaw battle that solved nothing, came to no conclusion, and served only to weaken both sides and, eventually, to kill them.

At first, the Seleucids got the worst of it. In 246 B.C., the third Ptolemy ascended the throne and almost immediately the "Third Syrian War" broke out between the two Macedonian kingdoms. Ptolemy III led his army into Asia and defeated Seleucus II, who then ruled the Seleucid Empire. Ptolemy's army marched into Mesopotamia itself and for a few giddy moments actually occupied Seleucia. It was the high point of the Ptolemaic kingdom.

Wisely, Ptolemy III made no attempt to hold his gains. His secure hold on Egypt, he felt, was not worth risking for the illusion of wider Empire. He retreated.

The Seleucid Empire had been shaken apart in the process, however, and the provinces in the far east went out of control. While the Seleucid monarch foolishly fought for a few miles of Mediterranean shore, enormous provinces broke away in the east.

Farthest to the east was the province of Bactria (roughly equivalent in location to the modern nation of Afghanistan). About 250 B.C., its governor, Diodotus (dy-od'oh-tus), declared himself independent of the Seleucid monarch.

Immediately to its west lay the province of Parthia (in what is now northeastern Iran). It, too, at this time declared itself independent under its governor, Arshak, better known to us by the Greek version of the name, which was Arsaces (ahr'suh-seez).

In the fashion of the eastern monarchies, Arsaces I of Parthia claimed descent from the previous royal line of the Achaemenids. He traced his ancestry to Artaxerxes II who, a century and a half before, had been victorious at the Battle of Cunaxa. It was false, of course, but it pleased his subjects and made them the more willing to fight for him.

For a generation, the Seleucids were helpless to do much about this. They were too occupied with trifles in the west. In 223 B.C., however, Antiochus III (an-ty'oh-kus) came to the throne. He met defeat in 217 B.C. in a war against Ptolemy IV and, in disgust, turned eastward. There over the space of a dozen years, he concentrated his considerable talent. He suppressed revolts, restored authority, and reached understandings with Parthia and Bactria. He left them a certain amount of home rule but forced them to acknowledge Seleucid overlordship.

In 204 B.C., Antiochus III returned to Mesopotamia as, a century and a quarter before, Alexander had returned; and with, it seemed, the same result — a completely conquered east.

Antiochus, therefore, had himself called Antiochus the Great (in imitation of Alexander), and it is by this name that he is known to history.

Unfortunately, having gained all this, Antiochus fell prey again to the lure of the west. Soon after Antiochus' return, Ptolemy IV died and the new king, Ptolemy V, was only a young child. Here was Antiochus' chance to avenge his earlier defeat and to settle matters with Egypt once and for all. Antiochus III invaded Egypt and by 200 B.C. was sufficiently the victor to be able to seize parts of Asia Minor and all of Judea. For the first time, the Seleucids controlled the entire Fertile Crescent.

By that time, however, the most powerful nation in the Mediterranean region was a newcomer — Rome. For two centuries it had been expanding constantly. It had come to control all of Italy and the surrounding islands and had just defeated the north African city of Carthage utterly. The western Mediterranean was a Roman lake and now the city was ready to cross swords with the various Macedonian monarchies.

Had Antiochus III decided his future lay in the east, had he strengthened himself there, the Seleucid Empire might have become the rival and peer of Rome. Later eastern empires succeeded in doing this.

Unfortunately, Antiochus took entirely too seriously his self-description as "Great" and the deadly lure of the west was too strong. He was willing to fight Rome and was smashed, first in Greece, and then in Asia Minor. He had to abandon his holdings in Asia Minor and he had to pay an enormous indemnity. Worse yet, the eastern portion of the empire which he had, with such painful effort, subdued, broke away again.

The occasion of Antiochus III's death was a melancholy indication of the extent of his defeat, and brought with it, at the same time, a whiff of the long-gone past. He was killed by a mob that was exasperated at his attempt to loot a temple to get the gold he needed to meet the indemnity payments to Rome. The place of his death is given in the Greek histories as Elymais (el''ih-may'is). That is actually the Greek form of Elam, so that Antiochus III died where Ashurbanipal had won As-

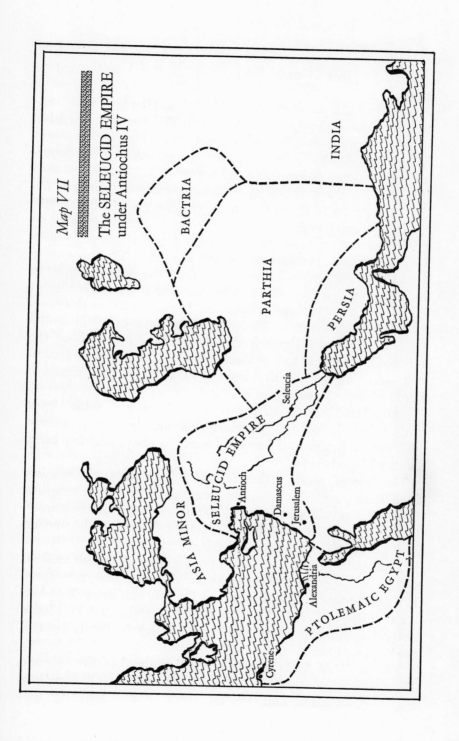

Map VII

The SELEUCID EMPIRE
under Antiochus IV

BACTRIA

INDIA

PARTHIA

PERSIA

Seleucia

SELEUCID EMPIRE

ASIA MINOR

Antioch

Damascus

Jerusalem

Alexandria

Cyrene

PTOLEMAIC EGYPT

syria's last great victories and where Darius I had ruled in glory.

In 175 B.C., a younger son of Antiochus III reached the Seleucid throne and reigned as Antiochus IV. He was a capable man who was ruined by lack of judgment. He was a fervent believer in Greek culture and made every attempt to encourage the growing Hellenization of his subjects. Thus, he established Greek theaters and gymnasiums at various points in his dominion, even in the fading town of Babylon which was still lingering its way to death.

He was led by his eagerness to use force where persuasion was insufficient, particularly against the Jews. The Jews were far more resistant to Hellenization than the other peoples in his kingdom and they rose in rebellion, under the leadership of a group of five brothers, collectively known today as the Maccabees (mak′uh-beez). The picture we have today of Antiochus IV is chiefly through the Jewish books describing the rebellion. Needless to say, Antiochus IV is pictured as a monster, something after the fashion in which some American books picture George III of England.

Antiochus IV also attempted to settle matters with Egypt and defeated Ptolemy VI easily. Rome, however, ordered him out of Egypt and he was forced to obey, slinking away like a whipped dog.

The loss of prestige that followed from his backing away from Rome, and the expenses incurred by trying to suppress the Jewish revolt, weakened him tremendously, and he turned to the east. There, he felt, he could get the money he needed and restore the reputation he had lost.

To a certain extent, he did. Like his father, he repressed revolts and began to make the Seleucid power felt once more. Perhaps he would have completed the job, and even done better than his father, had he lived long enough. But he died a natural death (apparently of tuberculosis) in Persia beyond the Zagros Mountains.

The death of Antiochus IV marked the end of the Seleucid Empire as a great power, though it was yet to make gestures eastward. Parthia and Bactria were now completely and permanently independent and each was marked by a thin layer of Hellenism over a base of Iranian peasantry.

Bactria, although the farther east, was the more Greek of the two. For a while it flourished and even seemed to be on the point of expanding; even while Antiochus IV was failing and dying in Persia, Bactrian leaders were pushing their armies and influence into India.

But Bactria was too far removed from the centers of civilization to be able to survive long. The surrounding sea of barbarism slowly closed in, and by a century later the last remnant of decaying Greek culture in central Asia was washed away.

The future of the Iranian peoples, whose realm had so rudely been broken down by the volcanic force of Alexander the Great, lay with Parthia.

8

THE PARTHIANS

EXIT THE SELEUCIDS

The Parthians, like the Medes and Persians, were an Iranian people. The Parthian homeland lay directly to the east of Media and it was mentioned first in the records of Darius I. It may even be that Parthia is but a dialect-form of the word Persia.

Alexander the Great passed through Parthia on his conquering journey and it remained under Seleucid domination (with considerable home rule) for a century and a half. This was not enough to change the basic ways of the people who remained Iranian in language and Zoroastrian in religion.

The upper classes, however, were only mildly Zorastrian and picked up a strong Greek tinge. Greek remained the official language of the Parthian aristocracy and they were enthusiastic over the literary products of Greece. They were particularly interested in the legends of Heracles, or Hercules (as he is more familiarly known to us), and established what was virtually a Hercules cult.

The rulers of Parthia are referred to as the "Arsacids" because all descended from Arshak or Arsaces I, under whom Parthia first obtained a measure of self-rule under the Seleucids. At first, successive Parthian monarchs all took Arsaces as the throne name, but were also known by their proper names. Thus, Arsaces VI is better known as Mithradates I (mith"ruh-day'teez). This last name shows the Zoroastrian background of even the Hellenist monarchs of the land for it means "gift of Mithras," where Mithras is a Zoroastrian symbol of the sun.

Mithradates I succeeded to the throne in 171 B.C. and adopted a vigorous expansionist policy from the first. While Antiochus IV lived and marched eastward, Mithradates stayed on the defensive toward the Seleucids, but pushed eastward himself into Bactria. Then, when Antiochus IV died, he looked westward as well.

The province of Media, which lay between Parthia and Mesopotamia, declared its independence after Antiochus IV was gone. The Seleucids, in a steep decline, could do nothing about that, but Parthia, on the rise, could. Westward it pushed its influence and by 150 B.C., Parthia had absorbed Media completely and we can now begin to talk of the Parthian Empire.

Nor did matters stop there. Various members of the Seleucid royal house were fighting each other desperately in Syria. Mithradates therefore extended the westward push and in 147 B.C., took Mesopotamia together with its proud capital of Seleucia that Seleucus I had founded a century and a half before.

Mithradates tried to reassure the Greek colonists and upper classes of Mesopotamia that the Parthian take-over did not mean an end to Hellenism. He emphasized his own attitude by calling himself Mithradates Philhellene ("Mithradates, the admirer of Greece"). Indeed, he and his successors were more Greek than the Greeks themselves. Where the Greeks had actively attempted to keep the old Babylonian culture alive, the Parthians did not trouble. The last of the ways of Sumer and Akkad, of Sargon and Hammurabi, died out under their rule. The last cuneiform text we have dates from two centuries after the Parthian coming, and beyond that is nothing. The last trace of living Babylonian culture, mortally wounded by Xerxes, was gone.

The Jews of Mesopotamia, on the other hand, benefiting by the Parthian lukewarmness on behalf of an ordinarily intolerant Zoroastrianism, flourished.

Nevertheless, the Greek cities of Media and Mesopotamia viewed their new Parthian master with great misgiving (and perhaps with some snobbishness) and longed for the Seleucids back again. They sent prayerful petitions to that effect to Antioch and on two different occasions, Seleucid monarchs actually tried their luck at eastern conquest.

In 140 B.C., the Seleucid king, Demetrius II (deh-mee′tree-us), invaded the Parthian dominions. He won several battles, but in 139 B.C. he was ambushed with his army. The army was destroyed and Demetrius was taken prisoner.

Mithradates died in 138 B.C. In his thirty-three-year rule, he had converted his province into an Empire controlling a stretch of territory running for more than 1500 miles from west to east. It made up the northern half of the territory of the old Persian Empire from the Euphrates eastward. (The southern half, consisting of the provinces on the Persian Gulf and the Indian Ocean — notably the heartland of Persia itself — clung to a more old-fashioned Zoroastrianism and never formed a clear part of the Parthian domain.)

With Mithradates gone, the Seleucids tried again. Demetrius' younger brother, Antiochus VII, was king. He invaded Mesopotamia in 130 B.C., defeated the Parthians and for a while was in control of the land of the two rivers again. But it was a flash in the pan, nothing more. The Parthians retreated into Media, Antiochus followed, was defeated in battle, and killed.

The Parthians then liberated Demetrius II so that he might return to Antioch and rule his land. Someone who had felt Parthian imprisonment, they felt, would be in no hurry to try again. Nor was he. For the few decades that the Seleucid Empire continued to exist, none of its remaining monarchs ever budged out of Syria.

In 129 B.C., the Parthians decided to establish a new capital in the western portion of the realm. (They were Hellenic enough to feel the lure of the west, just as the Seleucids had.) Seleucia already existed but it was a little too Greek, perhaps. Instead, they chose a suburb that lay eastward, just across the Tigris from Seleucia. The suburb was named Ctesiphon (tes'ih-fon).

Ctesiphon was to remain the capital of an Iranian power (both that of Parthia and of the regime that followed it) for eight centuries. It grew, naturally, until it rivaled and even surpassed Seleucia, the two forming a kind of "twin-city," one Greek and one Iranian, representing a fusion of the two cultures such as Alexander the Great might have admired.

ENTER ROME

With the Seleucids out of the game, another power arose in far northern Mesopotamia, along the foothills of the Caucasus, where once Urartu had existed.

After Urartu had been destroyed by the Medes, a new people, the Armenians, made their appearance in the area, moving eastward into it from Asia Minor. They were subject first to the Medes, then to the Persians, then to the Seleucids. After Antiochus III had been defeated by the Romans, however, they began to take their first steps toward independence.

The expansion of the Parthians had brought about their contact with Armenia and, for a while, it looked as though Armenia, like Media and Mesopotamia, would slide down the Parthian gullet. Indeed, Mithradates II of Parthia, a capable monarch who reigned from 124 to 87 B.C., attempted just that.

In 95 B.C. he set up a puppet of his own, Tigranes (ty-gray'-nees), as king of Armenia, and counted that land as his own thereafter. He called himself Mithradates the Great, and adopted the old Achaemenid title of "King of Kings" (or "Great King") signifying that he was the greatest and most powerful ruler in the world.

But when Mithradates II died, Parthia succumbed to a disease that afflicted it periodically — dynastic squabbling. All monarchies have their periodic dynastic troubles but Parthia was worse than most in this respect. For one thing, it was a feudal empire in which the great landowners were so powerful as to be almost independent of the crown. Naturally, they were always at odds with each other and always ready to back different claimants to the throne. Such claimants were always present in quantity, for the Parthians had the custom of passing the crown from brother to brother and there were always many brothers to make the claim.

While the Parthians were thus preoccupied, Tigranes shook loose and under him Armenia reached a peak of power. Tigranes pushed southward into Asia Minor and Syria, penetrated Mesopotamia and ravaged Media. He adopted in his turn the glowing titles of Tigranes the Great and King of Kings.

His capital was at Artaxata (ahr-tak'suh-tuh), in the Caucasian country, about 250 miles north of where once Nineveh had stood. Now, however, Tigranes, too, felt the lure of the west and he built himself a new capital, just north of the upper Tigris river near the eastern edge of the Asia Minor peninsula. This he called Tigranocerta (ty-gray"noh-sur'tuh).

The stage seemed set now for a replay of the ancient duel between Assyria and Urartu, with a recovering Parthia playing the part of the former and Armenia that of the latter. The trouble was that there was a third party in the field that was stronger than either. This was Rome.

A century before, when Rome had defeated Antiochus III and had faced down Antiochus IV, it had had as yet no actual foothold in the east. By Tigranes' time, however, Rome had annexed the western portion of Asia Minor as well as all of Greece and Macedonia. It was supreme throughout the entire Mediterranean.

Pontus, a kingdom of eastern Asia Minor, dared pick a

quarrel with the great western power, however, and for a while even managed to make headway against Rome. The king of Pontus was Mithradates VI (a breath of Iranianism in that name, even though Pontus was thoroughly Hellenized), and he was the father-in-law of Tigranes.

Rome, which was distracted by civil wars of its own, finally decided to put its full strength into Asia Minor, and sent a general named Lucullus (lyoo-kul′us) to take care of the matter. Lucullus was a dour and capable soldier and he marched eastward and crushed Pontus. Mithradates fled to the court of his son-in-law at Tigranocerta.

Tigranes the self-styled Great, took that title as seriously, as had Antiochus the self-styled Great a century and a quarter earlier. Tigranes, like Antiochus, felt his Greatness required him to oppose Rome. He did so, and the result was the same for Tigranes as it had been for Antiochus. In 69 B.C., Lucullus had penetrated to Tigranocerta and defeated Tigranes there. It was the first time (but would not be the last) that a Roman army had penetrated into Mesopotamia. The next year, Lucullus pushed further and defeated Tigranes again at Artaxata, the older capital.

It might have been the end for Tigranes, but Lucullus was a martinet who was detested by his troops. They rebelled and would follow him no more. He was recalled to Rome and Tigranes had a short breathing space.

Lucullus was soon replaced by another, and more popular, Roman general, Pompey (pom′pee). In 66 B.C., Pompey penetrated Armenia, reached Artaxata, and actually captured Tigranes himself. Tigranes' dreams of glory thus fell even lower than had those of Antiochus III who, at least, had kept his freedom.

Pompey, doubtful of Rome's ability to hold Armenia's mountainous territory in the long run, was content to let Tigranes remain king on the payment of a huge indemnity and on the understanding that his role was to be that of a Roman puppet. Under those terms, Tigranes remained king for the final decade of his life. He had had an odd career, for he began and ended his reign as a puppet (Parthian at first and Roman at last) and in between had had a couple of decades of great power.

Pompey turned south into Syria where, in 64 B.C., he put a final end to the last small remnant of the once-mighty Seleucid Empire, annexing it as the Roman province of Syria. He also annexed the Jewish kingdom which had gained a short-lived independence under the Maccabees.

THE ARMORED HORSEMEN

Parthia watched all this with considerable anxiety. Its old enemy, the Seleucid Empire, had become a Roman province. Its newer enemy, Armenia, had become a Roman puppet. Nothing now stood between Parthia itself and Rome's inexorable eastward drive.

Parthia did all it could to keep the peace, but Rome was quite uninterested in reaching any understanding. For a century and a half, it had been expanding with spectacular success, spreading out all over the Mediterranean with scarcely a defeat to check it.* Since it had supplanted the last Seleucid monarch, Antiochus XIII, in 64 B.C., there were some Romans who felt they had inherited the task of restoring the Iranian east to western rule.

This feeling came to a head about ten years after the absorption of the Seleucid Empire, when Pompey joined with two others to dominate Rome in a three-man dicatorship. One of his allies was Julius Caesar, Rome's cleverest politician, and the other was Marcus Crassus, Rome's richest businessman.

Pompey had already gained his military laurels in the east; Caesar had gone off to Gaul (modern France) to win battles and renown; it seemed to Crassus that it was only fair that he, too, should become a great warrior. He decided, therefore,

* For the story of Rome's expansion, see my book *The Roman Republic* (Houghton Mifflin, 1966).

to take up the task of winning back the lost provinces of the Seleucid Empire.

The occasion seemed right, too, for Phraates III (fruh-ay'-teez) of Parthia, who had worked ably and desperately for peace with Rome, was dead. He had been murdered by his two sons, who, as was natural for members of the Parthian ruling house, promptly fell to quarreling.

In 54 B.C., therefore, Crassus left Rome and Italy for the east, setting off, in all self-confidence, to begin a war of pure aggression against a power that had in no way offended Rome and had, indeed, done everything it could to avoid doing so.

The two armies, Roman and Parthian, were oddly unmatched. The Romans had developed the "legion," an organization of foot soldiers that had great flexibility. It did not have the formidable weight and power of the phalanx, but the phalanx could work best only on open and unbroken land, where it could maneuver as a close-knit large unit, while the legion could break apart and come together again without damage. On several occasions, the legion met the phalanx and, in the end, it was the versatility of the legion that won out over the sheer weight of the phalanx.

The Parthians, on the other hand, had developed cavalry to a new pitch of skill. The horses of the Iranian tribes were still the largest and best in the world, and the Parthian horsemen maneuvered their mounts with an ease that won the awed admiration of those who had to face them. Theirs was the hit-and-run tactic brought to perfection. They swept down suddenly upon an unprepared enemy, did their deadly work, then raced away to strike somewhere else.

There is the story, too, that when the Parthians were in quick retreat and the enemy was chasing wildly after in helpless anger at the sudden attack and sudden flight — the horsemen would, on signal, turn on their horses to send one last flight of arrows over their shoulders. This "Parthian shot," falling suddenly and unexpectedly on their pursuers, would often do more damange than anything that had preceded.

In addition, the Parthians had developed a heavy-armored cavalry as well. These were the "cataphracts" (from Greek

words meaning "wholly enclosed"). Such horsemen were en-
cased in armor, on horses who were sometimes armored as
well. To bear the weight of all the armor, a horse had to be
large and well-muscled. Such horses were available to the
Parthians, but rarely to their enemies.

The heavy cavalry was not speedy, but it didn't have to be.
It could come lumbering down upon an enemy line as a sort
of mounted phalanx, with heavy clublike spears. Or, when
equipped with bows they could riddle the enemy lines while
themselves almost immune to the return fire of the opposing
archers.

So terrifying were the Parthian horsemen that they became
the very representative of the fearsome warrior to the provinces to the west. In the Biblical book of Revelation, for instance, the catastrophe of war is symbolized by the picture of
a mounted Parthian bowman.

A great deal depended, of course, on the intelligence and
inspiration of the respective commanders. Roman generals
had been victorious over novel weapons before. They had
beaten elephants when they had none of their own, and they
had built ships and manned them with raw recruits in order
to defeat a seasoned naval power.

This time, however, the Romans were under a severe handi-
cap. Crassus was a by-the-book soldier, as Clearchus of the
Ten Thousand had been, three and a half centuries before.
He was completely helpless at the task of adapting to unexpected conditions.

Moreover, he lacked the advantage of facing a divided enemy. With the Roman invasion pending, Parthia managed to
pull out of the civil war when one of the feuding brothers
seized sole control and ruled as Orodes II.

Crassus landed in Syria, crossed the Euphrates and entered
Mesopotamia. Several of the Greek towns there welcomed him
eagerly, and when he returned to Syria for the winter, his self-
confidence had reached new heights.

The Parthians were correspondingly disheartened. A dele-
gation reached Antioch to dicker with Crassus and to make
any reasonable peace agreement. Crassus, however, must

have had Alexander the Great in mind. Alexander consistently rejected all compromise and drove hard after total victory and achieved it. This has been a glittering goal for army leaders since, and many a general has tried to use Alexander's methods without his genius and paid dearly for it.

Crassus told the Parthians proudly that he would discuss peace terms in Seleucia and they left empty-handed and angry.

In 53 B.C. Crassus crossed the Euphrates again. No army appeared to dispute the passage, and Crassus was advised by his lieutenants to follow the river downstream as the Ten Thousand had done. Crassus, however, wanted to advance into the heart of Parthia, Alexander-like, and eagerly agreed to follow an Arab who offered to lead him across the Mesopotamian plains to a point where the Romans could surprise the Parthian army and destroy them.

The Arab did lead them to the Parthian army, but he was in the pay of the Parthians and their army was ready for the meeting. The Parthians were waiting in the vicinity of Carrhae (kahr'ee). This is the Greek version of Haran, where two thousand years before Abraham's family had dwelt, and where five and a half centuries before, Assyria had made its last stand.

Only a small part of the Parthian host was visible, and the Romans poured onward, thinking in good truth that they had achieved a surprise. When they had committed themselves to the battle, however, those in view, who seemed ordinary horsemen, threw off their cloaks and revealed the armor beneath. They were the deadly cataphracts!

Before the Romans were well aware that they were in a major battle with themselves having been surprised, the Parthian bows were twanging and the Romans were dying on every hand. Crassus, in desperation, ordered his own cavalry, under his son Publius Crassus, to attack and try to drive the Parthians off.

The Roman cavalry charged and the Parthians retreated at once, shooting over their shoulders. The lightly armed, and therefore fleeter, Romans, were catching up when they realized they were being led into the rest of the Parthian army, with its own light cavalry far outnumbering the Roman, and far more skillful unit for unit.

The Romans fought with dogged tenacity, but it was a massacre, and in the end they died almost to a man. Publius Crassus also died, and the Parthians cut off his head and stuck it on the point of a lance. The Parthian cavalry then reformed their ranks and rode back to the main Roman army with young Crassus' head held high.

Roman morale sank at the sight, although Crassus rose to the occasion by calling out to the army, "The loss is mine, not yours."

The battle continued, with the Romans again getting the worse of it, and the next day Crassus was forced to retreat. The Parthians dogged and hounded his steps and Crassus himself was finally killed. Finally, the Parthians seized the battle flags of the Roman legions; a great disgrace in Roman eyes.

Only one man in four returned to Syria from this disastrous expedition. Worse for Rome than the defeat itself was Parthia's triumphant realization that the Romans could be defeated.

By virtue of their victory at Carrhae, Parthia now approached the peak of its power. Not only had it held off Rome, but it had now developed an important middleman position between Rome and another great empire thousands of miles away — a position that was highly profitable.

In the first century B.C., while Rome was consolidating its hold on the Mediterranean, the far eastern realm of China was under the firm and enlightened rule of the Han dynasty. In China, the production of silk from the cocoons of the silkworm had been developed but the process was kept a national secret. It was a source of great wealth for China, for all wanted the glossiness of the most beautiful natural fiber known, either then or now. At this peak for both empires, China and Parthia almost touched in central Asia.

Merchants bearing silk, worked their way westward across central Asia, reaching Parthia. Parthia charged a full middleman's share, and passed it on to Rome, where the upper classes had to pay a pound of gold for a pound of silk, and were glad to do it.

The Romans of this period found silk a mysterious substance indeed. Most thought it was obtained from a tree, though the Greek philosopher, Aristotle, three centuries before, had spoken of worms that produced fibers. It wasn't till centuries later that the methods of silk production, as distinguished from silk itself, reached the west.

STAND-OFF

It was now the turn of Rome to fall into civil war. Caesar and Pompey fell out, and in the war that followed it was Caesar who was victorious. By 44 B.C., he had crushed all his enemies and was dictator of all the Roman realm. He began to plan a campaign against Parthia to wipe out the disgrace of Carrhae.

Perhaps he might have carried that through, for he was a very capable general, but before he could set forth he was assassinated by republicans who feared he was planning to make himself king. Once again, the civil wars began. Fighting against the armies led by the assassins were Mark Antony, Caesar's faithful lieutenant, and the young Octavian, Caesar's grandnephew and adopted son.

In 42 B.C., the republican army was smashed in Greece, and most of the surviving republican leaders hastened to make their submission to the victors. One did not. He was Quintus Labienus (lab"ee-ee'nus), who fled to Parthia and offered his services to Orodes. Those services were accepted and in 40 B.C. he led a Parthian army into the eastern provinces of a still distracted Rome. Under his leadership, the Parthians took over Syria and Judea and moved deep into Asia Minor.

The Parthian moment of glory, with their standards flying in Antioch and Jerusalem, was a brief one. The Romans were rallying. One of Mark Antony's generals, Bassus Ventidius (ven-tih'dee-us), advanced into Syria and, in two successive campaigns in 39 B.C. and 38 B.C. defeated the Parthians, who were forced to retire behind the Euphrates.

In 37 B.C., Orodes II, whose reign had witnessed Parthia

at the peak of its power, met the Parthian royal death. He was killed by his son, who then reigned as Phraates IV.

The new Parthian king was able to repeat some of the successes of the old. After the defeat of the Republican army, Mark Antony and Octavian split the Roman realm between them, Mark Antony taking the east. It was now Mark Antony who dreamed of evening the score for Carrhae.

In 36 B.C., he therefore invaded Parthia but merely succeeded in adding a second disgrace. The Parthian forces avoided an open battle but harried the Romans in the mountains, pecking them to death. Mark Antony had to retreat and finally emerged from Parthia with most of his men gone and no battle fought. He had to try to make up for it by turning on Armenia and taking its king prisoner.

For centuries to follow, Armenia was to be a kind of Ping-Pong ball, shuttling between the powers to its west and east, never its own master, never securely on the one side or the other, always a battlefield for diplomats and armies.

The Roman civil wars finally ended in 31 B.C. when Octavian defeated Mark Antony in a huge naval battle. In secure and sole control of Rome, Octavian then spent years reorganizing the Roman government. He assumed the name Augustus, and what had been the Roman Republic became the Roman Empire, with Augustus as the first Emperor.

Many must have expected that now at last there would be the final showdown with Parthia. If so, they were disappointed. Augustus was a man of peace who wanted his Empire to establish itself behind safe, defensive lines and rest.*

As for Parthia, it would be enough to make use of the eternal civil wars there. Phraates IV was an unusually bloody king, even for a Parthian. He killed off his family wholesale, including his oldest son, in order to prevent any dangerous claimants to the throne. (As for killing his son, who should know better than he how dangerous sons are to fathers.) But rebellion arose anyhow and in 32 B.C. Phraates was pushed off the throne by a member of the royal family who had managed to survive.

* For the details of his career and of those of his successors, see my book, *The Roman Empire* (Houghton Mifflin, 1967).

The new king was Tiridates II (tir″ih-day′teez). Phraates IV
fled, but continued to fight.

Augustus refrained from helping Tiridates and negotiated
instead with old Phraates IV. When the old king was maneuvered back to the throne by 20 B.C. with a minimum involve-
ment of Roman troops, he showed his gratitude by returning
the battle flags captured from Crassus' legions.

In a formal sense, the disgrace had been eradicated, but
many Romans must have felt that this was a shopkeeper's way
of doing it; that the proper Roman style would have been to
smash the Parthians in battle. (Unfortunately, it is part of
the continuing madness of mankind, that it sees something
contemptible in winning a point by negotiation rather than
war.)

In return for the battle flags, Augustus sent Phraates a gift
that turned out to be deadly (though that was something Augustus could not have foreseen). It was merely a beautiful
slave girl, Musa, whom Phraates added to his harem.

She quickly became his favorite wife, had a son, and persuaded Phraates to send his older surviving children to Rome.
Phraates did as she suggested, the more readily since sons
were a dangerous luxury to a Parthian king. When that was
done, Musa waited for her own son to grow up. Once he was a
teen-ager, she poisoned Phraates IV and her son became king
as Phraates V in 2 B.C.

The Augustan policy of peace did not last, unfortunately.
The Parthians were careful not to invade Roman territory,
and Rome was careful to make no incursions into Parthia —
but there was always Armenia. The two powers took turns in
placing puppets on the Armenian throne, and armies marched
and countermarched across the country.

After a half century of incredible dynastic confusion, a
strong king finally found himself on the Parthian throne in
51.* This was Vologesus I (vol″oh-gee′zus). Determined to

---

* It is customary to give dates in terms of the birth of Jesus. Earlier
dates are given as "B.C.," later ones as "A.D." In this book, I will
not use A.D. Any date given without initials can be assumed to be
A.D.

end the stand-off, he placed his brother, Tiridates, on the Armenian throne.

In 54, a young Emperor, Nero, succeeded to the Roman throne, and he was not going to let that Armenian move pass uncountered. He sent Rome's most capable general, Gnaeus Domitius Corbulo (kawr'byoo-loh) to Asia Minor.

Corbulo suggested a compromise. Let Tiridates remain on the throne, but let him swear allegiance to Rome rather than Parthia. A land that was formally a Roman puppet but was ruled by a Parthian king, could scarcely lean too far toward either side and both competing powers should be satisfied.

Parthia turned this down and Corbulo invaded Armenia in 58 and made his way to Artaxata, where, a century and a quarter before, Lucullus had stood. It was not until 63, however, that Corbulo, plagued with jealousy in Rome and obdurate resistance in Ctesiphon, could enforce his compromise. Tiridates remained king, but under Rome. Had this been agreed to at the start, nine years of war would have been saved.

Corbulo got no good out of this. The Emperor Nero was a suspicious tyrant who saw conspirators everywhere. In 67, rather than send Corbulo to Judea, where a great revolt was starting, he sent the general an order to kill himself. Corbulo obeyed, muttering "Rightly served!" meaning that he deserved to die for not having rebelled against the tyrant while he had his army behind him.

That didn't help Nero, either. He sent another general Vespasian (ves-pay'zhan) to Judea, but was assassinated in 68. After some confusion, Vespasian became Emperor (as Corbulo might have done, had he lived).

The Jewish rebellion was crushed in 70, and Vespasian established friendly relations with Vologesus of Parthia, who reigned till 77.

ROME AT THE GULF

For a generation thereafter, Parthia remains sunk in the obscurity of civil war. All we have to go on as the record of that period are some coins bearing the names of kings, and some isolated and very casual literary references.

It was not until 109 that Parthia could draw its breath and in that year Osroes I (oz-roh′eez) established himself as sole ruler of the land. Despite Parthia's war-weariness, Osroes took it upon himself, in a fit of stupidity, to break the compromise that had kept the peace with Rome since the time of Corbulo. He replaced the Armenian ruler with one who acknowledged Parthian rather than Roman supremacy.

As it happened, Trajan (tray′jan) was Roman Emperor at the time. He was one of Rome's best and most capable Emperors and the first ruler since Julius Caesar to have a strong urge to initiate an expansionist policy, and the ability to carry one through. He fought two tremendous wars against the hardy and ably-led tribes of Dacia (the territory now occupied by the modern nation of Rumania) and added that land to the Empire.

Perhaps Osroes counted on Rome being occupied in Dacia, but if so, he counted wrongly. Trajan adjusted affairs elsewhere and moved into Asia Minor. Osroes, who by now understood the situation and realized he was in absolutely no position to fight Rome, offered to back down.

Trajan, however, was having none of that. He was strong and Parthia weak, and he wanted total victory. He therefore occupied Armenia and made it a Roman province outright.

He wanted more, too. In 115, he turned south into Mesopotamia and annexed its northern section to Rome. The area in which Crassus had fought and died nearly two centuries before was now Roman and was to remain Roman for several centuries. In 116, Trajan crossed the Tigris and annexed a region beyond that as the "province of Assyria."

Roman ships were then launched on the Euphrates and the Tigris. Like Sennacherib's fleet, eight centuries before, they worked their way downstream. The twin city of Seleucia-Ctesiphon fell into Roman hands. The ruins of Babylon (which Trajan saw as a tiny, miserable village) felt the tramp of the Roman legions and finally, the Roman Emperor stood on the Persian Gulf.

No Roman general had penetrated that far eastward ever before. No Roman general was ever to penetrate that far again.

For one brief moment, the entire Fertile Crescent was Roman, and at that moment, in 117, the Roman Empire stood at its maximum extent. From the western tip of Spain to the Persian Gulf, it stretched out over 3200 miles.

And still Trajan was not satisfied. He looked out across the Persian Gulf and is said to have said mournfully, "If only I were younger!"

But he was not. He was sixty-four and feeling his age. Even if he had been as young as Alexander, though, he might still not have been able to go farther, for troubles were gathering about him.

For all the impressiveness of his advance, he was in danger. The fortress of Hatra, between the rivers and about 60 miles south of where Nineveh had once stood, held out against him and posed a perpetual danger to his line of communications. The Parthians had retreated before him and their army was still intact in the mountains to the east. At home the Jews in Cyrene had broken out in a wild and dangerous revolt.

Trajan simply had to return, whatever his age. He didn't make it. He was sick even as he left, and he died in Asia Minor, while still on the march back.

Hadrian, his successor, was a man of peace. Sensibly, he decided that Trajan's conquests could not be maintained without continuous fighting, so he gave most of them up and patched up a peace with Parthia on the basis of the old Corbulo compromise.

Yet half a century later, Trajan's adventure was reenacted in such a way that each participant paid a higher price than before.

In 161, Hadrian died, and two rulers succeeded as Roman co-Emperors. Of these, one, Marcus Aurelius, was a philosopher, and the other, Lucius Verus, a pleasure-seeker.

The Parthian monarch of the time was Vologesus III, and it seemed to him that two monarchs were bound to turn on each other in civil war. It would be safe for him, therefore (or so he reasoned), to break the Corbulo compromise. He seized Armenia.

Marcus Aurelius, however, was not just a philosopher. He was an able man and a warrior. He sent Lucius Verus to the east along with a very capable general, Avidius Cassius. Cassius followed Trajan's route, storming southward through Mesopotamia.

In 165, he took Seleucia. Seleucia was still a Greek city, still large and populous. It was, in fact, the largest Greek-speaking city outside the Roman Empire, with a population, even then, of perhaps 400,000. Cassius, for no reason except to indulge his own feeling of victory, ordered the city burned. This was done, and Seleucia never recovered. As a great city, it came to an end almost five centuries after it had been founded. The cause of Hellenism in the east was mortally wounded as well.

Cassius next took Ctesiphon across the river and destroyed the royal palace but left the city itself reasonably intact.

In return for the gratuitous piece of criminal destruction at Seleucia, Parthia had an unwitting and horrible revenge. An epidemic of smallpox had been working its way through Asia and had reached Parthia. The Roman soldiers sickened in sufficient quantities to force a withdrawal from Seleucia.

The retreating soldiers carried the disease back with them to all parts of the Empire and through the years 166 and 167, it killed countless Romans. The plague weakened the Empire more than a full-scale enemy invasion might have. Indeed, there are many who feel that the Roman decline can be dated from this plague; that the Empire was so weakened that it could never make a true recovery from the evils that were to come upon it in ensuing decades.

One more Roman invasion of Mesopotamia was to come. In 192, the son of Marcus Aurelius, who succeeded him as Emperor, was assassinated. In the years of anarchy and civil war that followed, Parthia, now ruled by Vologesus IV, decided it was a good time for an adventure. Vologesus sent a Parthian army into those northwestern Mesopotamian provinces that had been Roman since Trajan's time, eighty years before.

But Rome settled down, and Septimius Severus (seh-vee′ rus) was firmly on the throne by 197. He at once hurried east and, for the third time, a Roman army flooded down Mesopotamia. Again Roman legions passed the site of Babylon, but this time there was nothing there, not one occupied hovel marked the place where once nearly a million people had swarmed.

In 198 the Roman army took Ctesiphon for the third time in eighty years. Severus sacked it thoroughly, killing the men and carrying the women and children off into slavery.

But Rome was weaker than it had been under Trajan and under Marcus Aurelius. It was harder to support an army so far from home and a shortage of supplies forced Severus to turn back. On his way home, he laid siege to Hatra, which had stubbornly resisted him as once it had resisted Trajan.

Severus was not successful. He was forced to retreat from Hatra with considerable loss of face and with some bloody memories of the Parthian archers.

His son, Caracalla (kar″uh-kal′uh), returned to the Parthian scene in 217. He campaigned in northern Mesopotamia, reaching the Tigris and might have done more, but was assassinated.

9

THE SASSANIDS

RE-ENTER THE PERSIANS

The repeated Roman victories, the threefold loss of the capital, the endless dynastic squabbling, finally brought an end to the Parthian Empire. Its subjects must have been ready for any other native dynasty who could bring order and efficient government to the land.

Salvation came from Persis, the Persian heartland, from which, eight centuries before, Cyrus had come to put an end to a north Iranian dynasty.

Persia had never bowed to Parthian overlordship but had clung to a precarious independence and to an old-fashioned Iranianism, resisting the lure of Hellenism all through the Seleucid and Parthian period. To all Iranians who deplored the Hellenic prejudices of their upper classes and who recognized in Hellenism (whether Greek, Macedonian, or Roman) their chief enemy over a period of seven centuries, Persia seemed the answer.

They had to be patient, though, to wait for the right Persian to appear. The land was split up into principalities and was weak through most of the Parthian period. The region about Persepolis came under the control of a shepherd (according to legend) called Sassan, about the time of Marcus Aurelius. His descendants are named, in his honor, the Sassanids (sas′ uh-nidz).

In 211 a disputed succession left Sassan's grandson, Ardashir (ahr′duh-shir) on the throne. (The name is a late Persian form of the old royal name, Artaxerxes.)

Ardashir began to consolidate his power over all Persia, and by 224 he was the national champion of Iranianism. He marched against Artabanus IV (ahr″tuh-bay′nus) who was then the Parthian king. For four years, Ardashir gained strength as Artabanus lost it, until finally, Artabanus tried to carry the fight into Persian territory. In one last battle at Hormuz (hawr′muz) on the seacoast at the mouth of the Persian Gulf, Ardashir defeated and killed this last of the Parthian kings, and in 228 occupied Ctesiphon. The empire was his. Only Hatra, that stubborn bastion of Parthianism held out for nearly twenty years until it was finally taken by Ardashir's son.

Thus ended a line that had ruled over sections of Iranian territory for nearly five centuries and over Mesopotamia for three and a half. This line, the Arsacids, was not, however, entirely extinct. By the Corbulo compromise, an Arsacid still ruled in Armenia and the line continued to rule there for generations more.

The accession of Ardashir represents, in some ways, only a change in dynasty, for the land remained essentially the same in people, language, and custom. Indeed, Persian legend grew busy and told tales tending to prove that Ardashir was an Arsacid on his mother's side, as once similar legends had connected Cyrus with the Median royal family.

Nevertheless, as in the case of Cyrus, the empire receives a new name at this point; indeed, almost the same new name. Because Ardashir came from Persia, one speaks of the land under this new dynasty as a Persian Empire again. To distinguish it from the earlier one of the Achaemenids, one can call it the "New Persian Empire" or the "Neo-Persian Empire." It seems best, however, to name it for the dynasty and call it the "Sassanid Empire." There is then no confusion possible.

This change was, from the Roman standpoint, all to the bad. The Sassanid Empire was larger than the Parthian Empire and the accession of Persia and other southern provinces strengthened it. Under the new dynasty, Persia enjoyed a revival, both political and spiritual, and just at this time, the Romans sank into a period of civil war and anarchy that, for fifty years, made them resemble the Parthians at their worst.

Just as the Romans, on occasion, hankered for the full inheritance of Alexander the Great, so the new dynasty, mindful of its Persian origin, felt that the full inheritance of Darius I belonged to itself. Of that inheritance, Asia Minor, Syria, and Egypt were Roman and had been Roman for centuries. The outlook, therefore, did not look good for real peace, and there never was any between Rome and Persia, only occasional truces.

Ardashir and his son and successor, Shapur I (shah-poor'), took advantage of Roman disorders to raid westward year after year. In 251, the Persians were in full control of Armenia and not long after they took Syria and drove into Antioch itself.

In 258, the Roman Emperor of the moment, Valerian, marched eastward to try to retrieve the situation. It didn't look good. The Roman Empire seemed as though it might fall apart at any moment. Emperor was following emperor at an average rate of one every two years; the provinces were riddled with disaffection and rebellion; and Valerian himself was worn out with five years of Emperorship that had consisted of nothing but warfare against the savage German tribes north of the Roman borders.

For a while, he drove the Persians back, but in 260, he was trapped at Edessa (ee-des'uh), a city in northwestern Mesopotamia, just twenty-five miles north of ill-fated Carrhae. We don't know the details of the battle, but apparently the Romans were caught by surprise and a large army of them was wiped out.

Worse yet — far worse from a propaganda standpoint — the Emperor Valerian was taken alive. He was the first Roman Emperor ever to be taken prisoner by an enemy and he remained a prisoner for the rest of his life, though no one knows exactly when he died.

(Stories went about later that Valerian was brutally mistreated as a prisoner. One favorite tale is that whenever Shapur wished to mount a horse, Valerian was forced to get on his hands and knees and serve as a mounting block. This, however, has all the earmarks of an "atrocity tale." Generally, important captives, taken in war, are well treated for it often happens that it is useful to release them at some later time, and a released ruler might as well have reasonably kindly feelings for his ex-captors when that happens.)

The capture of Valerian and the destruction of his army opened Asia Minor to Shapur. In fact, there was apparently nothing to stop him and for a moment, indeed, it seemed that the Empire of Darius I would be restored. That something *did* happen to stop the Persians is one of the surprises in which history so often abounds.

There was a city called Palmyra in the Syrian desert, about ninety miles south of Thapsacus on the Euphrates. It was near the limit of the Roman power and, in the period of anarchy into which Rome had fallen, it was virtually independent and under the rule of a native Arab chieftain named Odenathus (od"uh-nay'thus).

He reasoned that a weak Rome would give him no trouble, but that if Shapur conquered Syria, a strong Persia would. He therefore attacked Shapur. He could not attack him on equal terms, of course, since he was a small city against an Empire, but he didn't have to. Shapur's main forces were in Asia Minor, for the Persian was expecting no trouble in his rear. Odenathus supplied some, striking for the Euphrates and cutting down the light holding forces Shapur had left there. In 263, Odenathus was raiding into Mesopotamia and even threatening Ctesiphon.

Shapur was forced to retreat and Rome had a breathing spell in which she could recover.

Shapur's final years were spent in building activities, in which he made lavish use of the men he had carried off from the Roman provinces. He used prisoners from Antioch to build a city he called (in Persian) "better-than-Antioch."

THE PULL OF THE PAST

If Ardashir was the founder, or Cyrus, of the Sassanid Empire, Shapur was the organizer, or Darius, of it. His thirty-year rule was one of consolidation and, furthermore, of a deliberate return to the past.

Shapur himself patronized Greek scholars and placed Greek in his inscriptions but that was a personal predilection. Officially, he discouraged Hellenism, and his successors made no use of Greek. In every way, Shapur tried to remind the people of the past and pretend that the old Persian Empire of the Achaemenids had never passed away but had merely been driven underground for five centuries. In imitation of Darius, for instance, he deliberately set up mountainside inscriptions detailing his capture of the Roman Emperor, Valerian.

Ancient Iranianism was encouraged also in its religious aspect. Zoroastrianism had remained strong in the hearts of the Iranian peasantry, despite the Hellenism of the upper classes, and now it was to receive the full royal blessing. The entire weight of the government backed the Zoroastrian priesthood and non-Zoroastrians (the Jews in Mesopotamia, for instance) found that the easygoing Parthian days had come to an end.

The Zoroastrian writings were gathered, edited, revised, and compiled into a combination scripture and prayer book that has survived in its Sassanid form ever since. This they called the "Avesta," though it is best known to us as the "Zend-Avesta" ("interpretation of the Avesta"), the name originally given to a commentary on the Avesta rather than to the writings itself.

Zoroastrianism did not confine its influence to Persia only. During the period when Hellenism and Iranianism were mingling, religious influence flowed in both directions. In the Zoroastrian world picture, for instance, one of the important subordinates of Ahura Mazda was Mithras. He gradually grew more important in certain of the legends and came to represent the life-giving sun. Usually, he was pictured as a young man slaying a bull representing the darkness.

During the second century A.D., when Roman soldiers marched the length of Mesopotamia three times, they brought back the cult of Mithras, which underwent some changes as a result of contact with Hellenism. It became a soldier's religion, essentially, one that was closed to women. Converts entered by mysterious rites that involved bathing in the blood of a freshly killed bull. Indeed, Mithraism became far more popular and important in Rome than it possibly could become in Persia under the hostile eyes of the orthodox Zoroastrian priesthood.

As Persia grew strong and Rome weak, Mithraism grew stronger in Rome and even received Imperial sponsorship. In 274, not long after Shapur had very nearly ripped away the easternmost third of the Roman Empire, the Emperor, Aurelian (aw-ree'lee-an), established an official cult of "Sol Invictus" ("the unconquerable sun"), a form of Mithraism. December 25, the day of the sun's birth — when the noonday sun, according to Rome's Julian calendar, reached its lowest point at the winter solstice and began to rise again — became an important holiday.

Mithraism seemed to be more successful than a competing religion of Judean origin — Christianity. Christianity was pacifist in philosophy and refused to accept Emperor-worship. A religion which seemed hostile to the Imperial cult and to soldiers seemed dangerous indeed, particularly when Rome was so ringed with enemies outside and so filled with disaffection inside. Where the Mithraists were supported, therefore, the Christians were persecuted.

However, Christianity permitted women to participate in its

rites, and it showed no compunction about borrowing popular aspects of other religions. (It accepted December 25, for instance, as the birth of its founder, Jesus.) Many a Mithraist had a Christian wife who brought up the children as Christians. For this reason (and others) Christianity slowly gained at the expense of Mithraism.

In Shapur's time, a religious novelty appeared in the shape of a new prophet, Mani (mah'nee). He was to Zoroastrianism, in a way, what Jesus was to Judaism. That is, he began with Zoroastrian beliefs but claimed a new revelation that further explained and modified these beliefs.

Mani was born about 215 in Mesopotamia and, as is usually the case with founders of religions or empires, legends cluster about him. He was supposed to have been an Arsacid. He was supposed to have preached publicly for the first time on the very day of the coronation of Shapur I in 241. He was supposed to have had visions of angels and to have traveled widely; to India, for instance.

His doctrines centered on Zoroastrian dualism; that is, on the opposing armies of good and evil; and he went on to evolve a very complex set of symbolic myths centering about it. He claimed there were many prophets, including not only Zoroaster, but Buddha and Jesus as well. He himself, Mani, was, however, the latest and last of them. With this in mind, Mani included certain Buddhist and Christian viewpoints in his doctrines. This further complicated his already complex views.

Mani was supposed to have deliberately written down his own doctrines in order that they might not be distorted by later followers. (Perhaps he had the case of Jesus in mind.) In his writings, he tells of the organization of Heaven and Hell, of the creation of the world and of man, and, among other things, does not neglect to describe the role played in all this by Jesus (according to his own view).

He taught the necessity of withdrawal from the world, since the world was very largely in the power of evil, and it was almost impossible to deal with that evil without being corrupted. Naturally, those who were most pious withdrew completely and could not earn a living. Those who were a stage less pious were expected to stay in the world sufficiently to earn a living both for themselves and for the most pious whom they were to support.

Shapur was attracted to the teachings of Mani and, while he reigned, Mani could teach freely under his protection. This protection was needed, for Mani was no more popular among the conservative Zoroastrian priesthood than Jesus had been among the conservative Judean priesthood. Indeed, after Shapur's death in 272, Mani found himself in gathering danger. In 274, in the reign of Shapur's younger son, Varahran I (vah-rah-rahn'),* he was imprisoned and, soon after, he was dead.

That, however, was by no means the end of his doctrines. They flourished particularly in Mesopotamia where, perhaps, they served as a kind of nationalistic reaction toward the triumphant Iranian doctrine of Zoroastrianism. Perhaps the natives of what had once been Babylonia remembered dimly a time when they had had a great religion of their own, and were ready to adopt almost anything new (and remember that Mani himself was a native Mesopotamian) that would mark them off again.

The followers of Mani underwent a series of bitter persecutions and were gradually driven out to the very borders and beyond. By 600, they were concentrated in the extreme northeast of the Sassanid dominions, but had made their influence felt as far eastward as China.

Meanwhile, Mani's doctrines traveled westward, too, and entered the Roman Empire. There, Mani was known by a Greek version of his name, Manichaeus (man"ih-kee'us) and his doctrines were known as Manichaeism.

Manichaeism grew quite popular and by about 400 constituted a serious rival to Christianity. St. Augustine was a Manichaean before his conversion to Christianity. The Christian leaders persecuted the cult as enthusiastically as the Zoroastrians did, however, and gradually it died out in Europe, too. The works of Mani — the sacred scriptures of Manichaeism —

---

* This name is better known to us in its Arabic version of Bahram (bah-rahm').

were lost and are known to us only through quotation and commentary by its enemies.

Nevertheless, the belief survived in odd places in both Europe and Asia well into the Middle Ages. Certain Christian heresies of medieval times were strongly Manichaean in their beliefs.

ROMAN RECOVERY

Shapur's failure to seize the eastern portion of the Roman Empire was a fatal one for Persia, for it gave Rome a chance to recover. The opportunity to strike a finishing blow at Rome was not to come again for three centuries.

The two enemies now settled down to a long tug-of-war curiously like that which had previously occupied the Parthians and Romans.

The old points at issue had been replaced by others. Armenia, it is true, was still a buffer territory coveted by both powers, but to it now had been added northwestern Mesopotamia. Since Trajan's time, it had remained, more or less, in Roman hands, but Persia could not help but covet the region that contained Carrhae where once so signal a defeat had been handed the Roman forces.

As for the Romans, they had evened the score for Crassus by taking Ctesiphon three times. Since then, however, the new disgrace of Valerian's capture at Edessa had arisen and the Romans yearned to even that score, too.

It was not long after Shapur's death that the situation grew acute. In 284, Diocletian (dy"oh-klee'shan) became the Roman Emperor and he ended the half-century of anarchy. He reorganized the government and associated with himself several strong men to share the tasks of government. One of these was Galerius (guh-leer'ee-us).

Meanwhile, a new king had gained the throne in Persia. He was Narsah (nahr'suh), the youngest son of old Shapur I. Following his father's expansionist policy, and perhaps not

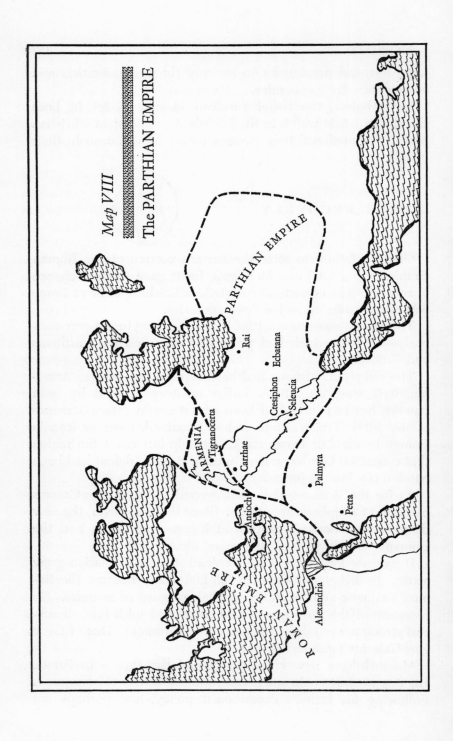

Map VIII
The PARTHIAN EMPIRE

PARTHIAN EMPIRE

Rai •

Ecbatana •

Ctesiphon •
Seleucia •

ARMENIA
Tigranocerta •
Carrhae •

Palmyra •

Antioch •

Petra •

ROMAN EMPIRE

Alexandria •

quite realizing that the situation had changed in Rome, Narsah invaded and occupied parts of Armenia.

Diocletian promptly sent Galerius eastward. In 297, Galerius took his army into Mesopotamia, and met the Persians near ill-starred Carrhae. It was doubly ill-starred now, for Galerius met with a serious reverse and had to retreat.

Diocletian, however, had a grim and determined faith in Galerius' ability. He sent him forward in a second campaign, this time into Armenia. There, Galerius justified Diocletian's faith. He not only defeated Narsah and drove him out of Armenia, but in doing so he nearly annihilated the Persian army. What is more, he cut off Narsah's auxiliary columns, and when he came to look over the prisoners he found that among them was Narsah's harem — his wife and children. (It was customary for Iranian potentates to take their harem with them on the march.)

This almost evened the score with respect to Valerian's capture. Furthermore, it gave Galerius a perfect way of putting the screws on Narsah. The Persian king felt affection for his family, presumably, and, in addition, was keenly aware of the loss of face that would follow if he left his family imprisoned. So he bartered for them, and for their return he gave up all claims to Armenia and northwestern Mesopotamia; he even ceded additional territory. He got his family back and there was peace for forty years between Persia and Rome.

This war had an important effect on Rome. Galerius returned to find himself high in favor with Diocletian. It so happened that Galerius was strongly anti-Christian and he used his war-won prestige to persuade Diocletian to set in motion a general persecution of Christians throughout the Empire. It was the worst persecution the Christians had to undergo.

For Persia, however, the period of peace that follows is a dim one. Unfortunately, the histories and documents we must depend on are largely of Roman origin. This means that the periods when Persia fought with Rome are therefore much better known than the periods of peace in between. Furthermore, Persian activities against Rome are better known than its adventures and misadventures on other frontiers.

For instance, Shapur I had expanded eastward as well as westward. At the Parthian height, he had absorbed the territory of the old kingdom of Bactria, and its eastern border had almost reached the western border of China. During the first century A.D., however, the nomadic Kushan tribes had flooded in from central Asia and had taken over what had once been Bactria and is now the modern nation of Afghanistan. The Kushans held their independence throughout the decline of the Parthian Empire, and it was only with the new vigor of the Sassanids that they gave in. Shapur I struck eastward and absorbed them into his empire. In addition, Persia had to withstand periodic raids from Arabic principalities to the southwest. All such events on the eastern and southern borders are seen through a cloudy haze.

Equally mist-ridden are internal affairs. Under Varahran II, a predecessor of Narsah, Zoroastrianism reached a peak of fanaticism and the last traces of Hellenism in Mesopotamia were wiped out. On the other hand, under Narsah's son, Hormizdas II (hawr′miz-das), who reigned from 301 to 309, there was an attempt to procure social justice. The arbitrary powers of the rich landowning aristocracy came under attack.

The great magnates naturally resented this. It is logical for the king to oppose these magnates (in all countries, not in Persia alone), for they tend to be a turbulent lot who hamper the king's policies. On the other hand, if they are ever aggrieved enough to unite against the king, they usually have sufficient power to destroy him. Any king attempting to fight a too powerful aristocracy must keep that in mind and, at least at first, win victories by playing off factions, one against the other.

Hormizdas II did not, apparently, deal cleverly in this respect. His death seems to have come early and may have been hastened. Certainly, the nobles were in power after his death and the royal family was hounded almost into extinction. The son who ought to have succeeded to the throne was killed, another was blinded, a third was imprisoned.

Yet it didn't seem safe to try to do without a Sassanid on the throne altogether. The dynasty had been sufficiently successful and orthodox in its century of power to gain the affection of the people generally and of the priesthood in particular. Any noble who attempted to take the rule would suffer the automatic hostility of the people, priests, and, in addition, of the other nobles.

Someone had a stroke of genius. Hormizdas' wife was pregnant when the king had died, and it was suggested that the unborn child, if a boy, be declared king. There is even a story that the crown was placed on the queen's swollen abdomen while the nobles knelt in homage.

The purpose was clear. A Sassanid would remain on the throne to make everything legal. He would be a baby, however, and the nobles would remain in control. The baby would grow up, of course, but there would be ways of keeping him under control — or worse.

So it happened that when the infant (who was indeed a boy) was born, he was already king. He reigned as Shapur II and while he was a child, the nobles ruled and a rare mess they made of it — as a bunch of quarreling nobles are bound to do. Each would be interested in his own power, his own lands, and the common good would be lost in the shuffle. Arabic raids were particularly destructive in the minority of Shapur II, and Mesopotamia was ravaged by them, even to the point of a sack of Ctesiphon.

The nobles had miscalculated one point — the character of Shapur II. He matured quickly and he had ability. By the time he was seventeen, while the nobles still thought of him as a child, he was a man in all but years. Moving quickly, he seized control of the government, and had the army and the populace shouting deliriously as he sat in triumph on the throne.

He then converted the momentary enthusiasm into firm homage by launching a punitive expedition against the Arabs. He spread fire and destruction far and wide and utterly smashed the Arab raiders. Persia rang with pride at the deeds of its new, young king and his throne was secure. He was to have long life, too, and, considering that he was king at birth, he ended up with a reign of seventy years!

Only once in history since has that record been surpassed,
and that by Louis XIV of France who, thirteen and a half centuries later, was to rule for seventy-two years.

THE CHRISTIAN ENEMY

As Shapur looked about the world, now that he was fully
master of Persia, he must have noted the crucial change that
took place during the generation of peace with Rome. The
persecution of Christianity, which had begun in Rome in the
aftermath of their great victory over the Persians in the time
of Galerius, had petered out without accomplishing its aim of
crushing the new religion.

A later Emperor, Constantine I, who began his rule in 306,
saw virtue in rallying the Christian population of the Empire
to his side, against other claimants who were violently anti-
Christian. In the end, he won out and by 324 he was ruling
over the entire Empire, which he was in the process of making
officially Christian. It was this new Christian Rome which
Shapur found himself facing.

Until that point, Persia had been reasonably tolerant of
Christians. Christianity had spread among the population of
Mesopotamia, and it had been there that Manichaeism, that
curious amalgam of Zorastrianism and Christianity, had flourished.

Christianity had also spread in Armenia. Indeed, the first
ruler to turn Christian in all the world was an Arsacid. Not
Constantine of Rome but Tiridates III of Armenia was the
first Christian monarch. Tiridates was converted in 294.

As long as Rome was anti-Christian, the Christians of Persia
gave loyal service. Indeed, a number of them were refugees
from Roman persecution and these could be counted on, as
refugees always can be, to be furiously hostile to the nation

from which they had fled. (Much more hostile, usually, than its merely foreign enemies.)

But now what a change had taken place. Rome was officially Christian. Its emperor took tender care of the bishops and guided their councils. Rome, from being the cruel persecutor, had become the kindly father. This meant that every Christian inside the Persian realm had become, virtually overnight, a potential fifth columnist. It meant that Armenia, so long suspended midway between Rome on one side and Parthia-Persia on the other, was suddenly very likely to swing to Rome entirely for religious reasons.

Persia had to react. She tightened her own Zoroastrian orthodoxy and declared war on heresy. This in itself made a renewed war with Rome likely, a war made one notch more horrible by religious fervor on each side.

Shapur II waited for Constantine to die. The Roman Empire was left to his three sons, when he died in 337, and Shapur calculated that an empire ruled by three was weaker than an empire ruled by one. Immediately after Constantine's death, he therefore began a war against Constantius, that one of Constantine's sons who ruled in the East.

Naturally, this war was promptly and loudly opposed by Persia's Christians. The bishop of Ctesiphon denounced Shapur virulently. It was an honest thing to do, but foolhardy. Shapur was not playing games. His persecution of Christians intensified to the point where they were all but wiped out.

Constantius was not a great soldier and he lost consistently in open battle. On the other hand, the Romans had fortified key towns in northwestern Mesopotamia, and these fortified points consistently resisted siege. Notable among these Roman strong points was Nisibis (nis'ih-bis), about 120 miles east of Carrhae, which never fell to Shapur.

A remarkable young man, however, was to be found in the Roman far west. He was Julian, a cousin of Constantius, who, alone of all Constantius' relatives, still remained alive. (Constantius had himself seen to the slaughter of most of them, for being Christian had not altered the old habit whereby absolute monarchs killed other members of the family to prevent civil war. Julian, long fearful of death, was not impressed with Christian love and mercy, and despite a Christian education, turned secretly pagan.)

By leaving Julian alive, Constantius had let live one too many, for the young man, while still in his twenties, was winning remarkable victories over German tribes who had invaded Gaul. He was doing this even while Constantius was drearily fighting in Mesopotamia without displaying a spark of military talent. So popular was Julian with his troops that when the jealous Constantius tried to weaken him by withdrawing some of his legions, the soldiers proclaimed him Emperor and forced him to march eastward.

Constantius died before the civil war could really be joined and in 361, Julian ruled Rome.

It would have paid Julian to make a reasonable peace with Persia. The religious motive for war had vanished, for as soon as he was Emperor, Julian openly admitted himself to be a pagan. (The indignant Christians called him "Julian the Apostate.") He was, indeed, anxious to weaken the Christians without actively persecuting them, and surely he might have done that best by making friends with Persia against the common enemy.

Unfortunately for himself, Julian had an even more enticing goal than the weakening of Christianity. His victories in Gaul had been much like those of Julius Caesar and he may have had visions of proving himself a new Alexander the Great. He was, after all, still a young man, barely thirty.

Following the footsteps of Trajan, Julian marched into Mesopotamia and led his army down the Euphrates, taking cities with an elaborate display of effective siege machinery. He reached Ctesiphon at last. For the fourth time, this capital witnessed the approach of a Roman army.

The first three times the city had fallen, but now it seemed determined not to. It closed its gates, manned its walls, and breathed defiance. This was disturbing. The fact that a second army, that was supposed to have marched down the Tigris and joined Julian at Ctesiphon, did not do so, but apparently dawdled on the road, was even more disturbing.

Julian was in no mood to settle down to a long siege of Ctesiphon. The city had been taken three times before without that feat destroying the enemy, so its capture was no end in itself. Besides, Shapur's army was still intact somewhere to the east, and a siege would seriously weaken the Romans and make them sitting ducks for a counterattack.

Julian did, therefore, what he thought Alexander the Great would have done. He burned his river fleet, cut loose from his bases, and launched his army into the Iranian east, there to find the Persians and destroy them.

But to be an Alexander, it helps to fight a Darius III, and Shapur wasn't going to oblige. He gathered his army about him and retreated. He had no intention of risking it in the field against this talented Roman general until the invader had been cut down to size. He followed a policy which, in modern times, has been called "scorched earth."

Wherever Julian went he found nothing but smoldering ruins. There was no food, no shelter, and worst of all, no enemy to fight. He was in the position not of Alexander in Persia, seven centuries before, but of Napoleon in Russia, fourteen centuries later.

Julian was stymied. Too late, he realized he had underestimated his wily opponent. He turned back, intent only on reaching safety, before exposure, starvation, and disease prepared the way for a Persian slaughter of his troops.

Once he began to retreat, the Persians appeared, but only in the distance and at the flanks. They cut off stragglers and mounted hit-and-run attacks. Julian's army bled at a hundred small wounds, but the resolute Emperor was able to hold it together.

Unfortunately, he was vulnerable within as well as without. The fact that he was a pagan did not sit well with those of his officers and men who were Christians. It became entirely too easy to whisper that Julian was being driven by God to madness and ruin as punishment for his apostasy, and that the army would be destroyed with him if they did nothing to prevent it.

Toward the end of June, 363, during a skirmish with the Persians, a spear struck him and while it did not kill him at once, it was obvious that he would not live long. The army's officers, who gathered at once to choose a new Emperor, said it was a Persian spear, but there is a good possibility that it wasn't. It might have been a Roman spear, cast by a Christian arm.

Julian died after a reign of less than two years. He and Alexander were the same age at their death, but there the resemblance stopped. A general named Jovian was chosen as the new Emperor. He was Christian, but that was his only merit.

Jovian had to return to Asia Minor as rapidly as possible in order that his election might be confirmed, but Shapur II wasn't letting the army go that easily. If they wanted out, they had better come to some agreement, and Shapur II had the exact terms all spelled out; they had only to sign.

Jovian did sign, and by that signature, the victory of Galerius, seventy years before, was completely nullified. All the territory ceded to Rome by Narsah was restored, and Armenia was admitted to be in the Persian sphere of influence. In addition (and most disgracefully) several of the fortified points in upper Mesopotamia, including Nisibis which for so long and so valiantly had resisted Shapur's armies, were handed over.

All this gained Jovian nothing, for he died on his way back and never did get to be confirmed and crowned.

Shapur had considerable difficulty, by the way, in enforcing his newly won but only theoretical control over Armenia. An attempt to crush Christianity in that mountainous country failed utterly and, for a dozen years, Shapur had to fight Roman intrigue which kept the Armenians in a constant state of rebellion against him. In the end, however, Shapur bought Armenia's submission by paying the price of tolerating Armenian Christianity. (Armenians remain Christian, by and large, to this day despite centuries of sometimes-hideous persecution; a stubborn feat matched only by Europe's Jews.)

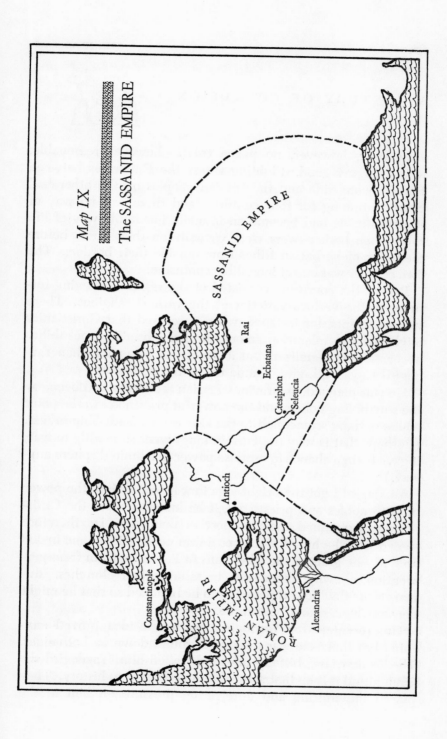

Map IX

The SASSANID EMPIRE

SASSANID EMPIRE

Rai

Ecbatana

Ctesiphon
Seleucia

Antioch

Constantinople

ROMAN EMPIRE

Alexandria

A CENTURY OF CONFUSION

By now, however, no peace treaty, however reasonable, would do any good. Fighting across the Euphrates between Rome on one side and the Iranian peoples on the other had been continuing for four centuries and there was no way of stopping it. It had become an insanely inevitable way of life even when both powers were virtually on their knees before the influx of barbarian tribes from outside their borders. The fifth century was one of incredible confusion.

Part of the confusion consisted of the rapidly changing fortunes of the various varieties of the various religions. There were moments, for instance, when it seemed that Christianity might achieve toleration among the Persians. That possibility never quite materialized, but it almost came to pass when Yazdegird I (yaz″dih-gird′) came to the throne in 399.

He was plagued, as previous Persian monarchs had been, by the squabbling nobles and the powerful priesthood to the point where nothing seemed left to the king except leadership in war. (Perhaps that is why the Persian kings went so readily to war; it gave them a chance to exercise power in a limited sphere anyway.)

Yazdegird I got the bright idea that he could limit the power of both nobles and priesthood, if he leaned toward the Christians and obtained their support in that way. He therefore signed what he hoped would be a firm peace with Rome in 408 and, in 409, granted the Christians in Persia freedom from persecution, allowing them even to rebuild their churches. Rumors arose that he was planning to be baptized so that he might become the Persian Constantine.

Unfortunately for Yazdegird, his bright idea proved anything but that. He was promptly ground down on both sides. The Zoroastrians, bitterly offended, called him "Yazdegird the Sinner" and it is by that name that he is known to history. They placed unremitting and unrelenting pressure on him to the point where the assassin's knife must have seemed to glitter ominously in his mind's eye.

He might have endured, if he could have felt sure of the backing of a Christian priesthood. These, however, filled with the wine of sudden freedom and conscious of mighty Rome at their back, proved quite intransigent. They made it increasingly plain that as far as they were concerned, toleration and even a royal conversion was not enough. Persia had to be Christian entirely, and Zoroastrianism must, in the end, be utterly stamped out.

Yazdegird, faced with a religious totalitarianism in either direction, chose the one he knew, and returned to the old ways. By 416, Christianity was under the Zoroastrian yoke again.

Nevertheless, Yazdegird remained unforgiven. In 420, he was assassinated and none of his sons was allowed, at first, to succeed him.

The confusion was increased by the growing influence of forces hitherto insignificant. Until now, the Arab tribes had satisfied themselves with occasional raids — notably during Shapur II's minority. Since about 200, however, there had been growing up the kingdom of Hira (hee'ruh) southwest of the Euphrates River and along the southern shores of the Persian Gulf. This was governed by the Lakhmids, an Arab dynasty that recognized the overlordship of the Sassanids, when they came to power. They enjoyed a considerable degree of self-government, however, and became a center of Arab culture. Much poetry dates from this period and, according to legend, it was in Hira that the Arab script was first developed.

By 400, Hira was a cultured and powerful state, strong enough to make its influence felt in a confused Persia. One son of Yazdegird I had been brought up in Hira, and its Arab ruler saw quite well that a prince friendly to himself would be ideal as Persian monarch. He supported the prince with sufficient backing in the way of money and soldiers to make it possible for him to seat himself on the throne and rule as Varahran V.

Varahran V had learned culture and pleasure in Hira and retained that love as Persian king. He was charming about it, rather than dissolute. At least, later legend gloried in his successes as a hunter and lover and wove tall tales about him with the same kind of affection for his weaknesses that a later people poured forth on Henry IV of France. His legends continued popular in later centuries, and he became better known by the Arabic version of his name, Bahram Gor ("Varahran the Wild Ass"), because he loved to hunt that fleet animal across the broad steppes, and perhaps because he himself was as wild and free as that animal.

It is to this Varahran that a certain verse in Edward Fitzgerald's translation of Omar Khayyam's *Rubaiyat* (written about seven centuries after Varahran's time) refers. In the eighteenth quatrain, Omar sighs over vanished greatness and the emptiness of worldly glory:

> They say the Lion and the Lizard keep
> The Courts where Jamshyd gloried and drank deep.
>   And Bahram, that great Hunter — the Wild Ass
> Stamps o'er his Head, but cannot break his sleep.

Varahran V inherited the persecution program of Yazdegird's last years and even had a little try at a war with Rome, in 421. The excuse was that Rome was harboring Christian refugees from Persia. But Persia suffered defeat and the civilized Varahran decided that this particular game was not worth the candle.

He attempted a peace that seemed, on the face of it, a model of logic and reasonableness. Persia agreed to tolerate Christians and Rome agreed to tolerate Zoroastrians. (The Zoroastrian priests must have been quick to point out, in exasperation, that where there were many Christians in Persia, there were few Zoroastrians in Rome, so that the agreement was entirely one-sided.)

To be sure, Varaharan experienced some military successes. It was in his time that a nomadic people from central Asia, the Huns, were spreading westward over the Eurasian steppes and into northern and central Europe. They established a vast but short-lived empire that was one of the factors driving the German tribes into the Roman Empire; a drive that ripped the western half of that Empire to shreds. Varahran was able to take advantage of Rome's preoccupation with this deadly attack in the west. He took over outright control of the eastern portion of Armenia in 429, and this portion was known as "Persarmenia" thereafter.

(Nevertheless, while the western half of the Roman Empire was in a state of virtual collapse at this time, the eastern portion of the Empire remained intact in all its parts, and the frontier against Persia remained as firm as ever. Except for its strengthened grip on part of Armenia, Persia did not benefit from the western "fall of Rome.")

Nor was Persia entirely immune to the type of outside attack that was destroying the western half of Rome. The Hephthalites, a people related to the Huns, were swarming into the eastern provinces of the Sassanid Empire. Varahran's armies dealt severely with them, however, throwing them back. For a while, at least, the Sassanids maintained themselves far more successfully against nomadic attack from without than the Romans did.

With the death of Varahran V in 439, the status of the Christians slipped again. His son, Yazdegird II, was entirely Zoroastrian, and Christianity was forced underground once more.

The Jews, too, encountered a newly intense opposition. True, the Sassanids did not allow them the freedom they had experienced under the Parthians, but their situation had not been entirely bad. There was no great Jewish power threatening Persia's frontiers, so the Jews were merely a religious threat, not, as was the case with the Christians, a political and military threat as well. The Jews were therefore, on and off, allowed considerable control over their own affairs under a self-styled "leader of the Jews in exile."

Indeed, Jewish intellectual life continued strong under the early Sassanids. Various commentaries and interpretations of the Mosaic law were produced by generations of scholarly rabbis in Mesopotamia, and slowly what is now known as the "Talmud of Babylon" was built up. This was much fuller than the "Talmud of Palestine" built up in the stricken land that had once been Judea.

The Talmud of Babylon, which has been of great influence

on Jewish religious thought ever since, came to a slow end in the
fifth century as gathering persecution by Yazdegird II pinched
off Jewish intellectual life for a season.

And even for the Persians themselves, there was a darkening.
After Yazdegird's death in 457, his son, Firuz (fee-rooz'),
had to face a massive Hephthalite invasion of Persia. In 484,
Firuz was defeated and killed by them, and the intensifying
havoc in Persia reached a crescendo of nearly two decades of
anarchy.

It was not till 501 that Firuz's son, Kavadh, was able to seize
firm hold of the throne in 501 (with Hephthalite help!) and begin to restore order to Persia. At least he was able to get it
back on its feet sufficiently to launch a war with Rome again
— the surest sign of national health in the insanity of the times.

THE HERETICS

The confusion of the century made itself shown in religion
as well. In the Roman Empire, for instance, the final victory
of Christianity did not mean there was to be no more religious strife at all. Periodically, certain doctrines were advanced
which did not meet with the favor of the majority of the bishops and were therefore declared to be heresies. These heresies sometimes persisted, and there would be mutual persecutions, as well as steadfastness to the point of martyrdom. Christian fought Christian as relentlessly as they had earlier fought
paganism.

There was a priest named Nestorius, for instance, who, in
428, became the Patriarch of Constantinople and was therefore
the most powerful single priest in the Roman Empire. He held
that Jesus was made up of two natures, a human and a divine.
The details of his doctrine met with violent resistance on the
part of those who thought that the nature of Jesus was both
human and divine, embodied in a single nature.

A gathering of bishops in 431 voted down this "Nestorian" viewpoint, but it spread and became particularly strong in a theological school at Edessa in northwestern Mesopotamia. This Nestorian heresy thus came to serve as a form of nationalistic rebellion (as heresy often does). The orthodox Christians of the Roman Empire had Latin and Greek as their liturgical languages and were heavily Greek in culture. In Edessa, there was comparatively little Greek and a good deal of native Syrian flavor.

There were certain nationalistic tendencies among the Persian Christians, too. The Christians of Persia had been firmly withstanding persecution for a century and a quarter, but they were not a Greek-speaking church and they were not enthusiastic about being completely under the thumb of the Graeco-Latin Christians of Rome. Besides, if the Persian Church made it quite plain that it was not a mere puppet of the Roman Church it might cease to be viewed as a fifth column, and persecution might ease up.

The Nestorians of Edessa, faced with the persecution of the Christians of Rome and aware of the sympathy toward them of the Christians of Persia, slipped across the border.

The Persian kings, as, for instance, the ill-fated Firuz, were quite aware that a Christian heresy persecuted in Rome could be counted on to be loyal to Persia. He therefore encouraged the Nestorians as much as possible. It became very easy for Persian Christians to adhere to Nestorianism and they did. By 500, the Persian church was entirely Nestorian.

The same strategy worked in states subservient to Persia; in Armenia, for instance, or in the Arabic kingdom of Hira. Both became almost entirely Nestorian.

The Nestorian form of Christianity continued to be an important minority in Asia for many centuries. It even spread eastward into China.

The Nestorians, for all that they rebelled against the Hellenism of the Roman Church, could not help bringing the records of Greek learning with them; a learning that had vanished in Persia after the coming to power of the strongly Iranian Sassanids. In later years, when the Arabs controlled western Asia,

they picked up Greek science from the Nestorians and
preserved it through many centuries when it was all but dead
in Europe.

Zoroastrianism also bred its heresies. After all, Mani's doctrines had been one of them. Now, during the decades of Hephthalite confusion, a new heresy arose, fostered by a Zoroastrian priest named Mazdak. He preached a form of Manichaeism and advocated an ascetic and communistic way of life. He
denounced the vested property interests of the nobility and the
entrenched power of the priesthood. Naturally, he roused
the bitter enmity of these powerful elements.

Kavadh, whose reign brought an end to the period of
anarchy, felt a strong sympathy for Mazdakism. It might have
been a sincere belief in the ethics it preached or it might have
been the common royal feeling that anything that broke the
power of nobles and priests had to be all right.

But Mazdakism, like almost all puritan movements, tended
to be intolerant in small things as well as large. Mazdakite
spokesmen would denounce small pleasures as readily and as
bitterly as they would denounce huge injustices. Since few
people are without their pleasures, many who might have
been in sympathy with the broader aims balked at the details.
They were not willing to be freed of injustice at the price of losing their pleasures. Under such conditions the nobles and
priests found the very populace they oppressed on their side.
They could then easily force their way upon the king. Kavadh
was deposed and was not restored until he had promised to see
the light as far as Mazdakism was concerned and to be a good
Zoroastrian.

When Kavadh died, his oldest son, known to be a follower
of Mazdak, was barred from the throne. Instead, a younger son,
Chosrau I ("famous"), better known by the Greek version of
his name, Chosroes (koz′roh-eez) was made king in 531. Chosroes promptly had Mazdak and his chief followers put to death
and saw to it that their writings were destroyed. The cult did
not entirely to die (somehow cults hardly ever do), but it remained completely unimportant thereafter.

THE MOMENT OF ENLIGHTENMENT

Leaving aside this display of religious bigotry, undoubtedly forced on him by the nobles and priests as the price of the
crown, and forgetting also the almost routine slaughter of relatives to prevent civil war, Chosroes I was a civilized king. He
was perhaps the most enlightened of the Sassanids and was
called Chosroes Anushirvan ("of the immortal spirit") or Chosroes the Just.

In Kavadh's time, there had been a continuation of the en-
demic war with Rome, but in 527 a new and capable monarch,
Justinian I, was on the throne in Constantinople. (It was Constantinople that was now capital of the Roman Empire and had
been since Constantine's day two centuries before. The city of
Rome was actually under the control of German tribes at this
time.)

Justinian had the dream of regaining the western half of the
Empire from the Germans who held it. To do this, he needed
peace with Persia. As for Chosroes I, he strongly desired to reorganize the internal administration of Persia and he had the
sensible notion that such reforms could best be carried through
in times of peace.

With both sides willing, it was easy to sign what was called
"The Endless Peace" in 533.

Unfortunately, it is an irony of history that an "Endless Peace"
usually lasts a shorter time than just an ordinary peace. Within
seven years of the signing of that peace, Rome and Persia were
back at war.

The trouble was that Justinian was too victorious. His generals had quickly recaptured North Africa, Italy, and even parts
of Spain. It seemed to Chosroes that if Justinian continued in

this way, he would become so strong that he would be able to smash Persia. In this, he happened to be wrong, for Roman victories were not accomplished without cost, and Justinian's realm was being drained dry by the effort made to carry on wars against hard-fighting German tribes.

Nevertheless, it is easier for us to see this now than for Chosroes to see it then, and in 540, the endless wars of Persia and Rome began again. In the first stroke of the renewed war, Persia briefly occupied Antioch, but matters soon settled down to the usual stalemate.

During the interval of peace, though, a most ironic development took place.

Ever since the death of the Roman Emperor, Julian, a century and a half before, paganism in the Roman Empire had been declining steadily. It had long lost vitality and under Christian oppression those pagans that remained either turned Christian or waited halfheartedly for the passing of life.

Even in Athens, the stronghold of pagan philosophy, the light flickered and began to die. By the time Justinian became Emperor, the only philosophic school that remained in Athens was the Academy, which had been founded in 387 B.C. by the great Athenian philosopher, Plato. For nine hundred years, it had existed, but that existence now offended the pious Justinian, who ordered the Academy closed. The last pagan teachers found their harmless scholarship (heard by very few) forbidden, and themselves with no place to go.

Then came word of the new king of Persia, of his tolerance and enlightenment. Here was someone, it seemed, who might understand the Platonic teaching. So it was that the last pagan philosophers of Athens — the very Athens that had gained its greatest fame by its deathless stand against Perisan tyranny in the days of Darius and Xerxes — now fled to freedom in Persia.

To be sure, they found, once they got there, that matters were not as pleasant as they had hoped. They found the Persian court alien, Chosroes absorbed in other work and uninterested in sitting at their feet. Eventually they were homesick for Athens and the familiar surroundings of even a Christian Greece.

Chosroes here showed his essential decency. He was not insulted at this turn of events. Indeed, he made a special effort to get Justinian to take them back and leave them in peace (even though still not permitted to teach). In 549 he succeeded. The teachers went back, showering the magnanimous Persian with their gratitude, and when they died, Greek paganism, to all intents and purposes, died too.

Chosroes I reigned for nearly half a century, from 531 to 579, and Persia advanced greatly in his time. Chosroes reorganized the administration of the Empire, dividing it up into four chief districts. He arranged for a fixed land tax that was supervised by the priests and even ordered a census of date palms and olive trees in an attempt to make the tax rates fair. (It is always easier for people to pay a tax when they know how much it will be. Earlier the taxes had been quite variable, depending very much on the particular rapacity of the local officials. When this is true, every tax payment seems insupportably high, even when it is actually reasonable.)

Then, too, the century of confusion had taken its toll of the Mesopotamian irrigation network. The ravages of long-time neglect were also beginning to show. The changing course of the rivers, the gradual increase in the salt content of the soil, and the silting of the canals, was gradually undermining the so-long fabulous prosperity of Mesopotamia. Chosroes did what he could to repair what could be repaired and in his time Mesopotamia witnessed relief from the slow downhill slide.

Chosroes also saw to it that foreigners were protected (as in the case of the Greek philosophers) and continued to tolerate Nestorian Christianity.

There was considerable trade and cultural exchange with India. Indian literature and medical treatises entered Persia. There was also an additional import of particular value to many people throughout the western world thereafter.

The Indians, it seemed, played a subtle game involving pieces of different types moving on a squared board. It is thought that the game was invented in India; at least it can't be traced any further back with any reasonable certainty.

Chosroes' physician, after a journey to India on the service of the king, is supposed to have brought the game back with him. The Persian court was fascinated by it. From the Persians it was passed later to the Arabs, who in turn passed it on to the Spaniards and to the remnants of the Roman Empire. From there it spread all over the world.

The game, however, bears the marks, here in the west, of the time it spent in Persia. The piece representing the "king" is central to the game. The Persian word for king ("shah"), after undergoing numerous changes, gives the game its name in English — chess.

When the king is under attack, the player says "check" which also is derived from "shah." And when the game ends with the king on the point of inevitable capture, one says "checkmate" which comes from the Persian "shah mat" ("the king is dead").

Yet throughout Chosroes' long, prosperous, and generally constructive reign, the two most important developments for the future of Persia and the Middle East generally took place outside Persian borders and were little regarded at the time.

First, a new nomad people drifted southward out of central Asia and made their appearance on the northeast border of Persia. These new nomads were called by a name which to us has become "Turk," and in 560, the first mention of the Turks is to be found in the Persian records. (The name "Turkistan" or "land of the Turks" is still applied to large sections of central Asia, in an unofficial way.)

The Hephthalites were, at this time, in decay, and the Persians welcomed the coming of the Turks as their chance to put the final end to the earlier nomads. Persians and Turks formed an alliance against the Hephthalites who were crushed and who then disappeared from history. Once more, the Persian realm expanded into what is now Afghanistan.

This, however, left the Turks as Persia's new neighbors and they were no more comfortable in that role than the Hephthalites had been. It was the turn of the Roman Empire to make an alliance with them, and the turn of Persia to be caught between the two jaws.

Persia fought the Turks and Romans off and flattered itself, perhaps, that the Turks were but another group of nomads of the type that came and went. No one in the time of Chosroes could foresee that the Turks were more than that and that the time would come when they would dominate the east.

The second world-shaking event of the reign of Chosroes I was even less regarded at the time. Indeed, it took place without exciting any remark or even being known to anyone outside a distant town in Arabia. Nor could anyone, even in that town, have possibly imagined the consequences of that event. The town was Mecca (mek'uh) and, in 570 or thereabouts, a child was born there who was given the name (in the most familiar English spelling) of Mohammed.

THE MOMENT OF TRIUMPH

Ormizd IV, the son and successor of Chosroes I, mounted the throne in 579 and continued his father's policy of toleration of the Christians, who were steadily increasing in numbers and influence. This continued to stimulate the smothered fury of the Zoroastrian priesthood. They had been helpless to act against the strong Chosroes I, but his son, far less able, was easier game.

To do their work for them, the priests made use of Bahram Chobin. He was a general who had won victories over the Turks some years before but who had lost a battle against the Romans and who had then promptly been relieved of his post by Ormizd. Bahram Chobin was spoiling for revenge and was easily talked into arranging the assassination of the king. Ormizd's son, Chosroes II, became the new king in 589.

But Bahram Chobin, having been a victorious general, and

having become a king-maker, found his appetite only the more keen and decided to be king himself,.even though he was not a Sassanid.

Chosroes II, forced off the throne and certain of death if he stayed, managed to get away in 590 and fled to Persia's great enemy, the court at Constantinople.

Ruling in Constantinople at that time was Maurice, who would have welcomed a suspension of hostilities with Persia, since a new group of nomads, the Avars, were penetrating the Balkan peninsula and threatening the European provinces of the Empire.

It seemed to Maurice that if he could gain the gratitude of the young prince by replacing him on the throne, a period of peace might be assured. He therefore sent the Roman army eastward.

Maurice succeeded. Chosroes II regained the throne in 591 to the plaudits of the Persian populace who resented a non-Sassanid on the throne. Bahram Chobin fled to the Turks, whom he had handily defeated only a few years back, and who now returned the compliment by killing him.

As it happened, Maurice was right. Chosroes II did indeed display the kind of gratitude unusual in monarchs. While Maurice was on the throne, Persia kept the peace.

But then affairs altered abruptly. It seems that the Roman army on the Danube, led by a brutal and uneducated soldier named Phocas, grew tired of facing the formidable Avars. They rebelled in 602 and marched on Constantinople, declaring Phocas to be Emperor. Maurice and his sons were cruelly slaughtered by them.

When the news reached Chosroes II, he could argue at once that he owed a debt of gratitude to the Emperor who had been so foully murdered, and that all the laws of justice required him to march against Constantinople in order to exact vengeance.

In preparation for that work, he guarded his rear by wiping out the Arab kingdom of Hira whose Nestorianism gave him the necessary pretext. He might argue, after all, that Christian Hira might combine with Christian Rome against him.

That done, Chosroes II moved westward. Almost without trouble, he took all of northwestern Mesopotamia, which for over three centuries now, had steadfastly eluded the clutching fingers of Sassanid after Sassanid. He even drove into eastern Asia Minor.

It was clear by now that Phocas was not only cruel and ignorant, but that he was utterly incompetent as well. He could work up no effective resistance against the Persian advance, nor was he capable of handling the Avars. Constantinople, watching the Persians move closer from the east while the Avars approached from the north, went into a frenzy of panic. They rose in revolt, killed Phocas, and declared another general, Heraclius (her"uh-kly'us) Emperor in his place.

Had Chosroes II been consistent, the death of Phocas ought to have satisfied him and ended the war. However, the Persian monarch was riding the crest of a situation that was working all in his favor. His unexpected victories went to his head. If he had been sincere at first in considering his war to be one of just revenge, it now became one of unabashed conquest.

Undoubtedly, Roman provinces were virtually begging to be conquered. Following the Nestorian heresy, other sects had developed in the Roman Empire, and both Syria and Egypt were strongholds of one called Monophysitism. Indeed, Monophysitism was even spreading into Persia, gradually replacing Nestorianism.

Many of the Syrians and Egyptians could scarcely have helped notice that while the orthodox Christians who dominated the Church at Constantinople were intolerant of doctrines that deviated from theirs, the Persians were tolerating (rather spottily) the Christian heresies.

Chosroes II therefore found little difficulty in advancing over those provinces. In 611, he took Antioch; in 614 he took Damascus, and in 615, he took Jerusalem.

The capture of Jerusalem was a particularly heavy blow to the Romans. The very fount and origin of Christianity, the land which had felt the footsteps of Jesus, was under the control of a pagan horde. To make matters worse, Chosroes II calmly carried off the cross which all Christians believed to be the very one on which Jesus had been crucified (the "True Cross").

Chosroes II went further still. In 615 he entered Egypt and within the year had stamped his hold on the entire province. By 617, all of Asia Minor was his and Persian troops were camped in Chalcedon (kal'sih-don), a suburb of Constantinople just across the straits. Only a mile of water separated Chosroes II from Constantinople itself.

For a few glorious years, Persia stood on the dizzying height of utter triumph. Chosroes II had managed to do what had eluded all his Sassanid predecessors over the past four centuries. He had virtually restored the Empire of Darius I. Chosroes II called himself Chosroes Parviz ("Chosroes the Victorious") and certainly the name seemed justified.

Constantinople seemed through. The Persians were just across the strait and the Avars were at the walls. Only Heraclius, the Emperor, did not despair. Doggedly, he continued to try to reorganize the army and prepare the measures for a counterattack.

Heraclius had one strong weapon that Persia could not match; that was the control of the sea. Heraclius used the church wealth (reluctantly granted him under the pressure of absolute disaster) to outfit a fleet. In 622, he placed an army on board the ships and, abandoning his capital to its siege by the Persians and Avars, let the sea carry him close to the enemy's heart. Once, three and a half centuries before, the Persians had swarmed over Asia Minor, and Odenathus of Palmyra had brought them running back by striking in their rear. Heraclius planned to do the same.

He sailed through the Black Sea to Armenia and for years maneuvered through the Persian interior like another Alexander. Chosroes II was, in the end, forced, much against his will, to bring back his army from its advanced points and, eventually, to stake the game on a pitched battle.

In 627 the two armies met near Nineveh, of all places. Once more the ghosts of twelve and a half centuries past were to be disturbed by the noise and clash of tremendous battle. Under the inspired leadership of Heraclius who, according to the perhaps exaggerated tales, displayed the valor of a hero, the

Romans prevailed and the Persian army was cut to pieces. During the night, what was left of the Persians hastily retreated.

Heraclius then led his army through Mesopotamia, like Trajan reborn, repaying the devastation the Persians had visited upon Asia Minor. He marched to the very walls of Ctesiphon.

Chosroes' great gamble was played out and lost. The empire of old Darius had been won back, held for five years, and then lost. The Persian magnates, utterly disheartened by such a vast turn in fortune, had no wish to continue the war. When Chosroes showed no signs of wanting to make peace, even with Ctesiphon under siege, they first imprisoned him and then, in 628, executed him. Thus died Chosroes II after the passing of his moment of triumph.

The Persians were ready for peace on Heraclius' terms. Heraclius relentlessly ordered them out of every inch of territory they had taken, and forced the surrender of the True Cross.

In 629, with impressive and appropriate ceremonies, he supervised its restoration to its place in Jerusalem.

10

THE ARABS

HISTORY REPEATS ITSELF

Even while Chosroes II had lingered at the heights of his success, a message reached him from Arabia. Some Arab fanatic was ordering him to abandon his religion and accept instead that Arab as his prophet. The prophet was Mohammed. Chosroes II tore up the message and, in all likelihood, never thought of the matter again.

But while Chosroes sank from those heights, down the precipitous decline to disgrace and death, Mohammed was gradually uniting the hardy Arab tribes behind him and inspiring them with a fervent belief in a new religion, a complete confidence in the rightness of their cause, and of an instant reward in Paradise for those who fought and died in that cause.

The religion was called "Islam" ("submission" — to the will of Allah, the Arabic term for God), and its practitioners were Moslems ("ones who surrendered"). In the west we often speak of Mohammedans and Mohammedanism, but that is wrong.

As Arabia grew strong, Persia grew weak. After the death of Chosroes II, there was a period of anarchy, of successive kings proclaimed and deposed. Then in 632, Yazdegird III, a grandson of Chosroes II, was placed on the throne. He was only fifteen years old, and had no real power.

With an almost weird exactness, history was repeating itself. Two situations, separated by a thousand years, were virtual duplicates. Under the Sassanids (Achaemenids), the death of the conquering king, Chosroes II (Artaxerxes III), was followed by a few years of anarchy with the accession at last of the incompetent Yazdegird III (Darius III).

Under the Sassanids (Achaemenids), the accession of Yazdegird III (Darius III) came just as a new and unregarded nation, Arabia (Macedonia), had grown strong and was ready to begin a career of unparalleled conquest. In the year that Yazdegird III (Darius III) came to the throne, however, the brilliant newcomer, Mohammed (Philip of Macedon) died and the chance of conquest seemed ended before it had begun.

Here the parallel seems to break off. Philip of Macedon was succeeded by his son, the young genius, Alexander. Mohammed was succeeded by his aged father-in-law Abu Bekr (uh-boo''-bek'er). He was the first Khalifah ("successor"), a word with which we are more familiar in the spelling, Caliph.

Yet despite this, the parallelism continued. Abu Bekr sent another invitation to join Islam, one message going to Yazdegird III, the other to Heraclius. Both were disregarded. The Moslems therefore lunged forward on the attack.

They faced two enemies where Alexander the Great had faced but one, and it might have seemed to anyone with even a trifle of sense that the only way to win out over two enemies is to form an alliance with one against the other. Once one enemy is crushed, you can turn on the ally. This is standard operating procedure for any conqueror. Even Hitler made use of it, forming an alliance with the Soviet Union so that he could crush Poland and France, and then turning on his ally.

With sublime effrontery, however, the Arab tribes chose to attack both their great enemies simultaneously. Undoubtedly, the Arab rank and file attacked in the serene confidence that Allah was with them, but one might wonder if some of their leaders had correctly gauged the actual situation.

The Roman Empire and Persia had come through a bitter twenty-year war in which each, in turn, had laid waste the other. Both were worn out, converted by their exertions into a shell, still seemingly powerful without, but hollow at the core.

With almost insolent ease, the Arabs snatched from the Roman Empire those very provinces that had just been rescued from Persia. By 636, they had taken Judea and Syria, so that Jerusalem and the True Cross were lost again, this time permanently. By 640, they were overrunning Egypt.

Heraclius, in his declining years, saw his great victory completely wiped out and could not find it within himself to rise once more in counterattack. Like the Empire itself, the great effort of the 620's had reduced him to a shell. He died in 641, an Alexander who had lived too long.

To be sure, Constantinople did not lose everything. It retained Asia Minor and its European provinces, and against these the Arab armies dashed themselves in vain. After the Arab conquests, however, one can no longer really speak of the Roman Empire. The successors of Heraclius did so, to be sure, and called themselves Roman Emperors and their subjects the Roman people to the very end of their history. Historians generally, however, term the lands ruled by Constantinople after the time of Heraclius the "Byzantine Empire" from Byzantium, the old Greek name for Constantinople.

Meanwhile, the Arabs were also attacking Persia. They had a grievance ready-made, for Chosroes II, a quarter-century before, had crushed the Arabic kingdom of Hira. The Arabs announced themselves Hira's avengers, and an army was sent northeastward, taking Hira and moving on toward the Euphrates.

The astonished and indignant Persians, who were just in the process of crowning Yazdegird III, hastily gathered an army with which to chastise the nomads, and defeated them roundly in 634 at what is called the "Battle of the Bridge." The

Arabs did not accept defeat, but filled with confidence at the gathering victory against the Romans on the other flank, they sent a larger army into Persia.

In 637, the main armies finally clashed at Kadisiya (kah″dih-see′uh) on the Euphrates, about fifty miles south of where Babylon had once stood. Once again, the hoary land of Mesopotamia was to witness one of the important battles of man.

The numbers of the opposing forces were about equal, though the Arabs were animated by the knowledge of their just-concluded conquest of Syria, and the Persians were depressed by the same knowledge. The battle continued indecisively for at least two days, the Arabs being saved from defeat at one point by the providential arrival of six thousand reinforcements from Syria.

On the third morning, a sandstorm arose and, by the luck of the wind, blew into the faces of the Persians. The Persians, unable to see, broke, and that was the end. The Arabs dashed forward and the break became a rout. They then advanced rapidly into the heart of Mesopotamia and took Ctesiphon.

One last attempt was made by despairing Persia. As after Issus, the Persians had made their final stand at Gaugamela; so now after Kadisiya, the Persians made their final stand at Nehavend, about fifty miles south of Ecbatana, which had once been the capital of Media. Here, in 642, the Arabs won another great victory, greater than their first (as Gaugamela had been greater than Issus).

Yazdegird III fled again, as Darius III had, making his way deep into the northeast corner of his land and appealing even to the Emperor of distant China for help. He was killed finally in 651, after a reign of nineteen years of almost unrelieved flight and defeat.

Only a quarter-century after Chosroes II stood on the shores of the straits and saw the spires of Constantinople glisten in the sun across a mere mile of water, his Empire had disappeared forever from the map.

The conquest of Persia by the Macedonians had left Zoroastrianism alive and gave it a chance for an ultimate comeback. The conquest by the Arabs was another affair.

Officially, the Moslems tolerated Zoroastrians, as they tolerated Christians in the provinces they had taken from the Roman Empire. However, Zoroastrians and Christians alike had to pay a special tax which Mohammedans did not. (This trick of letting minority religions buy toleration at a reasonable rate was learned by Islam from the example set by the Zoroastrians themselves.)

The financial inducement to save money by turning Moslem worked better than force would have. Persia turned quickly from Zoroastrianism to Islam (and Syria and Egypt turned just as quickly from Christianity).

Not all Zoroastrians turned Moslem, of course. (Nor did all Christians, for that matter.) Dwindling colonies of Zoroastrians persisted in Iran and eventually some of them, according to their own traditions, concentrated in Hormuz on the Persian Gulf. (This was the city where Ardashir had won his battle over the last Parthian king and established the Sassanid Empire some five centuries before.) Some time after 700, these Zoroastrian relics left Persia altogether and crossed to India.

Their descendants still exist in India, to the number of about 130,000, and are called "Parsees." They still maintain their ancient ways and still number the years from the reign of Yazdegird III.

As for the Jews of Mesopotamia, they, too, were tolerated by the Moslems in return for the payment of a tax. Unlike the Zoroastrians, they were used to this. It mattered little to them that the Moslem had replaced the Zoroastrian as the Gentile ruler. They continued as before, therefore, and, under the relatively mild rule of the early Moslems, even flourished in a peace and prosperity such as they had not seen since the times of the Maccabees, nearly a thousand years before.

THE FACTIONS OF ISLAM

Mesopotamia and Persia did not melt completely into the Moslem world. Just as the non-Greek provinces of the Roman

Empire found a nationalistic refuge in Christian heresy, so the non-Arab provinces of the Moslem Empire found one in Islamic heresies.

It came about as follows. In 644, just after the conquest of Persia, a new caliph was selected, Othman (ooth-mahn'). He was an elderly man who was a son-in-law of Mohammed and who was a member of a noble Meccan family, the Omayyads (oh-my'adz). Under him, other members of the family seemed to be getting far more than their fair share of government office, and imperial loot and discontent arose.

There were troop mutinies and, in 656, a contingent of soldiers from Egypt found the Caliph in his house in Arabia and killed him. They then supervised the selection of a successor, who turned out to be Ali, another son-in-law of Mohammed.

However, Ali was not recognized by partisans of the Omayyads, who undoubtedly felt (and with apparent justice) that the election could scarcely be a free one with Othman's assassins overseeing it.

The leader of the Omayyad party was the governor of Syria, Mauwiya (moo-ah'wee-yah). Ali, on the other hand, received his chief support in Mesopotamia. Indeed, Ali made his capital in the city of Kufa (koo'fuh), which had been founded by the Arabs in 638, soon after the battle of Kadisiya. It stood on the Euphrates about forty miles downstream from where Babylon had once stood.

The civil war was, therefore, between Syria and Mesopotamia, the former representing the Arabic core of the new Empire, while the latter represented Persian culture.

The war continued drearily, with Ali steadily losing support, until in 661, a conspiracy was formed among certain groups who were tired of the war. They felt that by killing the principals on both sides, a peace could be arranged. Part of the plan misfired, however; Muawiya escaped and only Ali was assassinated.

Muawiya at once managed to establish himself as Caliph and secured himself by refusing to make his capital in turbulent Arabia, but moving it into his own Syria. The central city of the entire Moslem world became Damascus, which thus reached its peak point in history. It had not been the capital of a completely independent state in fourteen centuries, and even then it had only been the capital of Biblical Syria, a small kingdom no more powerful than Israel.

The line of rulers who governed from Damascus in the following century is referred to as the Omayyad Caliphate.

The followers of Ali did not give in entirely to the new state of affairs. They represented, in part, the Persian reaction to Arabic domination, and they tried to rally round Ali's older son, Hassan (ha-san'). Hassan, unfortunately for the group, was a studious pious man with no love for battle. He quickly abdicated.

The party of Ali nevertheless held out in Kufa and when Muawiya died in 680, they invited Hosein (hoo-sine'), Ali's younger son, to lead them in a drive for the Caliphate. He came to Kufa, but in a battle with the Omayyad forces, he was abandoned by his own followers and was killed in battle at Kerbela (kur'-beh-lah), just west of Kufa, on October 10, 680. In 700, the party of Ali tried again and failed. In 740, they tried still again, under a grandson of Hosein, and failed still again.

Despite these repeated failures, the party survived and came to be known as the Shiites (shee'ites), from an Arabic word meaning "partisan," that is, the partisans of Ali. To this day, the Shiites consider Ali and his sons to have been the true successors of Othaman, and all the caliphs from Muawiya on to have been usurpers. They keep the anniversary of Hosein's death as a day of mourning and consider Kerbela a holy city. Opposing the Shiites are the Sunnites, from an Arabic word meaning "tradition," that is, the followers of the orthodox tradition.

Shiism had a most checkered history in Islam, and there were times when its partisans controlled large provinces. To this very day, they make up the minority sect, including only about ten percent of all Moslems. Even so, Shiism remains the outlet for Persian nationalism, for it forms the ruling majority in the modern nations of Iraq (Mesopotamia) and Iran (Persia).

As long as the Arab conquests continued, the Omayyad Caliphate remained strong. By 717, the Moslem Empire spread from the eastern boundaries of Afghanistan to the Atlantic Ocean and even included Europe's Spanish peninsula. The empire had an extreme east-west width of 5000 miles, the largest tract of land the earth had, up to that time, ever seen under a single rule.

Yet even the Arabs finally found their limits. In 717, a tremendous attempt to take Constaninople by land and sea was beaten back. And in 732, the Arabic advance guard was smashed in central France. The first, irresistible wave of conquest was over. Islam was to continue winning victories for centuries, but under the Arabs those were to remain minor in nature thereafter, and when major victories were again won, they were to be under the leadership of other groups than the Arabs.

The factions opposing the Omayyads could now make themselves felt, for with the ceasing of rapid conquest, the popularity of the dynasty fell.

Chief among those opposing the Omayyads was another Meccan family of considerable prestige. This family traced its ancestry to al-Abbas, an uncle of Mohammed, and it is therefore known as the Abbasids (ab'uh-sidz).

The Abbasids were Sunnites, and they could therefore count on the support of all Sunnites who were tired of the Omayyads. They could also count on the automatic support of all Shiites who were ready to support even Sunnites against the hated Omayyads.

The Abbasids picked their time carefully, and gathered their partisans in the east. In 749, Abul-Abbas (uh-bool''ah-bahs'), then leader of the Abbasid family, arrived at Kufa and was there proclaimed Caliph.

The Omayyads did not take that without a fight. Their army rushed eastward, and battle was joined at the river Zab, a tributary of the Tigris. There, yet again in the unhallowed neighborhood of ancient Nineveh, now fourteen centuries dead, a battle of decision was fought. The Abbasid army won and, in 750, the Omayyad Caliphate came to an end.

(All the numerous members of the Omayyad family were

slaughtered with the exception of one who escaped and reached Spain. There for two and a half centuries, a brilliant Omayyad dynasty was to maintain itself independently of the rest of the Mohammedan world.)

BAGHDAD

The Abbasid dynasty at once removed the capital of Islam from Omayyad Syria. The center of Islamic power was transferred to Mesopotamia which once more became the ruling center of world empire.

However, Mesopotamia was also a center of Shiite strength, and the Abbasids could not afford to be too closely tied to a minority sect, for fear they would alienate the large body of Moslems elsewhere.

The second Abbasid Caliph, al-Mansur (al-man-soor′), therefore seized an opportunity for crushing the more extreme groups among the Shiites. They had found another leader in the form of Mohammed, a grandson of Hassan, and he led al-Mansur a wearisome chase for a while and even conquered the holy city of Mecca. In the end, however, he met the usual fate of the family of Ali; he and his brother, Ibrahim, were killed in battle.

Such events made Kufa increasingly uncomfortable as a capital, and al-Mansur determined to build a new one for himself. In 762, he chose the site occupied by the then-unimportant village of Baghdad, situated on the right bank of the Tigris about 20 miles north of Ctesiphon.

The building of Baghdad meant the slow death of Ctesiphon which, for seven centuries, had been the seat of the Arsacids and the Sassanids. Indeed, Ctesiphon was used as a source of building materials for the construction of Baghdad and the visible relic of the old Sassanid dynasty melted away.

Baghdad was to be the largest city Mesopotamia ever saw, larger even than Babylon in its prime. At its height, Baghdad was estimated to have had a population of two million, and for a time it was to be the greatest city of the world. The Caliph ruling over Baghdad extended the sway of his scepter to Afghanistan in the east and to modern Algeria in the west. (Morocco and Spain, still farther west, never acknowledged the Abbasid Caliphate.)

Al-Mansur's son, al-Mahdi (al-mah'dee), consolidated his leadership over Islam by recognizing the Sunnite doctrine as official. The Shiites, who were vividly conscious of their own role in having helped establish the Abbasid dynasty on the throne, had to retire into sullen and irreconcilable opposition.

Baghdad's most glamorous and legendary period began in 786, when the son of al-Mahdi came to the throne. This was the famous Harun al-Rashid (hah-roon'al-ra-sheed') or "Aaron the Just."

Abbasid power approached its peak. Repeatedly, Harun attacked Asia Minor, though always, apparently, in response to some aggression by the Byzantine Empire. After one such aggression, Harun wrote a famous brief reply to the Byzantine Emperor: "I have received your letter, son of an infidel, and you shall not hear my reply, you shall see it."

Each of Harun's campaigns in Asia Minor was successful, and the Byzantines were forced, each time, to patch up a peace on whatever terms they could.

Harun even enters west European history for, in 807, he exchanged embassies, gifts, and flowery expressions of diplomatic praise, with Charlemagne (Charles the Great) who then controlled the section of Europe which includes the modern nations of France, Germany, and Italy.

Nor was this reasonless. There were at the time in the Mediterranean area four great powers. Of these, two were Christian: Charlemagne's western Empire and Constantinople's eastern Empire. The other two were Moslem; Harun al-Rashid's Abbasid Caliphate, and the Omayyad kingdom of Spain.

Charlemagne was at constant war with Omayyad Spain and was a rival of the Byzantine Emperor. Harun al-Rashid was at constant war with the Byzantines and was a rival of Omayyad Spain. Since Charlemagne and Harun shared common enemies, it was natural that they exhibit a mutual friendliness de-

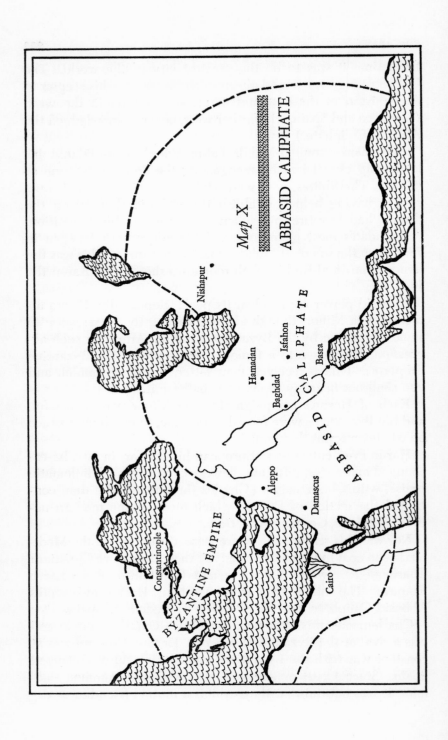

Map X

ABBASID CALIPHATE

Nishapur

Hamadan
Isfahan
Baghdad
Basra

Aleppo
Damascus

Cairo

Constantinople

BYZANTINE EMPIRE

ABBASID   CALIPHATE

spite the difference in religion. Such incidents, which are extremely common in history, have given rise to such sayings as "Politics make strange bedfellows."

Harun's success in warfare and his influence throughout the civilized world were matched by an enlightened government and a careful administration of taxation and finance. The result was that the Empire was prosperous and reasonably content.

Under the Abbasids, centered as they were in Mesopotamia, the purely Arabic leadership that had dominated the first century of Moslem power, while the capital had been at Mecca and at Damascus, began to fade. Instead, Moslem civilization began to take on a deeper and deeper Persian tinge. (Although, to be sure, the language of Mesopotamia slowly became Arabic, and has remained Arabic ever since.)

Thus, the chief advisers of the early Abbasids were members of a noble Persian family called the Barmecides (bahr'meh-sidez), who were patrons of arts and of literature. When Harun al-Rashid became Caliph, he made one of the family, Yahya, his vizier, or chief minister. And Yahya's son, Jafar, was Harun's boon companion.

As is true of any family that becomes too exclusively a favorite of the monarch, the Barmecides grew proud (or were deemed to have grown proud by their rivals). Their enemies multiplied and, eventually, Harun was persuaded that the Barmecides represented a danger to the throne. In 803, Jafar was executed without warning and others of the family put in prison. Yet though the Barmecides were gone, Persian influence remained and grew.

Harun's reputation with posterity, however, rests not with his real accomplishments at all, but with his role in legend. A century or so after his reign, some unnamed collectors began putting together wonder tales and adventure stories. The collection grew with time and came to include many legendary tales about the magnanimous and good-humored Harun who, with his friend, Jafar, would (according to the stories) wander about Baghdad in disguise to correct injustices and right wrongs.

The connecting thread that held the completely amorphous collection together was that of a queen, Scheherazade, who told the stories night after night for more than three years. This accounts for the popular title of the collection, *The Thousand and One Nights* or, even more popularly, *The Arabian Nights*. The collection was first brought to the west by a French traveler named Antoine Galland and was published in many volumes between 1704 and 1717. They became all the rage and the Baghdad of Harun al-Rashid became a fairy-tale city of purple-gold legend.

Harun's younger son, al-Mamun (al-ma-moon'), became Caliph in 813. He was a man of great culture and was utterly under Persian influence. Indeed, he spent the first few years of his reign in Persia and seemed to plan to make his capital there. It took a resentful uprising in Baghdad to bring him back.

In Baghdad, al-Mamun opened an academy which had, for its purpose, the translation and study of Greek works on science and philosophy, with Nestorian Christians engaged as translators. Al-Mamun also had an observatory built for the purpose of the study of astronomy.

World leadership in science, which had passed from Mesopotamia to Greece in the time after Nebuchadrezzar thirteen centuries before, now returned, at least temporarily, to Mesopotamia.

Jabir (jah'bir), who lived in Kufa and in Baghdad, in the time of Harun al-Rashid, was a pioneer alchemist (what we would today call "chemist") whose equal was not to be found before modern times. Al-Khwarizmi (al-kwah'riz-mee), who lived in Baghdad in al-Mamun's time, wrote on mathematics. The title of one of his books gives us the name "algebra" for one important branch of the subject. He also introduced a new way of symbolizing numbers, a way first introduced in India. This Indian method reached the west by way of the Moslems. Eventually, it replaced the cumbersome system of Roman numerals. The new method is still used today, and we still speak of "Arabic numerals."

During al-Mamun's reign, the Abbasids continued to gain

military success. The islands of Crete and Sicily were captured, for instance. All in all, it seems reasonable that this Caliph is called al-Mamun the Great, even though he is virtually unknown to the general public in contrast to his legendary father, Harun al-Rashid.

THE PUPPET CALIPHS

In 833, al-Mamun died and was succeeded by his brother, al-Mutasim (al-moo'tuh-sim). He made two far-reaching and disastrous mistakes.

He fell prey to the temptation of following the example of monarchs who, to insure their own security in troubled times, engage a bodyguard of soldiers intended to be loyal only to themselves. To make this bodyguard truly effective, it is best to select it from strange races and distant peoples who are apt to be out of sympathy with the population of the capital and are therefore unlikely to make common cause with them against the monarch.

Al-Mutasim selected soldiers from among the Turks for inclusion in the bodyguard. These were not subject to the Abbasids at all, nor were they as yet enlightened by a settled culture. In short, al-Mutasim cultivated what we might consider a "barbarian bodyguard."

Such barbarian bodyguards can be very effective tools in the hands of a strong monarch, but they can become masters under weak monarchs and sooner or later, a weak monarch is bound to turn up.

By al-Mutasim's time, Baghdad had grown into a large and turbulent metropolis that represented a constant danger to the monarch's peace of mind, even with Turkish soldiers standing between himself and the people. Al-Mutasim therefore chose a new capital and retired to Samarra (sa-mur'rah) on the Tigris, sixty-five miles upstream from Baghdad. Baghdad remained the effective capital of the Empire and Samarra was merely the royal residence. (It was like the relationship of Versailles to Paris in eighteenth-century France.)

This was pleasant for al-Mutasim, but again it was a deadly danger. The Caliph withdrew and fell out of touch with the empire. It became too easy for him to delegate authority and to remain flaccidly at home with his harem and his pleasures. He need be little concerned with disorders and rebellions in distant provinces or defeats on faraway borders, while his palace and his parks remained a heaven on earth.

Al-Mutasim's grandson, al-Mutawakkil, who came to the throne in 847, seems to have recognized the dangers. He tried to shift his capital back to Damascus, but that proved a most unpopular move and perhaps he himself longed for the comforts of Samarra, for he returned almost at once. He gave up, and occupied himself in building a new palace which the empire could ill afford, and in trying to demonstrate his orthodoxy by persecuting Jews, Christians, and Shiites.

Eventually, his eldest son grew tired of waiting for him to die and, in 861, organized a conspiracy and had his father murdered by the leaders of the Turkish guard.

That was it! The Turks found out they could kill Caliphs as well as subjects. There followed a decade of absolute anarchy while the Turks made and unmade Caliphs from among the various members of the Abbasid house. The Turks themselves were the real rulers, and were beginning to pass their offices down from father to son. There were several of these Turkish "dynasties" which increased the chaos but kept the Turks, through mutual squabbling, from getting as powerful as they might have become otherwise.

During this period, the provinces began to break away from the control of Baghdad. Theoretically, all the vast dominions of Harun al-Rashid still recognized the Caliph, but he became only a name to mention in prayers. The actual powers were held by a series of rulers called emirs. One of them controlled Tunis; another controlled Egypt and Syria; a third controlled much of Persia, and so on.

By 870, less than forty years after the death of the great al-

Mamun, the Caliph's direct power was largely confined to Mesopotamia itself.

Matters grew even worse, when Islam was riven by a new and dangerous sect. About 750, there had lived a man named Ismail (is"muh-eel) who was a great-great-grandson of Husayn, the Shiite martyr. In his name, an extreme Shiite sect was established and it is known as Ismailism.

Warlike bands of Ismailis began to take over portions of the Moslem Empire. In 929 some took over sections of Mesopotamia and Syria. Another group, claiming to be ruled by descendants of Fatima, the daughter of Mohammed (a dynasty therefore called the Fatimids), took over Egypt.

In this way everything was lost to the Abbasids but the name of Caliph. Mesopotamia, even Baghdad, was lost to them. They became purely religious figures without secular power at all; something like the Pope in modern times. In fact, Mesopotamia was now and then under the control of Shiite emirs who were tempted at times to abolish the Caliphate altogether.

Yet even while the Caliphate faded, and the great Abbasid Empire shattered and broke into a dozen pieces, Islamic intellectual advance continued and even reached new peaks.

About 900, for instance, al-Battani (al"bat-tah'nee) was at work at Rakkah (rok'kah), a town on the upper Euphrates, not far from where the old Sumerian town of Mari had existed twenty-five centuries before. It had been a favorite residence of Harun al-Rashid, but now it was the workplace of al-Battani, the greatest astronomer of the Middle Ages. He was not to be surpassed until the rebirth of science in Europe six centuries later.

The same might be said, in another field, of al-Razi, whose name is more familiar to us in its Latinized version as Rhazes (ray'zeez). In 900, he was chief physician of the hospital at Baghdad, and was one of the great influences on the development of medieval medicine in Europe as well as in the Moslem world.

But secular leadership and the imperial role was passing to a less civilized people.

11

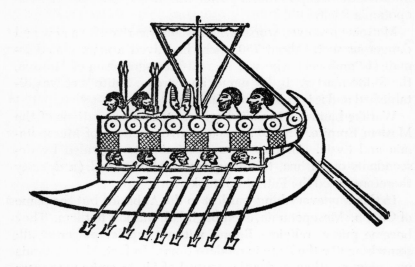

THE TURKS

THE HEIRS TAKE OVER

If the Moslem world was not utterly lost in the course of the fragmentation of the tenth century, it was partly because the Christian world was equally fragmented. After the death of Charlemagne, the western empire broke up into quarreling segments and all fell prey to the havoc caused by raiding Northmen or Vikings from Scandinavia. The Byzantine Empire, while remaining intact, spent its energies in religious disputes.

As the year 1000 approached, however, it might have seemed to an impartial observer that the Moslem world was in growing danger. The Byzantine Empire began to gain strength and under Basil II, who came to the throne in 976, it seemed almost to regain its youth.

But in the world of Islam, too, new champions had entered the ring. They were the Turks. Just as the German tribes outside the Roman Empire had accepted Christianity even while

remaining relatively uncivilized, so did the Turkish tribes accept Islam, and the Sunnite variety at that. In the centuries to
come, the Sunnite Turks were to prove themselves the heirs
of the Arabs and the new upholders of Islam against the Christian opposition.

During the tenth century, a group of Turks moved into the
far eastern reaches of the Islamic world and made their capital
in Ghazni (ghaz'nee), in what is now eastern Afghanistan.
Their power rapidly expanded and reached its peak in 1000
under its king Mahmud (mad-mood'). It reached from India
to the borders of Mesopotamia, and it was almost Persia brought
back to life again.

Indeed, Persian culture in its older Sassanid version had a
strong revival then, four centuries after its political death,
thanks particularly to a Persian poet who wrote under the pen-
name of Firdausi (fir-dow'see).

Firdausi wrote a long poem of 60,000 verses (seven times
the length of Homer's *Iliad*), detailing the history of the Persian kings from its legendary beginnings down to Chosroes II.
It was in pure Persian, not Arabic, and has remained the
great national poem of the nation and its preeminent literary
work ever since. (It was a factor in keeping Persian the language of modern Iran, and preventing replacement by Arabic.)

Its early legendary portions feature Rustem, a Hercules-like
figure of incredible strength and bravery, who seems to have
been inspired by the Hercules cult of the Parthians to begin
with. The best known and most affecting episode is the one in
which the aging Rustem manages, after a fierce battle, to kill a
young champion whom he then, and only then, recognizes as
his son, Sohrab. Alexander the Great is also introduced into the
epic but is given a Persian mother in order to soothe national
pride.

The great epic was presented to Mahmud of Ghazni in 1010,
but Mahmud was a fiercely ardent Sunnite, and Firdausi was a
Shiite. Mahmud therefore gave the poet an insultingly small
payment. Firdausi took his revenge by writing a contemptuous
satire against Mahmud and then, very prudently, fled the country as quickly as he could.

Even while Ghazni was rising toward empire, another tribe of Turks, ruled by a princeling named Seljuk (sel-jook'), settled at the northern borders of what had been the Abbasid realm. They, together with those who eventually joined them, are usually called the Seljuk Turks.

They drifted southward and served as mercenaries at first. In 1037, however, under Seljuk's grandson, Tughril Beg, they decided to strike out for power in their own name. Since Mahmud of Ghazni had died in 1033, and since his son was far less competent, the Seljuks bit deep into the eastern kingdom which dwindled rapidly after its single generation of glory.

Finally, in 1055, Tughril Beg marched into Shiite Mesopotamia which fell without a fight. Baghdad surrendered to him, and the joyful Caliph of the moment, freed from Shiite domination, bestowed upon the faithful Sunnite the one thing he had in his power to give — a title. He made Tughril Beg a sultan (a word originally meaning "dominion" and therefore proper to apply to a ruler). Turkish leaders held that title for over eight centuries.

In return, Tughril Beg left the Caliph in nominal control of Baghdad and Mesopotamia by rather ostentatiously refusing to place his capital there. He ruled from Ecbatana, a name that under Islamic rule had become distorted to Hamadan (ham'-uh-dan). Naturally, the Caliph didn't really rule, whatever Tughril Beg might pretend. He remained a Turkish puppet.

END AND BEGINNING OF A DUEL

Tughril Beg died in 1063, and was succeeded by Alp Arslan (ahlp-ahrs-lahn'), a second capable ruler. Almost at once he moved his troops northwest into Armenia. Now his western borders marched right down the line of the Byzantine border from the Black Sea to the Mediterranean. The stage was set for a renewal of the thousand-year-old feud of west versus east over the northwestern rim of Mesopotamia. It had been Rome versus first the Parthians, then the Sassanids. Then it had been the Byzantine heirs of Rome against first the Arabs and now the Turks.

It was the misfortune of the Byzantine Empire that the able and hard-driving Basil II had died without strong heirs. In the decades that followed, the period of their revival had faded and they were not quite ready to take on anyone as formidable as Alp Arslan.

Turks had already been raiding into Asia Minor in the 1050's and 1060's and had achieved considerable success. In particular, they had taken Manzikert, a city near Lake Van in the easternmost reaches of the Byzantine realm. (Lake Van had been the center of the ancient land of Urartu.)

In 1067, a capable general, Romanus Diogenes (roh-may'-nus-dy-oj'uh-neez), was in control of the Byzantine Empire, and Alp Arslan felt it better to avoid war with him. He was, in any case, much more interested in taking Syria from the Egyptian Fatimids, who were Shiite heretics, than in warring with mere Christians. He therefore patched up a truce with Romanus and left for the south.

Manzikert, however, was still in Turkish hands, and Romanus could not resist the temptation of trying to complete the job, truce or no truce. He advanced toward the city and when word of this reached Alp Arslan, he most reluctantly abandoned his Syrian venture and hurried northward.

The two armies met at Manzikert in 1071. Romanus had the larger army and rejected Alp Arslan's offer of a peaceful settlement. The Byzantine army, a solid mass of men, lunged confidently forward into the center of the Turkish line. The Turks gave way slowly, fighting with a minimum of effort while compelling the Byzantine footmen to sweat out most of an extraordinarily hot summer day.

When evening was falling, the Byzantines attempted to retreat into night quarters so that they might take up the fight again the next day, but by now they had advanced so far into the Turkish center that the enemy lines enclosed them on three sides like a large crescent. Alp Arslan, handling his men with superb skill, saw to it that the horns of the crescent consisted of fresh men, vigorous and unwearied. As they closed in strongly on either side, the Turkish cavalry chose the precise moment of confusion to come riding in so as to close the opening of the crescent.

The Byzantine army was wiped out and Romanus Diogenes taken prisoner. Alp Arslan, however, never got back to Syria after all. A revolt in the far east forced him to travel thither, and there he died the next year.

The defeat at Manzikert was the end of the Byzantine Empire as a great power. For four centuries, it had held off the forces of Islam, single-handedly, but it could do so no longer.

The Turks swarmed through Asia Minor, and were never again ejected. Rome's eleven-century struggle against the east was finally lost as Asia Minor became Turkish and Islamic and remained so down to this very day. The Byzantine Empire continued to live for some centuries, but only in the shadows. It was the Christians of western Europe that now stepped forward as the great opponents of Islam.

The Islamic world contributed to the rise of western Christendom (unwittingly, of course) by committing intellectual suicide. This was not evident at once, for Alp Arslan was followed, in 1072, by Malik Shah, the greatest of the Seljuks. He was more than merely a warrior. He built mosques out of respect for religion, and roads and canals out of respect for the world. He encouraged learning, too, and established schools in Baghdad.

Under him, a committee of scholars, including the Persian poet and astronomer, Omar Khayyam (oh'mahr-ky-ahm'), carried through a calendar reform, producing one that is, in some respects, superior to the one we now use. Omar Khayyam is best known for his series of four-line verses that were translated into English in 1859 by Edward Fitzgerald. They have been enormously popular in the English-speaking world ever since.

A generation later, however, another Persian made his mark. This was al-Ghazzali (al''ga-zah'lee) whose philosophical works, published soon after 1100, supported traditional Islamic doctrine against the pagan science of the Greeks. In the main, the Moslems followed him and Islamic science went into steep decline.

It happened that the greatest of all Islamic philosophers, the Spanish Moslem, ibn-Rushd, better known by his Latinized name of Averroes (uh-ver'oh-eez), produced his great interpretations of Aristotle about 1150. These were completely ignored by the now anti-science Moslems but were taken up with enthusiasm by western Christianity. Thus, while Islam declined into intellectual darkness, western Christianity began a rise that produced our world of today.

The new version of the east-west duel, the one involving the western branch of the Christian world, had its first episodes as a result of the military victories of Malik Shah.

In 1076, Malik Shah finally managed to snatch Syria from the Fatimids. He also gained Palestine, including the city of Jerusalem, and that made all the difference.

Under the relatively lax rule of the Abbasid Caliphs and of the Fatimids of Egypt, Christians from all parts of Europe were allowed to carry on pilgrimages to Jerusalem without serious interference. The Seljuk Turks, however, were filled with the fervor of the convert and were more easily offended by the sight of the infidel. Pilgrims began to suffer outrages and in the end this was to lead to western armies marching to the Holy Land in order to seek revenge.

Naturally, there were a great many sound social and economic reasons to explain why a huge western offensive against Islam should come about now, but what moved the common man of western Europe to support so desperate a venture was what we would now call "atrocity tales."

Pilgrims returning from Palestine (or claiming to have returned) wandered from hamlet to hamlet, freezing the blood of all who would listen with tales of Turkish cruelties. The most successful of these propagandists was one Peter the Hermit, who eventually helped lead a raggle-taggle army of peasants eastward to misery and death (which he himself somehow escaped).

In 1096, a real army, led by French noblemen, set out eastward, each wearing the insignia of a cloth cross sewn on his clothing. This was a symbol that he was fighting for Christianity against the Moslems. The movements are therefore called the "Crusades" from the Latin word for cross.

THE ASSASSINS

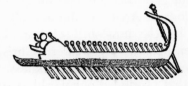

Had Malik Shah remained alive, or had he been followed by an equally capable successor, the Crusades would surely have failed at the outset.

That the Crusades experienced any success at all was due, chiefly, to internal squabbling in the Moslem world. The Turkish advance had meant a constant victory for the Sunnites over the Shiites, and it was time for a Shiite counterattack. The Ismaili extremists of the Shiite movement had supported the Fatimids against the Seljuk Turks but, in 1090, they struck out for themselves.

One of the Ismaili leaders, Hasan ibn al-Sabbah, seized a valley in the rough country south of the Caspian Sea, about seventy miles north of the Seljuk capital at Hamadan. Ringed by mountains, it was virtually impregnable, and al-Sabbah (as well as each of his successors in turn) became known as "the Old Man of the Mountain."

His followers were trained in absolute loyalty to the Old Man. It is said that he encouraged them to chew hashish (akin to what we now call marijuana) and then explained the drug-imposed hallucinations that followed as visions of heaven — a heaven they would enter immediately, if they fell in the line of duty. (This is, possibly, a propaganda story on the part of the sect's enemies.)

Because of this, the followers of the Old Man of the Mountains were called "Hashishin" ("hashish-smokers"). To Europeans, this became Assassins.

The method of operation of the new sect was simple, if terrifying. They did not act against the common people or attempt to organize armies. They organized secret agents, instead, whose mission it was to kill rulers, generals, and leaders. They struck at the heart and were virtually unstoppable, since a killer who is not in the least interested in getting away is almost sure to succeed sooner or later. It is only the difficulty of getting away that complicates most such plans. It is because of the activities of this sect that any political killing is now called an "assassination."

The prime targets of the Assassins were, of course, the Sunnite leaders, although the killers also aimed at those Shiites who were the wrong sort. (It is hard to satisfy an extremist.) Their first great coup was the assassination of Malik Shah himself in 1092.

The Seljuk realm fell apart almost at once as different members of the dynasty struggled for the throne. As is only too often the case, none of the contenders won outright, and while each one concentrated on his brothers, uncles, and cousins, the Crusaders fought their way into Syria and finally reached Jerusalem in 1099, subjecting it to a disgraceful sack.

The eastern shores of the Mediterranean were soon divided into West Christian states under the leadership of the "King of Jerusalem." A section of northwestern Mesopotamia was captured and was organized as the County of Edessa. For nearly fifty years, Christian barons ruled over the city where, eight centuries back, the Roman Emperor Valerian, had fallen prisoner to the Persians. This half-century period was the first time that western Christians ruled in any part of Mesopotamia. This was not to be repeated for nine more centuries.

While Crusaders and Turks fought it out bloodily, the Assassins dashed nimbly in and out, aiming at both with grim impartiality. The Turks tried to crush the Old Man of the Mountains by military force, but they were easily held off when they tried to penetrate the wild mountain ranges. And while the Assassins defended their fastness, they established subsidiary strongholds in Mesopotamia and Syria, and for a century and a half inflicted a unique reign of terror on Islam. No ruler in the Middle East could sleep in security.

The Seljuks, divided as they were, could not mount a thorough counterattack against the Crusaders. When the counterattack came it was led not by a Turk at all, but by a man of Armenian descent, who was born in Mesopotamia. He was Salah al-Din ("honor of the faith"), and he was born at Tikrit on the Tigris, halfway between Baghdad and the ancient ruins of Nineveh. A life of adventurous fighting against the Crusaders led him to the control of Egypt. In 1171, he abolished the Fatimid government and declared the return of Egypt to the Sunnite doctrine.

He reformed Egypt's government and economy and took over Syria as well. In 1187, he defeated the Crusaders and retook Jerusalem, quickly overrunning almost all the rest of the territory they had held.

It took another crusade, with England's Richard the Lion-Hearted as its leading light, to restore at least part of the Christian position. The Moslem champion won undying fame in legend under the Christian version of his name, Saladin (sal'-uh-din).

TERROR FROM CENTRAL ASIA

But while Christian and Moslem fought back and forth over the bloody fields of Palestine and Syria, a fresh and most monstrous invasion was being prepared by the Mongols of central Asia.

The groundwork for the Mongol impingement upon world history was laid in 1206, when their chieftain, Temujin (tem'-yoo-jin), succeeded in uniting the various tribes of Mongolia. He promptly took the name of Genghis Khan (jeng'gis-khahn'). The name means "universal king," and Genghis Khan must have taken the new title literally, for he immediately embarked on a program of unlimited conquest. It might seem to have been a rather foolish program, for the Mongols numbered not more than a million while surrounding them were mighty civilizations with advanced technologies.

Genghis Khan, however, surprised the world. He was an organizing genius who was centuries ahead of his time in military strategy. He was the first man who knew how to fight war on a truly continental scale; the first man to understand the "blitzkrieg" in its modern sense. His horsemen made independent sweeps for hundreds of miles to gather at some point picked out in advance, while signals and messengers kept the units in touch with each other. Virtually living on their shaggy ponies, the Mongols could cover ground at speeds that could not be matched under military conditions until the invention of the internal combustion engine.

Like the Assyrians, the Mongols made use of terror as a weapon; slaughtering in wholesale lots where even slight resistance was offered, but always saving technicians of all sorts and making use of their skills for the next conquest.

Genghis Khan died in 1227, but in the twenty-one years that he directed his armies, they had conquered half of China and smashed into eastern Persia.

Genghis Khan had a simple world outlook — nomadism was the proper way of life. Ideally, he would have like to flatten all cities and end all civilization. It was with difficulty that he was persuaded to leave the Chinese cities intact, the argument being that the clever city dwellers would be of use to him.

Having his citified base in the east, he was less careful of the settled areas in the west. Wholesale slaughter in Persia and the destruction of cities led to the falling apart of irrigation systems that were maintained only by closely cooperative work of settled populations. The painstaking labor of centuries was undone and areas made fertile by the unremitting labor of man fell back into semi-desert, with results felt even today, seven centuries later.

Genghis Khan was succeeded by his son Ogadai Khan (og'-uh-dy), who enlarged his father's capital in Karakorum (kar"-uh-kawr'um) which was almost dead center in what is now the Mongolian Peoples' Republic.

In 1236, an expeditionary force was sent against Europe and

victories were won rapidly. Russia and Poland were quickly taken and the Mongols, about to drive into the heart of Germany, were stopped only by the fortunate (for Europeans) death of Ogadai at the end of 1241. The Mongol generals had to return to Karakorum to participate in the election of a new khan.

There was some trouble here, but finally Mangu Khan, a grandson of Genghis, was established on the throne in 1251. During the decade of uncertainty, the vast Mongol Empire remained absolutely intact. No one dared budge against it. The Mongols called themselves Tatars, but to the prostrate Europeans this became Tartars — creatures from Tartarus (Hell).

With Mangu firmly on the throne, at last, the Mongol program of world conquest was renewed. Mangu's brother, Kublai (koo′bly), was entrusted with the task of subjugating what remained of China, while another brother, Hulagu (hoo-lah′-goo), was placed in charge of the campaign against the Moslem world.

Hulagu began his campaign at the end of 1255, moving southwestward from the Sea of Aral. He skirted the Caspian Sea and sent his men swarming into the secluded valley of the Old Man of the Mountains. The Assassins had been immune to the best armies and the most capable generals the Moslems had been able to send against them, but they were no more than child's play to the Mongols. The Mongols wiped them out and reduced them at a stroke to insignificance. Remnants of the Ismailis still exist to this day. Their leader, since 1800, has borne the title of Aga Khan, but these leaders are known today as playboys, rather than as feared assassins.

Hulagu's army then drove southward into Mesopotamia. Messengers sped ahead to call upon the Caliph to appear before Hulagu as a suppliant and to order the dismantling of Baghdad.

The Caliph was al-Mustasim. He had earlier refused to ally himself with the Mongols against the Assassins and now he refused to surrender. Where and how he gained the courage (or folly) to do this, we can't say. The Mongols were unper-

turbed by this defiance. In 1258, they swept aside the army
raised by the Caliph, plunged around and into Baghdad, and
subjected it to a savage sack that lasted for many days. Hundreds of thousands are supposed to have been slaughtered and
the accumulated treasures of centuries were indiscriminately
destroyed.

Al-Mustasim had the melancholy distinction of being the
last of the Abbasid Caliphs of Baghdad, a line that had had its
origin five centuries before. According to some tales, he was
strangled; according to others, he was kicked to death.

But though the Caliphate was at an end in Baghdad, it was
not completely wiped out. For purely propaganda purposes,
the rulers of Egypt picked up a member of the Abbasid family who had managed to escape the general destruction in
Baghdad and declared him Caliph. The Abbasid Caliphate in
Egypt was recognized only in that country, but it remained
there for two and a half centuries.

The Jewish community in Mesopotamia also came to a virtual end with the coming of the Mongols, after eighteen centuries of checkered history dating back to the time of Nebuchadrezzar. For some centuries, the community had been fading and Jewish intellectual leadership had shifted to other
parts of Islam, to Egypt and Spain. But now, it passes out of
history altogether.

The Caliphate and the Jewish community was not all that
came to an end in Mesopotamia. The destruction and depopu-
lation in the land meant that the canal system was disrupted
and destroyed. True, it had been in decay for a century, but
it might have been restored in time as it had on more than one
occasion in the past. What happened after the Mongol devastation put it beyond restoration.

One is staggered at the vandalism involved in this. Those
canals had supported a high civilization in Mesopotamia for
over five thousand years. Invasion, destruction, dark age, had
come and gone, but the canals had survived and the wealth
of Mesopotamia, however wasted and dissipated, had always
been recouped.

Now it could not. The canal system died and Mesopotamia

decayed into a grubby poverty that has remained with it down to the present. The glory had gone at last and has not yet returned.

In 1259, Mangu Khan died and Kublai succeeded. At his succession he ruled over the largest continuous Empire ever under the control of a single man. From the Pacific to central Europe, he controlled some 11,000,000 square miles, one-third the land surface of the Eastern Hemisphere. That record for continuous Empire has not been beaten to this very day.

But even as Kublai Khan ascended that unparalleled throne, the end came into view, when the insatiable Hulagu, having completed the conquest of Mesopotamia, moved into Syria.

Oddly enough, he was welcomed by some elements of the population. Hulagu's chief wife was a Nestorian Christian and the Mongol leaders generally were rather interested in Christianity. To the Christians in the Middle East, the Mongols seemed like potential allies against the Moslems.

But one Moslem power still stood in the way. Egypt was under the rule of the descendants of Saladin, but the actual control of the land was in the hands of a slave military caste called the Mamelukes (from an Arabic word meaning "slave"). The leader of the band, at the time the never-defeated Mongols were bearing down upon Egypt, was Baybars (by-bars'). He was a huge man of ferocity and almost maniacal courage. He led his Mamelukes into Syria, and near Damascus they met the Mongols. Baybars himself led the wild Mameluke charge that crushed the Mongol army in 1260!

It was the first defeat suffered by the Mongols anywhere in half a century of uninterrupted expansion. It saved Egypt, but it did far more than that. It taught the world that the riders from Hell, the demonic Tatars, could be defeated. The Mongol Empire expanded no more.

Persia and Mesopotamia remained under Hulagu, even after Baybars' victory had brought his advance to a halt. He was the "Il-Khan" ("regional governor") and his descendants are referred to as the Il-Khans in consequence.

The Il-Khans tended at first to be anti-Moslem. Hulagu's

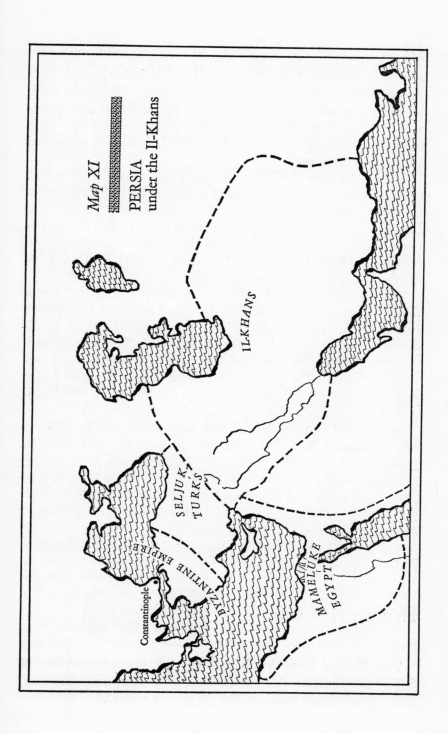

Map XI

PERSIA
under the Il-Khans

IL-KHANS

SELJUK TURKS

BYZANTINE EMPIRE

Constantinople

MAMELUKE EGYPT

son, who succeeded in 1265, was (like his father) married to a Christian; a Byzantine princess, in fact. Christians were looked upon with considerable favor in his realm and diplomatic connections with the Christian powers of Europe were attempted. The population of the land, however, remained stubbornly Moslem.

In 1295, a new Il-Khan, Ghazan, came to the throne and with him, at last, a generation of fighting the inevitable came to an end. He accepted conversion to Islam, and the cold war between the rulers and the ruled came to an end. He also declared his formal independence of the central Mongolian government. (Kublai Khan had just died in 1294, and with his death, Mongol unity disintegrated.)

The Mongol rule had softened by now. China had introduced paper currency, and it had worked well as a convenient substitute for metal coins where the population had confidence in such paper. An attempt was made by the now progressive Il-Khans to introduce the device into their own kingdom. It failed. The people would not accept strips of paper with writing upon it in exchange for valuable items, and financial chaos resulted. The experiment had to be ended.

Intellectual activity heightened, and under the Il-Khans, a scholar named Rashid al-Din was active. He was born in Hamadan about 1250, became a physician, served as vizier, and composed a history of the Mongols. In doing so, he wrote also about India and China and even about distant Europe — that is about all the peoples who had been touched by Mongol conquest or pressure. This amounted to an attempt at world history, the first time such a project had been undertaken in a reasonably modern sense.

THE OTTOMANS

The Mongol hurricane had destroyed the last remnants of Seljuk domination. A new Turkish tribe appeared, however, and gained dominance, as Mongol power waned.

The first important leader of this new tribe was Osman I (or Othman, in Arabic). The tribe under himself and his descendants are known as the Osmanli Turks or, more commonly (though incorrectly), the Ottoman Turks.

Othman assumed leadership in 1290 and began to extend his power over Asia Minor. Under his son, Orkhan I (awr-khahn'), who came to the throne in 1324, the rest of Asia Minor was taken. In 1345, Orkhan took advantage of a civil war among the Byzantines to cross over the straits, and thus the Turk entered Europe.

Turkish forces steadily reduced Byzantine power until it was confined to little more than the city of Constantinople. By 1391, indeed, the Ottoman sultan, Bayazid I (by-ah-zeed'), had Constantinople under virtual siege. He was on the point of taking it when a new and unexpected assault from the east distracted his attention.

The assault was that of a conqueror who claimed to be of the line of Genghis Khan, and indeed he seemed to have all the powers of the legendary Genghis. No one could stand against him. His name was Timur (tih-moor') but he was generally known as Timur-i-lenk ("Timur the Lame"), and this was distorted to Tamerlane by Europeans.

The center of his realm was at Samarkand (sam'er-kand) about 600 miles east of the Caspian, and he had made himself supreme among most of the surviving Mongol principalities. He even marched deep into Russia, occupying Moscow in 1382.

The Il-Khans of Persia had become so weakened and disrupted that they offered Timur no effective opposition. By 1395, he had taken all the Il-Khan dominion, then marched into India, took Delhi and sacked it.

He was nearly seventy by then, but the terrible old man did not let age stop him. In 1400, he invaded Syria and there outdid Hulagu's attempt of a century and a half before, for he met a Mameluke army, defeated it, and occupied Damascus.

He turned on Baghdad next, which was still holding out. In 1401, he took it, and if his sack was not as destructive as Hulagu's had been, it was because far less remained to destroy. Some 20,000 of its population were massacred.

Finally, Timur invaded Asia Minor and it was this that distracted Bayazid from his siege of Constantinople. In 1402, Timur met the Turkish army at Ankara, in mid-peninsula and smashed it. The Ottoman realm was shaken to its foundation and the tottering remnant of the Byzantine Empire was granted a last half-century of life.

Timur's rule extended roughly over the land that had once made up the Sassanid Empire. He now readied a vast expeditionary force which he led eastward toward the end of 1404 with the intention of conquering China. But he didn't make it. Age is the universal victor after all. Timur died within a month of setting out and his body was sent back to Samarkand.

For a century after Timur's death, there was confusion in the Middle East, while his descendants squabbled among themselves. Slowly, their power fragmented and declined and as it did so, that of the Ottoman Turks revived.

In 1451, Mohammed II was Sultan over a recovered Ottoman Empire. He laid siege to Constantinople and took it, at last, in 1453. The last Byzantine Emperor, Constantine XI, died bravely fighting. This brought to an end a line of rulers that traced itself back to Augustus, fifteen centuries before.

Constantinople became the capital of the Ottoman Empire under a new name, Istanbul, and it has been a Turkish city ever since.

It took longer for a revival to reach Persia. This revival came by way of a pious Shiite family known as the Safavids (sa''favidz') after its founder, Safi-al-Din, who lived in the time of Hulagu.

By 1501, a member of the family, Ismail, captured the city of Tabriz (tah-breez'), about 150 miles west of the Caspian Sea, and from there established his rule over Persia. The land had long been a battleground of ideas between the Sunnites and Shiites, and at this time the Sunnites were in the ascendancy. Ismail I, however, labored to bring his subjects to Shiism and succeeded. Since his time, Persia has been predominantly Shiite.

The Ottoman Empire, on the other hand, remained fanatically Sunnite, and the Persian rise was looked upon with great displeasure. In 1512, Selim I became the Ottoman Sultan. He was called "Selim the Grim" and he was indeed a grim warrior. In 1516 and 1517, he conquered Syria and Egypt, adding them to his dominion. In Egypt, he captured the last of the descendants of the Abbasid who had fled there from Baghdad after Hulagu's holocaust. According to the later story, Selim forced this last Abbasid to grant him the title of Caliph. The later Ottomans laid firm claim to this title as a result.

Selim had also measured swords with Ismail. The respective champions of Sunnism and Shiism met at Chaldiran (chahl"dih-rahn') in Armenia, on August 23, 1514. Selim won and took over control of the area west of the Caspian where, a dozen years before, Ismail had started his own career of conquest.

Ismail, however, endured. As Selim turned south to Syria and Egypt, Ismail managed to keep the Turks from any further advance eastward. He even managed to establish his power over Mesopotamia which, like Persia, became largely Shiite in consequence.

The duel that had so long been fought over Armenia and Mesopotamia between Roman and Persian, then between Christian and Moslem, was now renewed a third time on a new basis. It was Sunnite against Shiite, and it continued for four centuries.

12

THE EUROPEANS

THE RETURN OF THE WESTERNERS

But western Europe was making itself felt in the Middle
East once more. The last of the Crusaders had been hurled out
of Syria in 1291, but Europe had rebounded in a new fashion.
Slowly, under the leadership of her westernmost powers, Portugal and Spain, she was breeding a line of mariners who ventured far out into the ocean and who established political control over the lands they reached.

The most successful of the early Portuguese imperialists was
Affonso de Albuquerque (ahl''boo-kur'kee). He ranged all
the shores of the Indian Ocean and, in 1510, landed at the island of Ormuz at the mouth of the Persian Gulf. He staked
out mastery over parts of the adjoining mainland as well. Shah
Ismail protested this vigorously, but, engaged in a life-and-
death struggle with the Ottomans as he was, he could not
push matters farther than that.

Ismail was succeeded by his eleven-year-old son, Tahmasp

I, and while Persia underwent the uncertainties of a minority, it had to face the Ottoman Empire under its greatest ruler, Suleiman the Magnificent.

Suleiman defeated Persia time after time, forcing Tahmasp to move his capital eastward to Kazvin, near where the Assassins had had their stronghold four centuries before. What's more, Suleiman wrested Mesopotamia from the grip of the Persian Shahs.

In Tahmasp's reign, the first Englishman reached Persia. He was Anthony Jenkinson, in the employ of a company whose goal was to facilitate and extend trade between England and Russia. One possible route for such trade was overland across Persia, and in 1561, Jenkinson reached the Persian court at Kazvin in order to negotiate the establishment of such a trade route. He was not successful, for anti-Christian feeling in Persia was too strong.

In 1587, Abbas I became Shah. He was the most capable of the Safavid line and is sometimes called Abbas the Great. He labored to reform his army and make it more nearly the equal of the Turks. In this he had some unexpected aid. In 1598, some Englishmen arrived in his land, anxious to negotiate an alliance between Persia and Christian Europe against the Ottoman Empire. The leader of this English mission, Sir Robert Shirley, was a capable soldier.

Sir Robert remained in Abbas' service and helped him build up his army. The result was that in 1603, Abbas felt himself in a position to attack the Turks. He retook all the territory lost to Selim and Suleiman. In particular, he retook Mesopotamia and marched triumphantly into Baghdad.

The reign of Abbas I was one of prosperity for Persia. The Shah established a new and splendid capital at Isfahan (is'-fuh-han), three hundred miles south of Kazvin. He improved the road network of his realm and encouraged the establishment of English and Dutch trading posts.

He bitterly resented, however, the continuing presence of the Portuguese on the southern coast, where they had now been established for a century. With the aid of ships owned by the British trading company, he attacked the Portuguese in 1622 and drove them out at last. At the site he founded the city of Bandar Abbas, named for himself.

After Abbas' death in 1629, Persia rapidly declined, and it was her misfortune that one last capable ruler made his appearance on the Turkish throne. This was Murad IV, last of the Ottoman warrior sultans. No sooner was Abbas dead, when Murad went storming eastward, sacking Hamadan in 1630. In 1638, he took Baghdad. Once again, Mesopotamia became Turkish, and this time the change-over was permanent, in the sense that she never fell under Persian dominion again.

The next century saw even worse trouble from the east. There, Afghan tribes had gained their independence (and began the history of modern Afghanistan). In 1722, an Afghan army went careening into Persia and defeated a much larger Persian army. They took Isfahan and put an end to its century-long period of glory.

THE RUSSIANS

And while Persia was hounded west and east, she felt the beginning of a new kind of European pressure, overland and from the north, as the Russians, free at last of Mongol domination, came marching southward.

While Persia was reeling from the Afghan invasion, Russia was under its greatest Czar, Peter I. He chose the moment to move to the Caucasus and beyond, and for a while it looked as though Persia would vanish in a three-way split between Turk, Russ, and Afghan.

That this did not happen was the result of the sudden ap-

pearance of a capable general, Nadir Kuli (nah'dir). He was
a Sunnite Turk by descent but a Persian by ambition. He defeated the Afghans, held off the Ottoman Empire, and kept
Persia alive. In 1736, he deposed Abbas III, the last of the
Safavids (who had ruled Persia for two and a third centuries)
and made himself ruler outright, as Nadir Shah.

For a few years, Persia seemed a conquering power again.
Nadir invaded India in 1739, sacked Delhi, and carried off im-
mense wealth — reputed to amount to half a billion dollars.
He expanded into central Asia and even defeated the Turks
on the shores of the Black Sea. For a moment, the realm of
the Sassanids seemed restored.

However, even conquests cost money and can be more than
the economy of a nation can support. Besides, Nadir was trying to establish Sunnism as the official religion, and the Shiite
population fought against this with sullen fervor. There was
only one possible end — a drumbeat of rebellion and conspiracy and, in 1747, Nadir Shah was assassinated.

In the confused half-century that followed, the Persian capital shifted several times. In 1796, it was placed at Tehran (tah-
rahn') about 70 miles south of the Caspian. This city has remained the capital of Persia ever since.

By now, the chief pressures on Persia were from Europeans;
from the Russians in the north and the British (who had established themselves in India) in the southeast.

Persia fought a series of wars with Russia which, in general,
she lost, and Russian control seeped southward from the Caucasus. By 1828, the border between the two powers reached
the line that still exists today, about 70 miles north of Tabriz.

East of the Caspian Sea, however, the Russian southern
thrust continued. By 1853, Russian armies stood on the shores
of Lake Aral. By 1884, they had reached points 400 miles
south of that lake and established the present boundary between Persia and Russia.

Great Britain did her best to protect Persia against these
Russian advances, not so much out of disinterested love for
Persia, as out of fear of Russia. If Persia fell utterly under

Russian control, Britain's own rule over India might be threatened. Indeed, it was this rivalry between Britain and Russia in Asia that brought about the Crimean War of 1853 to 1856.

Throughout the second half of the nineteenth century, Persia could scarcely be considered independent. It was riddled by both Russian and British influences, each at war with the other, and with the interests of the Persians themselves counting for nothing.

About the only thing the Persians could do for themselves was to found a new religion. It came from Shiraz (shee-rahz'), about forty miles southwest of the site where once, two thousand years before, ancient Persepolis had stood.

In 1844, Mirza Ali Mohammed, a man of Shiraz, declared himself the Bab (that is "gateway") through which new divine revelations were to come. What he preached was a form of Shiism to which might be added certain aspects of Judaism and Christianity. His movement caught on, but promptly gained the disapproval of the orthodox Shiites. The Bab was executed in 1850, and his followers were bitterly persecuted and finally expelled from the land in 1864.

One of the followers of the Bab called himself Baha-ullah (bah-hah'oo-lah') or "splendor of God." He managed to make his way to Baghdad where he preached a somewhat new version of the religion, a version which became known, in his honor, as Bahaism (buh-hah'iz-um). It is even more eclectic than Babism, for it preaches the unity of all religions. It has no priesthood and no ritual, but confines itself to ethical teachings.

The Turkish government at Constantinople was no more pleased with the new doctrine than the Persians had been, and Baha-ullah was exiled to Palestine (which, under the Turks, was a scrubby, semi-desert, nearly abandoned land.) Baha-ullah died there in 1892, but the world headquarters of Bahaism remains in Haifa, Israel, to this day.

Up to the time of Baha-ullah's death, the new religion was confined to the Moslem world. In the 1890's, however, it began to spread westward, and it is stronger now in the United States than anywhere else in the world.

THE GERMANS

The British-Russian rivalry might have continued indefinitely, were it not that both Britain and Russia were coming face to face with a new enemy. In 1871, various German states had united to form the German Empire, which rapidly grew to be the most prosperous and strongest state, militarily, in Europe.

When William II became the German monarch in 1888, he foolishly initiated a flamboyant foreign policy that frightened the rest of the world. Russia feared the large and efficient army on its western border and Great Britain feared the new and technically advanced navy that Germany set about building.

With Britain and Russia both fearing Germany, the two old enemies could not help but draw together. In 1907, they came to an informal agreement. Part of this agreement dealt with Persia. Russia was to recognize Great Britain's exclusive control of the Persian Gulf coast of the land, and Britain was to recognize Russia's control of the Caspian coast. Between was a neutral strip that would keep the two influences sufficiently separate to prevent trouble.

This was a specific reply to the German effort to establish a Middle East hold of its own. Her influence was growing in Turkey (the remains of a much-shrunken Ottoman Empire), and in 1892 a German company had obtained permission to build a railroad across Asia Minor and into Mesopotamia to Baghdad.

Finally in 1914, when World War I broke out, with Germany on one side and Russia and Great Britain on the other, Turkey joined the Germans, but Persia declared itself neutral.

Persia, and the Middle East, generally, was important as a

route whereby Great Britain and Russia might make contact and outflank the German group of powers. In 1914, therefore, immediately after the Turks entered the war, the British landed a force at Basra, in Turkish territory, near the northern tip of the Persian Gulf. In the spring of 1915, the British forces began a march upstream, aimed at Baghdad.

By November, the British had reached the site of ancient Ctesiphon, and there they fought a battle with the Turks. But the advance had not been an easy one; heat and disease had had its toll; and even though the battle with the Turks was not an utter defeat, the British army was sufficiently weakened to make retreat advisable.

The British retired into Kut-al-Imara, a town on the Tigris about a hundred miles downstream from Baghdad. The Turks laid siege to it in December and for five months the British army (mostly Indians, as a matter of fact) festered and starved within the town, while three attempts to relieve them failed. On April 29, 1916, they were forced to surrender.

Toward the end of that year, the angry British assembled a larger and better-equipped army and drove into Mesopotamia again. In January, 1917, they fought the Turks at Kut-al-Imara, and this time they won a victory and took the city. By March 11, they were in Baghdad, and for the first time in the eleven-century history of that city, the capital of the Caliphs felt the tread of a conquering Christian army.

The war ended in 1918, with a complete victory for Great Britain and its allies (including the United States as an "associated power," but excluding Russia which had fallen into revolution and chaos, and had left the war).

Not long after the peace, the Ottoman Empire came to an end after six centuries of existence.

What non-Turkish subject peoples had remained by 1918 were now set free, but not entirely. Mesopotamia became, in theory, the independent nation of Iraq (ee-rahk') but in actual fact the British controlled the land under a "mandate" given it by the League of Nations (a loose union of nations founded after World War I).

The Iraqi did not like the arrangement and rebelled against

their new British masters in 1920, but were easily suppressed. In 1921, Faisal (fy'sal), of an important Arab family that had cooperated with the British during World War I, became king of Iraq. With a king of its own, Iraq felt itself to be more a self-respecting nation, and the land settled down to twenty years of reasonable cooperation with the British.

Persia, meanwhile, gained a truer measure of independence than it had had before. Russia, under its new revolutionary government, had all it could do to maintain its own territory intact. It could not possibly attempt imperialist adventures. Even Britain, having suffered from World War I, was less eager to extend its swollen Empire (making up a quarter of the Earth's land surface) any farther.

In 1921, a Persian army officer, Reza Khan, seized control of the Persian government, and in 1925, made himself Shah. Under him, Persia underwent a strong nationalist resurgence. British influence was lessened; treaties were signed with Russia (now the Soviet Union) and Turkey; the land was modernized. In 1935, it became officially Iran (ee-rahn'), the old Iranian name, rather than the Greek "Persia."

Through the 1930's, however, there was a growing disaffection in the Middle East. Jews were entering Palestine and were driving hard for the establishment of an independent Jewish state (a movement called "Zionism"). To this the various Moslem states of the Middle East were opposed. Since the Jews were supported, to some extent, by popular opinion in the West, the West grew unpopular among Arab nationalists — particularly since it was already unpopular as the colonial powers that kept the Arab states from enjoying complete independence.

Worse still, Germany experienced a revival in the 1930's and fell under the power of the demonic Adolf Hitler. His program included a fanatically anti-Jewish stand that pleased the anti-Zionist Arabs. Hitler bent every effort to influence the Middle East and draw its people to his side in the great war he was planning.

Thus, when World War II broke out in 1939, there followed Middle Eastern battles again.

Hitler's Germany won the first rounds in the war, utterly defeating France and reducing Great Britain to a desperate battle in isolation. The government of Iraq assumed that Great Britain was done, and thought the moment appropriate to establish their independence with German aid.

Britain, however, was not at all through. In May, 1941, British forces entered Iraq, bombed its airfields, and occupied Baghdad.

In June, 1941, the Germans invaded the Soviet Union, and once again Britain and Russia were associated against the common German enemy. Again it was necessary to establish a line of communication between the two nations and Persia seemed the obvious route. The Persian Shah, Reza Khan, was, however, distinctly pro-German in his sympathies.

Great Britain and the Soviet Union could not afford to stand on ceremony. They mounted a combined invasion of Iran in August, 1941, forced the Shah to abdicate, and established a solid line of communications across that land.

Slowly the tide began to turn, particularly after the United States was brought into the war as a result of the bombing of Pearl Harbor by Japan in December, 1941. In 1945, Germany was defeated a second time, far more disastrously than before.

ISRAEL

In theory, Iraq had become independent in 1932, and in that year it had been admitted into the League of Nations. Great Britain had still retained overriding influence, as the events of World War II demonstrated.

After the conclusion of World War II, however, Great Britain was no longer in a position to maintain her empire. Iraq's true independence dates from that time.

Postwar Iraq was influenced by three developments.

First, oil had become of paramount importance to the world's industrial powers. Automobiles, trucks, trains, ships, and airplanes ran by oil, and wars could not be fought without it. The Middle East, as it happened, was found to contain the world's greatest reservoir of oil, and the great industrial powers faced each other in fierce rivalry over stretches of territory that had little importance otherwise. More than half the national income of Iraq is derived from the sale of oil to outside powers nowadays.

Second, the industrial powers of the postwar world are, in essence, two in number — the United States and the Soviet Union. The two faced each other in a rivalry that was not quite open warfare but that expressed itself in every fashion but naked force. The rest of the world was forced to react, in one way or another, to this "cold war." Most nations had to choose sides.

The Arabic-speaking nations (the "Arab bloc") were pulled in both directions. On the one hand, the Soviet Union was a northern neighbor with an unfriendly history. Then, too, the rulers of the Arab bloc, benefiting by an archaic and unjust social and economic system, dreaded the possibility of being unseated in the name of Soviet-sponsored Communism. Add to this the fact that the United States was incomparably the richer of the two powers, the much better customer for oil, as well as the readier to make loans, and there seemed an apparently irresistible pull to join the American side of the cold war.

On the other hand, there was the third and most important influence upon postwar Iraq. The Jews had, after all, achieved their goal of founding an independent Jewish state. In 1948, they proclaimed the existence of the state of Israel in parts of Palestine. The Arab-bloc nations, including Iraq, reacted with extreme hostility and launched an attack upon it. They were defeated and Israel maintained its existence in triumph.

This but hardened Arab hostility, so that anti-Israel emotions dominated everything else among them. The United States was far more sympathetic to Israel than the Soviet Union was, and that, in the eyes of some Arab circles, seemed to be all that mattered. Egypt, under the dictatorial rule of Gamal Abdel Nasser (who gained control in 1954) began to edge closer to the Soviet Union.

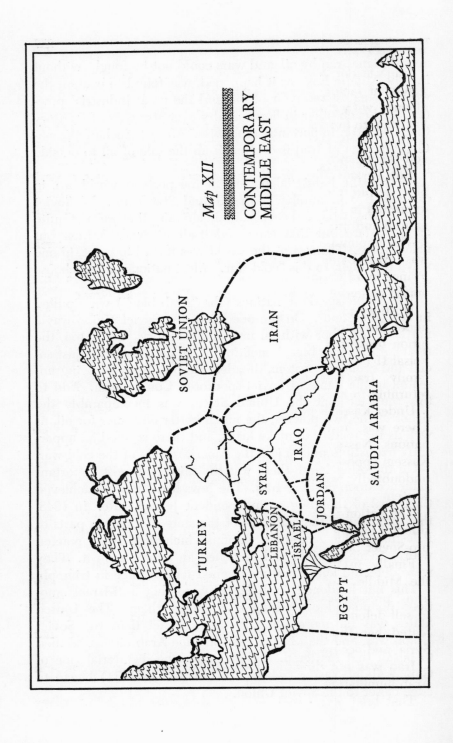

Map XII

CONTEMPORARY
MIDDLE EAST

SOVIET UNION

IRAN

TURKEY

SYRIA

IRAQ

LEBANON

ISRAEL

JORDAN

SAUDIA ARABIA

EGYPT

Iraq's leader, Nuri Pasha, to whom anti-Communism was the dominant factor, moved in the other direction. He joined in alliance with three other Islamic powers, Turkey, Iran, and Pakistan, to form a solid anti-Soviet barrier across the southern flank of the Soviet Union. Meetings were held at Baghdad, and the alliance was popularly known as the "Baghdad pact."

But Turkey, Iran, and Pakistan were not part of the Arab bloc, despite their Islamic character, and were not particularly interested in Israel. Iraq's membership in such a pact was unnatural and unpopular with much of her population.

The unpopularity of the pact among the Iraqi population was exacerbated in 1956, when Israel joined Britain and France in an assault on Egypt which was stopped only by the united action of the United States and the Soviet Union.

Hostility to the western powers grew steadily and in 1958, under the leadership of General Abdul Karim Kassem, a revolution broke out in Iraq. Nuri Pasha was killed and so were Feisal II (who had been king since 1953) and the entire royal family. Iraq became a republic and left the Baghdad Pact, returning to her anti-Israel position.

Under Kassem, Iraq swung much closer to the Soviet Union. There was, however, much internal friction within the Arab nations. Nasser drove for full leadership of the Arab bloc and Kassem opposed him in this. In 1963, a group of army officers, undoubtedly backed by Egypt, seized the government, killing Kassem.

The nation then swung closer to Egypt and to Nasser's position of having one's cake and eating it, too — that is, of being pro-Soviet but anti-Communist.

Finally, in June, 1967, the ticking time bomb exploded in the Middle East. The Arabic nations, supported by Soviet arms, pressed close about Israel, which suddenly struck back in self-defense. In a whirlwind six-day campaign, Israel defeated her three immediate neighbors, Egypt, Jordan, and Syria, and occupied sections of their territories.

Iraq was not directly involved, but shared in the general Arab humiliation.

That brief war somehow highlighted the tragic fall of the

land of the two rivers. It had given rise to the first farmers and city dwellers ten thousand years ago. It had given the world its first written language five thousand years ago. It had raised up empire after empire, and its cities had dominated the known world until a bare thousand years ago.

But to originate and continue so intricate a structure as civilization could not be done without a price. The accumulated wealth attracted the barbarous tribes on the outskirts, and time and again, the complex social structure of Mesopotamia was painfully and wastefully disorganized by barbarian invasions.

The swing of the pendulum from empire to barbarian inroad and back again, over and over, wasted the energies of the people, and the millennia of agriculture slowly wore out the land itself. The catastrophe of the Mongol destruction of the canals was only the last sudden act of a steady decline.

Meanwhile, the gains and advances that had been made originally along the Euphrates River had spread throughout the world in widening ripples. It was Sumerian writing that reached Egypt, and astronomy from Egypt and Babylonia that reached Greece, and learning from Greece (via the Arabic world of the Middle East) that reached the West at last.

And now Israel, which has fully accepted western technology, can hold at bay an Arabic world that outnumbers it some twenty to one but which has not fully accepted the western ways.

It would be a pity now if Iraq and the other Arabic nations, in their frustration, borrowed only the war weapons of the West. If they do so they may, in the end, defeat Israel by sheer weight, and gratify their own pride, but they will be left as miserable as before, for missiles and jet planes cannot, of themselves, cure the ingrained ills that beset the region.

We can hope that the ways of peace will attract the Arabic nations, for their territory and opportunities are broad enough for immeasurable advance, if the energies vented in spleen, are turned instead to a modernization of the technology, a restoration of the soil, and a renovation of the economic, social, and political structure of those great and venerable lands.

A TABLE OF DATES

NOTE: *Dates before 1000 B.C. are approximate*

B.C.

8500 Beginnings of agriculture northeast of Tigris River

5000 Agriculture along the upper Tigris and Euphrates Rivers

4500 Canal system begins along the lower Euphrates

4000 Sumerians enter lower Mesopotamia

3100 Invention of writing by Sumerians

3000 Akkadians enter Mesopotamia; Bronze comes into use

2800 The Great Flood

2700 Gilgamesh of Uruk

2550 Eannatum of Lagash; sets up "Stele of the Vultures"

2415 Urukagina of Lagash attempts reforms and fails

2400 Lugalzaggesi of Umma unifies Sumeria

2370 Sargon of Agade defeats Lugalzaggesi; sets up Akkadian Empire

2290 Naram-Sin; Akkadian Empire at peak

2215 Guti take Agade; destroy Akkadian Empire

B.C.

2150 Gudea of Lagash

2100 Ur-Nammu of Ur; oldest surviving law-code

2000 Elam conquers Ur and ends last period of Sumerian domination; Amorites infiltrate Mesopotamia and take Babylon; nomads of the steppe tame the horse

1950 Abraham leaves Ur

1900 Sumerian language and sense of nationality peter out

1850 Amorites take Asshur

1814 Shamshi-Adad I of Assyria; first Assyrian conqueror

1800 Horse-and-chariot comes into use; Hurrian tribes begin to raid Middle-Eastern civilizations

1792 Hammurabi of Babylon

1750 Death of Hammurabi after bringing Amorite Empire to peak of power and initiating greatness of Babylon

1700 Hittite Empire established

B.C.

in eastern Asia Minor; Kassites invade Mesopotamia

1595 Kassites take Babylon

1500 Phoenicians invent alphabet; Indo-European tribes (Medes) settle in mountains north and east of Mesopotamia; other tribes (Aryans) invade India. Kingdom of Mitanni established and dominates Assyria.

1479 Thutmose III of Egypt defeats Canaanites at Megiddo; goes on to defeat Mitanni and Hittites

1375 Hittites establish new Empire

1365 Ashur-uballit wins Assyrian independence of Mitanni

1300 Assyria absorbs Mitanni; iron-smelting discovered in Caucasus foothills

1275 Shalmaneser I establishes First Assyrian Empire

1245 Tukulti-Ninurta I (Nimrod); First Assyrian Empire at peak

1200 Invasion of Peoples of the Sea; Hittite Empire destroyed; First Assyrian Empire greatly weakened

1174 Elamites take Babylon and carry off law-code of Hammurabi

1124 Nebuchadrezzar I of Babylon

1115 Tiglath-Pileser I of Assyria; period of Assyrian revival

1100 Arameans infiltrate Fertile Crescent

B.C.

1050 Assyria declines again under Aramean pressures

1013 David of Judah establishes Israelite Empire over western half of Fertile Crescent

1000 Hurrian principalities north of Assyria unite to form kingdom of Urartu

973 Solomon of Israel

950 Chaldeans infiltrate Mesopotamia

933 Death of Solomon; Israelite Empire breaks up

900 Medes develop large breeds of horses capable of carrying armed warrior

889 Tukulti-Ninurta II of Assyria; Assyrian army begins to make use of iron and of siege machinery; Second Assyrian Empire

883 Ashurnasirpal II of Assyria; establishes Calah as capital; conducts wars of terror and cruelty; Second Assyrian Empire at peak

859 Shalmaneser III of Assyria

854 Israel and Syria unite to defeat Assyria at Karkar

810 Sammu-rammat of Assyria (Semiramis); Assyria in decline again

750 Urartu at its peak under Argistis I; Scythians invade regions north of Black Sea and begin to drive Cimmerians through the Caucasus

745 Tiglath-Pileser III of Assyria; establishes Third Assyrian Empire

729 Tiglath-Pileser III estab-

B.C.

lishes direct rule over Babylon

727 Shalmaneser V of Assyria

722 Sargon II of Assyria; takes Samaria and destroys kingdom of Israel

705 Sennacherib of Assyria; establishes Nineveh as capital

701 Sennacherib lays siege to Jerusalem but fails to take it

689 Sennacherib sacks Babylon

681 Esarhaddon of Assyria

673 Esarhaddon invades Egypt

671 Esarhaddon sacks Memphis in lower Egypt

669 Esarhaddon restores Bablon; Ashurbanipal of Assyria

661 Ashurbanipal sacks Thebes in Upper Egypt; Third Assyrian Empire at peak

652 Ashurbanipal in final victory over Cimmerians; Lydian kingdom established in western Asia Minor

648 Ashurbanipal defeats his brother Shamash-shumukin (Sardanapalus) in Babylon

639 Ashurbanipal takes and destroys Susa; Elamite history comes to end

625 Death of Ashurbanipal; Nabopolassar takes control of Babylon; Cyaxares rules over united Media

612 Nabopolassar takes and

B.C.

destroys Nineveh; establishes Chaldean Empire

608 Necho of Egypt defeats and kills Josiah of Judah at Megiddo

605 Nebuchadrezzar II of Chaldea defeats Necho and last Assyrian army; Assyria and Urartu disappear from history

587 Nebuchadrezzar II takes and destroys Jerusalem; carries Jews into Babylonian exile

585 Nebuchadrezzar II lays siege to Tyre; Chaldean Empire at peak

575 Zarathustra establishes Zoroastrian religion in Media

572 Nebuchadrezzar II forced to raise siege of Tyre

562 Death of Nebuchadrezzar II

559 Cyrus II of Persian principality of Anshan declares it independent of Media

550 Cyrus II takes Ecbatana, Median capital; Median Empire comes to end and Persian Empire takes its place

547 Cyrus II defeats Lydia; Lydian kingdom comes to end

539 Cyrus II takes Babylon; Chaldean Empire comes to end

538 Cyrus II allows Jews to return to Jerusalem

530 Cambyses of Persia

525 Cambyses takes Egypt

522 Darius I of Persia

B.C.

519 Darius I suppresses rebellion in Babylon

516 Jewish Temple rebuilt in Jerusalem

499 Revolt of Greek cities in Asia Minor crushed by Darius I; Persian Empire at peak

490 Athenians defeat Persians at Marathon

486 Xerxes I of Persia

484 Xerxes I sacks Babylon; final decline of city begins

480 Greeks defeat Persians at sea battle of Salamis

465 Artaxerxes I of Persia

424 Darius II of Persia

404 Artaxerxes II of Persia

401 Artaxerxes II defeats his younger brother, Cyrus, at Cunaxa

400 Ten thousand Greeks under Xenophon, retreating from Cunaxa, reach home safely

358 Artaxerxes III of Persia

338 Philip II of Macedon unites Greece, plans invasion of Persia

336 Philip II assassinated; Alexander III (the Great) succeeds to Macedonian throne; Darius III of Persia

334 Alexander the Great invades Persian Empire, defeats Persians at Granicus

333 Alexander the Great defeats Persians at Issus

331 Alexander the Great defeats Persians at Gaugamela

330 Darius III assassinated by

B.C.

his own men; Persian Empire comes to end

323 Alexander the Great dies in Babylon

312 Seleucus I, one of Alexander's generals, takes Babylon; founds Seleucid Empire; builds new capital at Seleucia, and Babylon quickly declines to village

250 Bactria under Diodotus I and Parthia under Arsaces I establish independence of Seleucid Empire

246 Ptolemy III of Egypt occupies Mesopotamia briefly

217 Antiochus III of Seleucid Empire temporarily reestablishes control over Parthia and Bactria: Seleucid Empire at peak

190 Antiochus III defeated by Romans

175 Antiochus IV of Seleucid Empire

171 Mithridates I of Parthia wins its final independence; establishes Parthian Empire

168 Jews rebel against Antiochus IV under Maccabees

150 Mithridates I takes Media from Seleucid Empire

147 Mithridates I takes Mesopotamia; Seleucid Empire confined to Syria

139 Parthians ambush Seleucid army and take Seleucid king, Demetrius II, prisoner

138 Death of Mithridates I

129 Parthians establish capital

B.C.

at Ctesiphon; Seleucia remains great and prosperous as Greek city

127 Antiochus VII of Seleucid Empire killed in battle against Parthians

95 Parthians set up Tigranes as king of Armenia

70 Tigranes most powerful monarch in west Asia. Armenia at peak

66 Roman general, Pompey, takes Tigranese prisoner

64 Pompey annexes Syria and Judea to Rome; Seleucid Empire at end

57 Orodes I of Parthia

53 Roman army under Crassus defeated by Parthians at Carrhae

40 Parthians briefly take Syria and Judea and invade Asia Minor. Parthian Empire at peak

38 Roman general, Ventidius, defeats Parthians; eastern provinces restored to Rome

20 Augustus, first Roman Emperor, makes compromise peace with Phraates IV of Parthia

A.D.

51 Vologesus I of Parthia

63 Vologesus I makes compromise peace with Roman general, Corbulo; Armenia as buffer between two powers

115 Roman Emperor Trajan conquers Mesopotamia; Roman Empire at peak

117 Roman Emperor Hadrian

A.D.

abandons Mesopotamia to Parthia

165 Roman general, Avidius Cassius, takes and destroys Seleucia

198 Roman Emperor, Septimius Severus, takes Ctesiphon; passes utterly deserted Babylon

200 Arabic kingdom of Hira established

228 Ardashir takes Ctesiphon, founds new (Sassanid) dynasty; Parthian Empire at end and replaced by Sassanid Persian Empire

240 Shapur I of Sassanid Empire; Manichaeism begins to spread

260 Roman Emperor, Valerian, taken prisoner at Edessa by Sassanids

274 Imprisonment and death of Mani, founder of Manichaeism

293 Narsah of Sassanid Empire

297 Roman Emperor, Galerius, defeats Narsah

301 Hormisdas II of Sassanid Empire; fails as reformer

309 Shapur II, ruler of Sassanid Empire at birth

337 Shapur II begins long war against Rome

361 Roman Emperor, Julian, invades Mesopotamia, lays siege to Ctesiphon

363 Julian killed in Mesopotamia

399 Yazdegird I of Sassanid Empire; sympathetic to Christianity at first

A.D.

420 Varahran V (Bahram Gor) of Sassanid Empire

429 Sassanid Empire gains control over eastern Armenia (Persarmenia)

439 Yazdegird II of Sassanid Empire; Christians persecuted

457 Firuz of Sassanid Empire

484 Firuz defeated and killed by raiding Hephthalite nomads: Anarchy in Sassanid Empire

501 Kavadh of Sassanid Empire; stability restored; Christianity in Empire almost entirely Nestorian; Zoroastrianism fights Mazdakite heresy

531 Chosroes I of Sassanid Empire; pagan Athenian philosophers flee to his court

549 Pagan Athenian philosophers return to Greece

589 Chosroes II of Sassanid Empire

603 Chosroes II destroys Arabic kingdom of Hira

615 Chosroes II takes Jerusalem

617 Chosroes II lays siege to Constantinople. Sassanid power at peak

622 Roman Emperor, Heraclius, counterattacks

627 Heraclius defeats Chosroes II near ruins of Nineveh

628 Death of Chosroes II

632 Yazdegird III of Sassanid Empire; Mohammed unites tribes of Arabia and dies

A.D.

637 Arabs defeat Sassanids at Kadisiya; take Asian provinces from Roman Empire, shrink its territory to what comes to be called Byzantine Empire

642 Arabs defeat Sassanids at Nehavend

651 Death of Yazdegird III; end of Sassanid Empire

661 Assassination of Ali; establishment of the Omayyad Caliphate; beginning of Shiite sect of Moslems

680 Omayyads defeat Shiites at Kerbelah; Omayyad Caliphate at peak

717 Arabic siege of Constantinople fails

750 Omayyad dynasty overthrown; Abbasid Caliphate established in its place; Ismailism founded

762 Abbasids establish capital at Baghdad; Ctesiphon begins its final decay

786 Harun al-Rashid as Abbasid Caliph

813 Al-Mamun as Abbasid Caliph; Abbasid Caliphate at peak

833 Al-Mutasim as Abbasid Caliph; employs Turkish bodyguard

861 Al-Mutasim assassinated; Caliphate quickly declines

900 Arabic and Persian science at height; Al-Battani greatest astronomer of the era and Al-Razi the greatest physician

1000 Turks under Ghazni rule

A.D.

over Persia; Firdausi writes Persian national epic

1037 Seljuk Turks under Tughril Beg take over Persia

1055 Tughril Beg conquers Mesopotamia

1063 Alp Arslan as Seljuk Sultan

1071 Alp Arslan defeats Byzantine Emperor, Romanus Diogenes, at Manzikert and takes over most of Asia Minor

1073 Malik Shah as Seljuk Sultan; Omar Khayyám writes poetry and reforms calendar

1076 Malik Shah takes Jerusalem; Seljuk power at peak

1090 Ismailis establish Assassin stronghold in mountains

1096 Western Europeans begin First Crusade against Moslems

1099 Crusaders take Jerusalem

1187 Saladin of Egypt and Syria retakes Jerusalem

1227 Death of Genghis Khan after conquest of northern half of China and eastern half of Persia

1255 Mongol general, Hulagu, invades Mesopotamia and destroys Assassin stronghold

1258 Hulagu sacks Baghdad, destroys canal system of Mesopotamia

1259 Kublai Khan as Mongol Khan; Mongol Empire at peak

1260 Mongols defeated by Mamelukes of Egypt;

A.D.

Mongol Il-Khans in power in Persia

1290 Othman becomes leader of a Turkish tribe, called Ottoman Turks after him; begins to spread through Asia Minor

1291 Last crusaders driven out of Asia

1295 Ghazan as Il-Khan; converted to Islam; Il-Khans at peak

1324 Orkhan I as Ottoman ruler

1345 Ottoman Turks cross Hellespont to establish first foothold in Europe

1389 Bayazid I as Ottoman ruler

1391 Ottoman Turks at outskirts of Constantinople

1395 Mongol conqueror, Tamerlane, defeats Il-Khans and puts an end to their dynasty

1401 Tamerlane takes and sacks Baghdad

1402 Tamerlane defeats Ottoman Turks at Ankara; takes Bayazid I prisoner

1404 Death of Tamerlane

1451 Mohammed II as Ottoman ruler

1453 Ottoman Turks take Constantinople; end of Byzantine Empire

1501 Ismail I takes Tabriz; founds Safavid dynasty ruling over Persia

1510 Portuguese explorer, Albuquerque, lands on island of Ormuz

1514 Ottoman Turks defeat Persians at Chaldiran and take over Mesopotamia;

A.D.

Ottoman Turkish Empire at peak

1524 Tahmasp I as Persian Shah

1561 English trader, Anthony Jenkinson, reaches Persia

1587 Abbas I as Persian Shah

1603 Abbas I retakes Mesopotamia from Turks; establishes capital at Isfahan; Safavid dynasty at peak

1629 Death of Abbas I

1638 Ottoman ruler, Murad IV, takes Mesopotamia once more

1722 Afghan invaders take and sack Isfahan

1736 Abbas III, last Safavid Shah, deposed; Nadir Shah rules Persia

1739 Nadir Shah invades India; sacks Delhi

1747 Nadir Shah assassinated

1796 Tehran becomes Persian capital

1844 Bahaism founded

1892 German company obtains permission to build railroad through Mesopotamia

1907 Great Britain and Russia divide Persia into spheres of influence

A.D.

1915 Great Britain invades Mesopotamia in course of World War I

1917 British take Baghdad

1918 British control Mesopotamia (Iraq) as a League of Nations mandate

1921 Faisal I of Iraq

1925 Reza Khan seizes throne of Persia

1932 Iraq becomes nominally independent; joins League of Nations

1935 Iran becomes official name of Persia

1941 British send force into Iraq in course of World War II; occupy Baghdad; British and Russians occupy Iran and force Reza Khan to abdicate

1948 Israel becomes independent nation

1956 Israel defeats Egypt in Sinai peninsula

1958 Revolution in Iraq; King Faisal II killed and a republic established under Kassem

1963 Kassem assassinated

1967 Israel defeats Arab nations in Six-Day War

INDEX

Abbas I, 249-250
Abbas III, 251
Abbasids, 221
  science under, 226
  at peak of power, 226-227
  decline of, 228
  end of, 240-241, 247
Abraham, 40-41, 113-114
Abu Bekr, 215
Abul-Abbas, 221
Academy, Plato's, 206
Achaemenids, 119
Adad-nirari II, 66-67
Adam and Eve, 22
Afghans, 250
Agade, 31
  destruction of, 35
Aga Khan, 240
Agriculture, 1-4
  irrigation and, 8
  religion and, 9-10
  Sumerian, 30
Ahab, 71-72
Ahasueras, 134
Ahriman, 125
Ahura Mazda, 125-126, 184
Akkad, 31
Akkadian Empire, 33-35
Akkadian language, 32
  decline of, 80-81
  death of, 122
  deciphering of, 132
Akkadians, 31
  religion of, 47-48
Al-Abbas, 221
Al-Battani, 229
Albuquerque, Affonso de, 248
Al-Din, Rashid, 244
Alexander the Great, 143 ff.
  in Babylon, 147-149
  death of, 149

Alexander's Empire, 148
  breakup of, 149-150
Alexandria, 151
Al-Ghazzali, 234-235
Ali, 219
Al-Khwarizmi, 226
Al-Mahdi, 223
Al-Mamun, 226
Al-Mansur, 222
Al-Mutasim, 227-228
Al-Mutawakkil, 228
Alp Arslan, 232-233
Alphabet, 18, 81
Al-Razi, 229
Al-Sabbah, Hasan ibn, 236
Amel-Marduk, 115
Amorite Empire, 45
  fall of, 57
Amorites, 42-43
Amraphel, 41, 44
Animal transport, 54-55
Anshan, 119
Antigonus, 151, 153
Antioch, 153
Antiochus III, 155-156
Antiochus IV, 158
Antiochus VII, 162
Antiochus XIII, 166
Anu, 46
Arab bloc, 257
Arabian Nights, The, 226
Arabic language, 225
Arabs, 191
  and Sassanid Empire, 199
  become Moslem, 214
  great offensive of, 215 ff.
Aramean language, 81, 122
Arameans, 65-66
Ararat, 60
Ardashir, 180
Argistis I, 78

Aristotle, 171, 235
Ark of the Covenant, 87
Armenia, 163
  at peak of power, 164
  taken by Trajan, 175
  and Christianity, 192, 203
  and Shapur II, 196
Arsaces I, 155
Arsaces VI, 161
Arsacids, 161
Artabanus IV, 180
Artaxata, 164
Artaxerxes I, 135-136
Artaxerxes II, 136-139
Artaxerxes III, 142
Aryans, 74
Ashur (city), 32, 39, 43, 60
  fall of, 101
Ashur (god), 49, 82
Ashurbanipal, 94
  library of, 95
  invades Egypt, 96
  conquers Elam, 97-98
  death of, 100
Ashurnasirpal II, 69-71
Ashur-uballit I, 58
Ashur-uballit II, 102-103
Assassins, 236-237
  end of, 240
Assyria, 32, 44
  religion of, 49
  Mitanni and, 55, 58
  Peoples of the Sea and, 62
  iron and, 67
  siege warfare and, 67-68
  royal hunters of, 69
  terror warfare and, 70-71
  legends of, 77-78, 96
  end of, 100-103
Assyrian Empire, 59, 64
Astyages, 118-120
Athena, 47
Athens, 47, 133, 136, 206
Atossa, 133
Augustine, Saint, 186
Augustus, 172-173
Aurelian, 184
Avars, 210
Averroes, 235
Avesta, 183-184

Bab, 252
Babel, 43
Babism, 252
Babylon, 45

Sumerian religion and, 48-49
  morality in, 53
  Kassite conquest of, 57
  legends of, 77
  Sennacherib and, 91-92
  Esarhaddon and, 92
  at peak of power, 107-109
  Hanging Gardens of, 109
  ziggurat of, 109
  science in, 110
  calendar of, 110-111
  Biblical view of, 111-112
  Cyrus and, 121
  Xerxes and, 134
  Alexander the Great and, 147
  Seleucus I and, 150-152
  end of, 152, 175
Bactria, 155, 159
Baghdad, 222
  under Turks, 232
  under Mongols, 241
  taken by Timur, 245
  taken by Safavids, 249
  taken by Ottomans, 250
  taken by British, 254
Baghdad pact, 259
Bahaism, 252
Baha-ullah, 252
Bahram Chobin, 209-210
Bahram Gor, 200
Bandar Abbas, 250
Bardiya, 124
Barmecides, 225
Basil II, 230
  death of, 233
Baybars, 242
Bel, 49
Belshazzar, 117
  death of, 121
Berossus, 152-153
Bible, 12, 21, 29, 40-41, 43, 49, 50, 56,
    60-61, 69, 72, 87, 102, 111-115,
    116-117, 121, 134, 168
  formation of, 113-115
Bisitun, 131
Borsippa, 48
Botta, Paul Emile, 86
Braidwood, Robert J., 3
Bridge, Battle of the, 216
Bronze, 23
Byzantine Empire, 216
  Abbasids and, 223
  Turks and, 233-234, 245
  end of, 246
Byzantium, 216

Caesar, Julius, 166
  assassination of, 171
Calah, 60, 69
Cambyses, 123
  death of, 124
Canaan, 6, 43
Canaanites, 43
Caracalla, 178
Carchemish, battle of, 104
Carrhae, battle of, 169-170
Cassius, Avidius, 177
Cataphracts, 167
Cavalry, armored, 167
Chaldean Empire, 104 ff.
  end of, 121
Chaldeans, 73, 81-82, 85
Chaldiran, battle of, 247
Chariots, 55
Charlemagne, 223
Chedorlaomer, 41
Cherubs, 87
Chess, 207-208
China, 170, 203, 217, 246
  under Mongols, 239-240
Chosroes I, 204-209
Chosroes II, 209
  victories of, 210-212
  defeat and death of, 212-213
Christianity, 184-185
  persecution of, 189
  Sassanid Empire and, 198-199
  heresies in, 202
Cimmerians, 84-85, 93
  end of, 96-97
Cities, 9
  siege of, 67-68
Civilization, 3
  barbarians and, 11
Clearchus, 137
  death of, 139
Code of Hammurabi, 49-53, 62
"Cold war," 257
Communism, 257
Constantine I, 192-193
Constantine XI, 246
Constantinople, 205
  Arab siege of, 221
  Turkish siege of, 245
  fall of, 246
Constantius, 193-194
Copper, 23
Corbulo, Gnaeus Domitius, 174
Crassus, Marcus, 166
  death of, 170
Crassus, Publius, 169-170

Creation myths, 46, 49
Crimean war, 252
Croesus, 120
Crusades, 235-236
  end of, 248
Ctesiphon, 163
  taken by Romans, 177
  taken by Sassanids, 180
  taken by Arabs, 217
  end of, 222
Cunaxa, battle of, 137-139
Cuneiform, 17, 32-33
  end of, 161-162
Cush, 60-61
Cyaxares, 101
Cylinder seal, 16
Cyprus, 83
Cyrus, 117
  birth legends of, 118
  Jews and, 121
  death of, 123
Cyrus the Younger, 136
  death of, 139

Dacia, 175
Damascus, 220, 245
Damascus, Kingdom of, 66
  end of, 80
Daniel, Biblical book of, 111-112, 117
Darius I, 125
  sacks Babylon, 127-128
  Jews and, 129
  Greece and, 130
  mountain inscription of, 131-132
  Athens and, 133
  death of, 133
Darius II, 136
Darius III, 143
  at Gaugamela, 145-146
  death of, 147
David, 66
Delhi, 245, 251
Demetrius II, 162
De Morgan, Jacques, 50
Diocletian, 187-189
Diodorus Siculus, 132
Diodotus, 155
Dur-Sharrukin, 85-86

Ea, 46
Eannatum, 25
Ecbatana, 120, 131-132
Eden, garden of, 87
Edessa, 203
  battle of, 181-182

Egypt, 17
  Old Kingdom of, 23
  Hyksos' conquest of, 56
  invades Asia, 57-58
  decline of, 61
  Assyria and, 88-89, 93, 96, 101-103
  and Nebuchadrezzar II, 107
  and Persia, 123-124, 133-135, 141-142
  under Ptolemy I, 150
  and Mongols, 242
  and Ottoman Turks, 247
  under Nasser, 257-259
Elam, 32, 41, 50
  Akkadians and, 33
  conquers Ur, 39
  sacks Babylon, 62
  Assyria and, 88, 90-93
  end of, 97-98
  language of, 132
Ellasar, 41
Elymais, 156
Enlil, 46
Eridu, 13, 20, 47
Esarhaddon, 92
  conquers Egypt, 93
  death of, 94
Eshnunna, 39
Esther, 134
Euphrates River, 6, 13-14, 20
Evil-Merodach, 116
Ezekiel, 112-113

Faisal I, 255
Faisal II, 259
Fatima, 229
Fatimids, 229
Fertile Crescent, 5-6, 156, 176
Firdausi, 231
Firuz, 202
Fitzgerald, Edward, 200, 234
Flood, The, 19-22

Galerius, 187-189
Galland, Antoine, 226
Gaugamela, battle of, 144-146
Gaumata, 124
Genghis Khan, 238-239
Germany, 253-256
Ghazan, 244
Ghazni, 231
Gilgamesh, 21-22, 25
Gods, 9-10
Great Britain, 251-256
Greeks, 61

  myths of, 46
  Babylon and, 109-111
  Persia and, 135
Gudea, 36
Guti, 35
Gyges, 97

Hades, 46
Hadrian, 176
Haifa, 252
Halaf period, 8
Hamadan, 232
Hammurabi, 44-45
  Code of, 49-53
Hanging Gardens, 109
Harran, 102-103, 116, 120
Harun al-Rashid, 223
  legends of, 225-226
Hassan, 220
Hassuna-Samarra period, 7
Hatra, 176, 178, 180
Hephthalites, 201
  end of, 208
Heraclius, 211-213
  death of, 216
Hercules, 21, 160
Herodotus, 89, 108, 124, 130
Hezekiah, 88-90
Hira, 199, 216
  Christianity and, 203
  end of, 210
Hitler, Adolf, 255-256
Hittites, 56-58
  end of, 62
  iron and, 64
Horites, 56
Hormizdas II, 190
Hormuz, 218
  battle of, 180
Horse, 54-55, 74-75
Hosein, 220
Hoshea, 82
Hulagu, 240, 242
Huns, 200
Hurrians, 55-56, 114
Hyksos, 56

Ibbi-Sin, 39
Ibn-Rushd, 235
Ibrahim, 222
Ideograph, 17
Il-Khans, 242-245
India, 74
  Persia and, 130
  Sassanids and, 207-208

Zoroastrianism in, 218
Timur and, 245
Nadir Shah and, 251
Indo-European languages, 56-57, 74
Ipsus, battle of, 153
Iran, 74, 255
Iranians, 74, 119
Iraq, 254-256, 259
Iron, 63-64
Assyria and, 67
Irrigation, 8, 84-85
Isaiah, 87
Isfahan, 249
Ishtar, 47
Ishtar Gate, 108
Isin, 39, 44
Islam, 214
heresies in, 219-220
Ismail, 229
Ismail I, 246-248
Ismailism, 229, 236
Isocrates, 142
Israel, 72, 78
end of, 82-83
"lost tribes" of, 83
Israel (modern), 257, 259
Israelite Empire, 66
Issus, battle of, 143
Istanbul, 246

Jabir, 226
Jacob's ladder, 113
Jafar, 225
Jarmo, 3-7
Jehu, 72
Jenkinson, Anthony, 249
Jeroboam II, 78-79
Jerusalem, 88-89
fall of, 105
Sassanids and, 211
Arabs and, 216
Turks and, 235, 238
Crusaders and, 237
Jesus, 81, 202
Jews, 105
in Babylonian Exile, 111-115
return from Exile, 121-122
Zoroastrianism and, 126
rebuild the Temple, 129
under the Seleucids, 158
under the Parthians, 162
under the Romans, 176
under the Sassanids, 201-202
under the Moslems, 218
under the Mongols, 241

and modern Israel, 255, 257
Josiah, 103
Jovian, 196
Judah, 83
Assyria and, 88-90
Egypt and, 103
Chaldea and, 105
Judaism, 112-115
Judea, 166, 174
Julian, 193
invades Mesopotamia, 194
death of, 196
Justinian I, 205-207

Kadisiya, battle of, 217
Karakorum, 239
Karkar, battle of, 71-72
Kassem, Abdul Karim, 259
Kassites, 57, 60
Kavadh, 202
Kerbela, battle of, 220
Kish, 24-25, 29, 31, 43
Kramer, Samuel N., 19
Kublai Khan, 240, 242, 244
Kufa, 219
Kushans, 190
Kut-al-Imara, 254

Labienus, Quintus, 171
Lagash, 25-27, 36
Larsa, 39, 43
in time of Nabonidus, 116
Law-codes, 38-39, 49-53
League of Nations, 254
Legion, Roman, 167
Library of Ashurbanipal, 95
Lucius Verus, 176-177
Lucullus, 165
Lugalzaggesi, 26-27
defeat of, 31
Lydia, 97
end of, 120
Lysimachus, 153

Maccabees, 158
Macedonia, 142
Magi, 124
Mahmud, 231
Malik Shah, 234-235
assassination of, 237
Mamelukes, 242
Manasseh, 90, 93
Mangu Khan, 240
Mani, 185-186
Manichaeism, 186-187

Manzikert, battle of, 233-234
Marathon, battle of, 133
Marcus Aurelius, 176-177
Marduk, 48-49, 82, 92, 109, 127, 134-135
Mari, 43
Mark Antony, 171-172
Maurice, 210
Mazdakism, 204
Mecca, 209
Medes, 74-75, 101
  Assyria and, 79
Media, 74
  taken by Parthia, 161
Median Empire, 104
  end of, 120
Megiddo, battle of, 103
Memphis, 108
Merodach-Baladan, 85, 88
Mesopotamia, 6
  taken by Trajan, 175-176
  end of canal system of, 241
Methusaleh, 21
Miletus, 109
Mitanni, 55-56
  decline of, 58
Mithradates I, 161-162
Mithradates II, 163-164
Mithradates VI, 164-165
Mithraism, 184-185
Mithras, 184
Mohammed, 209
  new religion of, 214
Mohammed (Shiite), 222
Mohammed II, 246
Mongol Empire, 240
  decline of, 244
Mongols, 238
  conquer China, 239
  conquer east Europe, 239-240
  wipe out Assassin, 240
  conquer Persia, 241
Monophysitism, 211
Moscow, 245
Moses, 31, 50
  law of, 114
Moslem Empire, 220-221
Moslems, 214
Muawiya, 219
Murad IV, 250
Musa, 173

Nabonidus, 116-117
  Cyrus and, 119-121
Nabopolassar, 100

Nabu, 48
Nadir Shah, 251
Nahum, 102
Naram-Sin, 33-34
Narsah, 187-189
Nasser, Gamal Abdel, 257-259
Nebuchadrezzar I, 62-63
Nebuchadrezzar II, 104 ff.
  Tyre and, 105-107
  invades Egypt, 107
  palace of, 108-109
  death of, 115
Nebuchadrezzar III, 127
Necho II, 103-104
Nehavend, battle of, 217
Neriglissar, 116
Nero, 174
Nestorianism, 202-204
Nestorius, 202
Nile River, 19
Nimrod, 60-61, 69
Nimrud, 61
Nineveh, 60
  legends concerning, 77
  as Assyrian capital, 87-88
  fall of, 102
  the Ten Thousand and, 140
Ninus, 77
Nippur, 13, 47
Nisibis, 193
Noah, 22, 29
Nuri Pasha, 259

Octavian, 171-172
Odenathus, 182
Ogdai Khan, 239-240
Old Man of the Mountain, 236
Omar Khayyam, 200, 234
Omayyads, 220-221
Orkhan I, 245
Ormizd IV, 209
Ormuz, 248
Orodes II, 168
  death of, 171-172
Osman I, 245
Osmanli Turks, 245
Osroes I, 175
Othman, 219
Ottoman Empire, 246
  end of, 254
Ottoman Turks, 245-247

Palestine, 252
Palmyra, 182
Papyrus, 17

Parsa, 131
Parsees, 218
Parthian Empire, 155, 160 ff.
  Rome and, 166 ff.
  at peak of power, 170
  end of, 180
Pasargadae, 119
Peoples of the Sea, 61-62
Perdiccas, 149-150
Persarmenia, 201
Persepolis, 131
  destruction of, 147
Persia, 119
  under Parthians, 162
  revival of, 179-180
  under Turks, 231
  Shiites and, 246
  European powers and, 248 ff.
  Anglo-Russian compromise over,
    253
  after World War I, 255
Persian Empire, 120
  religion of, 125-127
  organization of, 130
  Macedon and, 142-147
  fall of, 146-148
Persian Gulf, 13-14
Peter I, 250
Peter the Hermit, 235
Phalanx, Macedonian, 144
Philip II, 142-143
Philistines, 66
Phocas, 210-211
Phoenicians, 63, 81
Phraates III, 167
Phraates IV, 172-173
Phraates V, 173
Pictograph, 16
Planets, 110
Plato, 206
Pompey, 165-166
Pontus, 164-165
Portugal, 248
Poseidon, 46
Priests, 10, 16
Proto-literate period, 19
Proto-Semitic, 29
Psamtik I, 96
Ptolemy I, 150
Ptolemy III, 154-155
Ptolemy IV, 155-156
Ptolemy V, 156
Ptolemy VI, 158
Pulu, 82
Pythagoras, 110

Rakkah, 229
Rawlinson, Henry Creswicke, 132
Reza Khan, 255
Rhazes, 229
Richard the Lion-Hearted, 238
Rim-Sin, 44
Romanus Diogenes, 233-234
Rome, 108
  Antiochus III and, 156
  Antiochus IV and, 158
  Mithradates VI and, 165
  Parthians and, 166 ff.
  Armenia and, 174
  Sassanids and, 181 ff.
  Mithraism and, 184-185
  Manichaeism and, 186-187
  Christianity and, 189, 192
  end of paganism in, 206
Russia, 250-254
Rustem, 231

Sabbath, 114-115
Safavids, 246
  at peak of power, 249
  end of, 251
Safi-al-Din, 246
Saladin, 238
Samaria, 82-83
Samarkand, 245
Samarra, 227
Sammu-rammat, 77
Sardanapalus, 96-97
Sargon (of Agade), 30
  death of, 33
Sargon II, 82
  Urartu and, 84-85
  library of, 85
  capital of, 85
  death of, 86
Sargonids, 83
Sassan, 180
Sassanid Empire, 181 ff.
  Christianity and, 192-193, 198-199
  Arabs and, 199
  Nestorianism and, 203
  end of, 217
Sassanids, 180
Satan, 126
Scheherezade, 226
Scythians, 84, 101
Second Isaiah, 115, 121
Seleucia, 152
  taken by Ptolemy III, 155
  taken by Parthia, 161
  Ctesiphon and, 163

end of, 177
Seleucid Empire, 151
  at peak of power, 156
  end of, 166
Seleucids, 154
Seleucus I, 150
  founds Seleucia, 152
  founds Antioch, 153
  death of, 154
Seleucus II, 154
Selim I, 247
Seljuk, 232
Seljuk Turks, 232
  at peak of power, 234-235
  decline of, 237-238
Sem, 29
Semiramis, 77-78, 132
Semitic languages, 29
Sennacherib, 86
  palace of, 87
  invades Elam, 90-91
  death of, 92
Septimius Severus, 178
Shalmaneser I, 59-60
Shalmaneser III, 71-73
  death of, 76-77
Shalmaneser V, 82-83
Shamash, 47-48, 50
Shamash-shum-ukin, 94
  suicide of, 97
Shamshi-Adad, 43-44
Shapur I, 181
  Mani and, 185-186
Shapur II, 191
  Julian and, 195
Shem, 29
Sheol, 126
Shiites, 220, 229
  in Persia, 246
Shinar, 12
Shiraz, 252
Shirley, Sir Robert, 249
Silk, 170
Sin, 47
Sinai, Mount, 50
Sippar, 50
Slavery, 50-51
Smerdis, 124
Smith, George, 95
Sohrab, 231
Solomon, 66
Soviet Union, 255-259
Spain, 221-222
Sparta, 136
Stele of the Vultures, 25

Suleiman the Magnificent, 249
Sumer, 11
Sumeria, 11
Sumerian language, 19, 28
  decline of, 32
Sumerians, 11
  inventions of, 12-13
  end of, 39-40
  religion of, 45-49
  names of, 47-48
Sunnites, 220
Susa, 32, 50, 131
Susiana, 131
Syria, 6, 66, 71-72

Tabriz, 251
Tahmasp I, 248-249
Talmud, 201-202
Tamerlane, 245
Tatars, 240
Tehran, 251
Tell Halaf, 8
Tell Hassuna, 7
Tell el Ubaid, 11
Temujin, 238
Ten Thousand, retreat of, 139-140
Thales, 109
Thapachus, 137, 143
Thebes, 96, 108
Thutmose III, 58
Tiamat, 46, 113
Tiglath-Pileser I, 64-66
Tiglath-Pileser III, 79
  exile policy of, 80
  death of, 82
Tigranes, 163
  fall of, 165
Tigranocerta, 164
Tigris River, 6, 14, 20
Timur, 245-246
Tiridates I (Armenia), 174
Tiridates II (Parthia), 173
Tiridates III (Armenia), 192
Tower of Babel, 12, 113
Trajan, 175-176
Trapezus, 140
Troy, 62
Tughril Beg, 232
Tukulti-Ninurta I, 60, 77
Tukulti-Ninurta II, 67
Turkey, 253
Turkestan, 208
Turks, 208
  Abbasids and, 227-228
  in power, 230 ff.

Tyre, 105-107, 143

Ubaid period, 11
Umma, 25-27
United States, 252, 256-257
Ur, 20, 26, 47
  Second Dynasty of, 36
  Third Dynasty of, 37-41
  fall of, 39
  Kassite sack of, 57
  Nebuchadrezzar II and, 114
  Nabonidus and, 116
Ur-Nammu, 37-38
Urartu, 60
  iron and, 64
  Assyria and, 72-73
  at peak of power, 78
  Tiglath-Pileser III and, 80
  Cimmerians and, 84-85
  end of, 103-104
Uruk, 16, 26, 47
  writing and, 18
  First Dynasty of, 25
  Fourth Dynasty of, 36
  Fifth Dynasty of, 37
  under Seleucids, 151
Uruk period, 16
Urukagina, 26
Ut-napishtim, 21-22

Valerian, 181-182
Van, Lake, 73
Varahran I, 186
Varahran II, 190
Varahran V, 199-201
Ventidius, Bassus, 171
Vespasian, 174
Vologesus I, 173

Vologesus III, 176
Vologesus IV, 177

Warfare, 22-23
William II, 253
Woolley, Sir Charles Leonard, 20
World War I, 253-254
World War II, 255-256
Writing, 14-19

Xenophon, 139-140
Xerxes I, 133-135

Yahya, 225
Yazdegird I, 198-199
Yazdegird III, 215-217

Zagros Mountains, 11, 35
Zarathustra, 125
Zend-Avesta, 183-184
Zeus, 46
Ziggurats, 12
  of Ur, 38
  of Babylon, 109
Zionism, 255
Zopyrus, 127-128
Zoroaster, 125-126
Zoroastrianism, 127
    under Xerxes I, 133-134
    under Seleucids, 151
    under Parthia, 162
    under Sassanids, 183-186
    Manichaeism and, 186
    Christianity and, 198-199
    heresies of, 204
    under Moslems, 217-218
    in India, 218

R